Creating the Multiage Classroom

Sandra J. Stone

Illustrated by Yoshi Miyake

A GOOD YEAR BOOK™

Good Year Books
Tucson, Arizona

DEDICATION
To my children—
Jeff, John, Jason, and Brian

GOOD YEAR BOOKS
Our titles are available for most basic curriculum subjects plus many enrichment areas. For information on other Good Year Books and to place orders, contact your local bookseller or educational dealer, or visit our website at www.goodyearbooks.com. For a complete catalog, please contact:

Good Year Books
PO Box 91858
Tucson, AZ 85752-1858
www.goodyearbooks.com

Book design by Karen Kohn & Associates, Ltd.

Pages 20–22 contain excerpts from *Developmentally Appropriate Practice in Early Childhood Programs Serving Children from Birth Through Age 8* by Sue Bredekamp, editor. Copyright 1987 by the National Association for the Education of Young Children. Reprinted by permission.

Page 30 contains a philosophy statement reprinted courtesy of the Kentucky Department of Education. For ordering information, contact the Kentucky Department of Education Publications Center, 500 Metro Street, Frankfort, KY 40601.

Page 190 contains a chart reprinted by permission of Sandra J. Stone and the Association for Childhood Education International, 17904 Georgia Avenue, Suite 215, Olney, MD. Copyright 1995 by the Association.

Preface

The national school restructuring movement has spurred a surging interest in the multiage classroom from New York to Alaska. Across our nation, professionals turn to the multiage classroom as a viable and preferred option to traditional, same-age, same-grade classrooms. What is it about these classrooms that has piqued this sincere interest and inspired enthusiastic dedication to propagating the multiage philosophy within our educational system? What have we learned from past theories and recent research about how children learn to support instructional strategies appropriate for mixed-age learners? What benefits do mixed-age groupings offer that same-age groupings can't? How does one establish a multiage program that makes the most of its benefits?

This book answers these questions and supplies all the detailed practical information you will need to establish your multiage classroom. It should serve as a unique and helpful tool to encourage, excite, and enable you to implement a successful multiage program for young children in the primary grades.

Please note that for even treatment, the gender of children and the teacher in text alternates from chapter to chapter.

Acknowledgments

I wish to thank my husband, Bill, for all his work in helping me prepare this manuscript for publication. This book would not have been completed without his support. I also wish to acknowledge Dr. Reynaldo Gomez, Arizona State University, for informally introducing me to the concept of multiage classrooms. I am very grateful to Dr. Joan Moyer, Arizona State University, for giving me good advice as I began to implement my own multiage classroom.

Personally exploring the multiage classroom would not have been possible if it were not for an innovative and visionary principal—Dr. Paula Brimhall, Tempe Elementary District #3—and her ability to empower teachers to try new models of teaching. It was also my pleasure to work with two outstanding multiage teachers, Karen James and Frances Oberholtzer, who shared their expertise as we piloted primary multiage classrooms together.

Contents

From *Creating the Multiage Classroom* published by GoodYear Books. Copyright © 1996 Sandra J. Stone.

Forms and Assessments Throughout Book:

From *Creating the Multiage Classroom* published by GoodYear Books. Copyright © 1996 Sandra J. Stone.

Introduction

Simply defined, a *multiage classroom* is a mixed-age group of children that stays with the same teacher for several years. The children are randomly selected and balanced by age, ability, and gender. This grouping, deliberately made for the *benefit of children*, not for reasons of economics, curriculum, or convenience, comprises much more than school classmates, evolving instead into a true family of learners.

The multiage classroom is *not* a combination class where a teacher instructs two or three grade levels in their designated curricula. Ages and grades do not divide this community of learners within the classroom. Rather, in the multiage community, every child in the "family" can become a successful learner *on his own continuum of growth.* The multiage classroom supports this individual growth through a *process* approach to learning that is child centered rather than curriculum centered. The mixed-age environment requires teachers to facilitate the learning of each child rather than to instruct the class as a whole based on predetermined grade-level skills and content. As a result, the multiage classroom can turn the process of education into a wonderful and successful adventure in learning for both teacher and children.

The multiage concept is far from new. Children have long been educated in multiage groupings called *families*, where parents or other relatives made sure that children had the necessary skills to survive as well as to enjoy happy and productive lives. Parents who were able taught their children how to read and write. They educated them in life skills such as gardening, farming, sewing, and even washing dishes. Elders instructed children in religious beliefs and values. Youngsters learned informally, in the context of work and play, from adults and other children (*Gaustad 1992a*).

Studies of societies throughout the world show the natural occurrence of mixed-age children in play groups, where young children imitate and rely on the older ones. As children play and care for one another, they learn how to socialize, nurture each other, and be responsible.

Multiage education has long-established roots in the history of American pedagogy. Children in colonial and post-Revolutionary America were educated in informal mixed-age settings by families, tutors, and churches; no "system" of public schools or grading by age existed. Although laws passed in Massachusetts as early as 1642 required towns to establish and support schools, they were only built when enough students justified hiring a teacher. The resulting one-room schoolhouses were based on multiage groupings out of necessity, practicing what we now call "innovations": individualized instruction, independent study, cross-age tutoring, peer tutoring, flexible scheduling, and continuous progress *(Barker 1986; Beckner 1983; Hauschnerr 1988; Kindley 1985; James 1990)*. Because it met the economic and organizational needs of small, rural communities and supported children's learning in all areas of development, the one-room schoolhouse became a fixture on the American landscape.

With the advent of the Industrial Revolution and large-scale urban growth in the mid-eighteenth century, American attitudes toward education began to shift. The graded, curriculum-centered approach advocated by educator Horace Mann was deemed the most efficient way to prepare students to fit into an industrialized society. In practice the system had close parallels with successful manufacturing methodologies. In his quest for a return to child-centered education, *John Dewey (1899)* criticized such an approach for its "mechanical massing of children and its uniform curriculum and methods." The graded system prevailed, however, to become the basis of "traditional" American education.

In the late 1950s and early 1960s, reform advocates stimulated a reevaluation of teaching methods. The nongraded school movement sought changes in the curriculum and the structure of knowledge for teaching and learning *(Rippa 1988)*. In 1959, Goodlad and Anderson challenged age segregation in their book *The Nongraded School*. They decried "homogeneous" grouping and made a strong case for multiage grouping. Reform called for schools to be reorganized into "multigrades" or "nongraded classrooms" that depended on team teaching so that each child could progress according to his or her abilities. Schools were redesigned to accommodate new instructional demands. For example, large-group instruction took up 40 percent of the students' time. These large-group sessions required space for 125 to 135 students at once. An additional 20 percent of the students' time was spent in small groups and 40 percent in independent study *(Rippa 1988)*.

From *Creating the Multiage Classroom* published by GoodYear Books. Copyright © 1996 Sandra J. Stone.

The nongraded school movement influenced thousands of school districts, but it was "not powerful enough to overcome organizational structures which were politically safe and administratively convenient" *(Pratt 1986)*. Although innovative, its methods were associated with a lack of structure. *Goodlad and Anderson (1987, x)* comment that "the 1970s witnessed the beginning of a return to the traditional ways of thinking about schooling from which we had sought to depart." As *Gaustad (1992a, 9)* notes, "starting in the early seventies, dissatisfaction with ineffective reforms prompted a return to traditional graded teaching methods. In the eighties, improvement fueled a full-fledged 'back to basics' movement. In this climate, only a few scattered schools and classrooms maintained the nongraded approach." Even so, multiage classrooms did not cease to exist; they remained a reality for many small, rural school districts in the United States as well as in many schools around the world *(Miller 1990)*.

In the 1990s, we saw a resurgence of reform challenging schools to restructure and empowering teachers to "create the schools of tomorrow." The Kentucky Education Reform Acts (KERA) were passed by the state legislature on July 13, 1990. This landmark legislation mandated the implementation of ungraded primary programs in kindergarten through third grade beginning in September 1992 and completed in 1996. Kentucky based its reform on a solid understanding of early childhood and multiage practices and provided substantial inservice for its teachers and familiarized parents and communities with the benefits of its primary multiage program. Kentucky's efforts to better the education of young children led the way for other states considering multiage programs. The state legislatures of Florida and Louisiana called for implementation of multigrade programs. In 1990 the Mississippi state legislature mandated that elementary mixed-aged classrooms be phased in over several years. Later, in June 1991, the Oregon Education Act for the Twenty-first Century called for major restructuring of Oregon schools and the development of a model for ungraded primary classrooms.

In the 2000s, we are still seeing schools across the United States choose multiage education. Multiage classrooms now exist in nearly every state in the United States (public, charter, and private schools). The Standards Movement, based on a graded system, and high-stakes testing made an impact on the growth of multiage schools in the early 2000s, but interestingly, the multiage movement has steadily moved forward. The National Multiage Institute at Northern Arizona University in Flagstaff, Arizona, has become the leader in training teachers from all over the United States and many countries in multiage practices.

Internationally, multiage education is also continuing to grow. The United States Department of Defense Dependent Schools (DoDDS) chose multiage classrooms for primary ages (K–3) for their reduced class size initiative funded by the U.S. Congress in the late 1990s. Now in the mid-2000s, multiage classrooms are thriving in DoDDS in Europe and Asia. International schools in Japan and Italy have successfully created their entire schools around multiage concepts. The Netherlands Antilles federal government mandated a change from a traditional graded system and have engaged in completely changing their nation's schools to a child-centered, mixed-aged approach, implementing the changes beginning in 2004. Nova Scotia, Canada, is steadily progressing toward changing many of its schools to a multiage approach. In Australia the regional Multiage Association of Queensland reorganized in 2004 to create a national multiage association in which multiage schools are prevalent. Historically, New Zealand had already successfully organized its schools into mixed-aged groupings and is continuing to promote mixed-aged learning into this millennium.

Multiage classrooms occupy the "cutting edge" of changing schools to fit children. Their presence on the forefront of educational practice is backed by quality research, developmentally appropriate practice, and major changes in instructional strategies, environment, and assessment

FOUNDATIONS FOR SUCCESS

The successful multiage classroom depends on a series of basic organizational and philosophical principles of how children learn and what are the developmentally appropriate practices. Let's first examine the characteristic organization and philosophy of a typical multiage setting.

Organization and Philosophy of a Multiage Classroom

MIXED AGES. In a primary multiage classroom, the most common age groups are four through six years, five through seven years, and six through eight years. Some multiage classrooms group two age levels together, such as kindergarten and first graders or first and second graders. Three age levels, however, afford more opportunities for interaction between ages. Additionally, with three ages in the same room, the teacher is less tempted to teach grade-level curriculum.

THREE YEARS WITH THE SAME TEACHER. In the ideal primary multiage classroom, the same group of children stays together for at least three years with the same teacher. This three-year span offers a greater opportunity for establishing the group as a "family" of learners and gives each child a three year time frame for development.

Over the years, the teacher can attend to each child's progress through the learning processes. For example, in writing, the teacher can see the child begin with scribbling at five and end with writing complete stories at seven. The teacher does not have to dissect the child's learning into curricular pieces; he is now able to support the growth from year to year, supporting each child's natural learning rate with the gift of time.

The teacher also knows each student's academic, social, emotional, and physical strengths and is therefore able to offer the greatest support. He knows how to work best with each child. This gives the teacher the confidence to say to each student, "The better I know you, the better I am able to guide your learning." In return, the child grows more comfortable and secure with her "guide" through the learning processes.

FAMILY UNIT. A primary goal of the multiage classroom is to establish a community of learners. This "family" unit should support and nurture each of its members. It includes the teacher, the children, and the parents as well. Throughout the extended life of a multiage classroom, teachers and parents have more time to get to know one another and become true partners in their children's education. Thus, parents become an integral part of the classroom community.

HETEROGENEOUS. Multiage classrooms should strike a heterogeneous balance of gender and ability within each age level. Each age group should be roughly equal in number.

RESPECT FOR THE INDIVIDUAL. The organization of the multiage classroom is based upon the philosophy of respect for the individual. Each child's learning rate and style is honored and supported.

From *Creating the Multiage Classroom* published by GoodYear Books. Copyright © 1996 Sandra J. Stone.

FOCUS ON SUCCESS. In the multiage classroom, each child's progress is viewed in terms of success rather than failure. The multiage philosophy rejects a "deficit model" that focuses on what a child doesn't know, rather than on what she does know. This focus on success keeps the child engaged in the learning processes. Because the teacher knows the child's strengths, he can support her and challenge her appropriately. The child is able to say, "I can do this! I can read this book. I can solve this problem. I can play this game." The multiage classroom provides repeated success for all children in the classroom no matter where they are on their continuum of learning.

The multiage classroom provides a positive learning environment. Most teachers strive for a positive learning environment in their classrooms. However, the structure of schools with same-age classrooms and expectations often interferes with the good intentions of classroom teachers. Multiage classrooms embrace a structure and philosophy that creates a positive learning environment for supporting children's achievement and self-esteem.

Without labels, retention, and grade levels, children are free to learn at their own pace and to take risks that include learning from mistakes. Multiage opportunities for social interaction and cross-age learning enable children to learn in an emotionally secure environment. With the focus on success rather than failure, children see themselves as capable individuals. Children should enjoy learning, and in a multiage classroom they come to know it as a labor of discovery, exploration, play, excitement, and joy. Learning does not just mean getting ready for the next grade. To become life-long learners, children must see their work as rewarding, meaningful, and absolutely enjoyable.

"The multiage philosophy rejects a 'deficit model' that focuses on what a child doesn't know, rather than on what she does know. This focus on success keeps the child engaged in the learning processes."

CROSS-AGE LEARNING. One basic multiage premise holds that in mixed-age groupings, younger students benefit from collaborating with older children who model more sophisticated approaches to learning. And older children benefit by modeling teachers in their roles as mentors to younger children. Vygotsky *(1976)* envisions a "zone of proximal development." This zone is the distance between the actual development of the child and the level of potential development that can be enhanced by adults or more capable peers. In the context of social interactions, adults or more capable peers can encourage children to use more sophisticated approaches to tasks through the process of "scaffolding" *(Meltzer 1991, 179)*. Meltzer suggests that adults or more capable peers can give children temporary support to help them accomplish tasks beyond their current independent capabilities. For example, during journal writing, the presence of an older child might prompt a younger child to use words, spellings, or concepts of print that the younger child would not ordinarily use on her own.

Parents responding to one year-end survey indicated that they were pleased by the fact that "the younger children learn from the older children." This phenomenon recurs over and over in the multiage classroom where children look to each other and not just to the teacher for learning opportunities.

"Children look to each other and not just to the teacher for learning opportunities."

MENTORING/LEADERSHIP.
Mentoring is another cross-age learning dynamic that occurs in the multiage classroom, where older children sometimes take the initiative to "teach" their younger classmates. For instance, an older student might decide to conference with younger children during journal writing just as the teacher would. After completing her own writing, the older child invites the younger children to conference with her. Such peer mentoring is an exciting experience for both the younger and older children.

Eventually, every child in a multiage classroom has the opportunity to be both "pupil" and "mentor," since younger children get their opportunity to mentor as they mature.

Mentoring directly benefits the mentors as well. For example, an older, insecure reader who mentors a younger nonreader boosts her own self-esteem. This could not occur in a same-age classroom where the insecure student would be labeled a poor reader by classmates and denied the opportunity to be someone of importance.

As social mentors, older children in multiage classrooms escort younger children to the cafeteria or the nurse's office and create learning and play groups. Mixed-age groups of children offer all older children the opportunity to play esteem-building leadership roles academically and socially. The social and emotional benefits of mentoring for younger and older children cannot be overstated.

AUTONOMOUS LEARNERS.

The multiage classroom develops self-directing, autonomous individuals *(Anderson & Pavan 1993)*. Autonomy is a critical issue in multiage classrooms where it is imperative that children take charge of their own learning. The structure of multiage classrooms invites children to participate in their own learning and offers them numerous opportunities for choices. As independent learners, children do not have to wait for the teacher to tell them what to do. Children become active and enthusiastic participants in their own learning, enjoying their "ownership" of the processes of learning to read, write, and solve problems.

Encouraging and nurturing the development of self-directed, autonomous individuals lays an important foundation, not only for the children, but also for the successful multiage classroom. Among self-directed learners, the teacher can become a true facilitator. He is free to work with small groups and individuals, to conference with children about their learning progress, and to mentor and guide the children in his care. Relieved of "herding" children through the curriculum, he can enjoy watching them make choices and set goals, knowing that they are on their way to becoming lifelong learners.

FLEXIBLE GROUPINGS.

Traditionally, children have been placed in ability groups for math and reading. These groups usually remain static for an entire year. In the multiage classroom, groups are flexible and based on need, interest, or topic. The teacher or students can create groups, and the multiage teacher facilitates the groups to meet the collective needs of the children. When the needs are met, a group is disbanded. The "group" may number from one child to many children.

From *Creating the Multiage Classroom* published by GoodYear Books. Copyright © 1996 Sandra J. Stone.

Grouping can be another way to label children. In the multiage classroom, ability grouping is not used to define a child's learning capabilities as students are not placed in traditional low, medium, and high groups. Consider Thomas, who was transferred into a multiage classroom from a traditional first-grade classroom. From conferencing with Thomas's mother, the teacher found that Thomas was in the low reading group. Thomas was very well aware of his inadequacies in reading. From the first day, when Thomas was called to a reading group, he asked, "What group am I in?" The teacher replied, "I don't know. You are just in a group, and we are reading." Every time Thomas was called to a group to read, he would ask the same question. After several weeks, Thomas stopped asking the question and began to enjoy reading and learning.

Flexible groupings also offer children ample occasions to interact with older and younger classmates. All groups, whether convened by teacher or students, or whether based on need, interest, or topic, comprise mixed ages. Grouping in multiage classrooms are never formed solely by age or grade level.

NO RETENTION OR PROMOTION. Multiage classrooms do not depend on retention or promotion. Continuous learning and success for each child is the focus.

The research on retention of young children *(Smith & Shepard 1987)* paints a gloomy picture. Children regard being retained as equal with the stress of a divorce or a death in the family. Yet, this emotionally devastating practice is still propagated today as beneficial for "helping children to catch up." Retention is a by-product of traditional classrooms where the expectations are the same for all children; yet we clearly know that all children do not learn at the same rate.

NO LABELING. Because each child in the multiage classroom is respected as an individual and supported with the opportunity for continuous learning, grade labels are unnecessary. In same-grade classes, children are typically labeled as "below grade level," "on grade level," and "above grade level." This creates a dilemma for young children, especially those who are "below grade level." These children do not see themselves as "fitting in" *(Mitchell 1990)*. They feel that "something is wrong with them."

When expectations are the same for all children, labeling inevitably occurs. In the multiage classroom, the focus shifts from getting every child to the same level of performance to encouraging each child's individual development.

From Creating the Multiage Classroom published by GoodYear Books. Copyright © 1996 Sandra J. Stone.

CHILD-CENTERED. Multiage education offers child-centered, not curriculum-centered learning. Because learning is a personal construction of knowledge, multiage curriculum goals and plans are selected based on individual needs, strengths, and interests. Teachers develop a child-centered curriculum rather than insisting that every child master a predetermined curriculum regardless of their needs.

AUTHENTIC ASSESSMENT. In the multiage classroom, teachers use qualitative reporting tools such as portfolios, anecdotal records, observations, journals, and videotapes. Standardized tests, teacher-made tests, and textbook tests are not used; children are not labeled by grades. Some multiage teachers record each child's growth on a developmental continuum or use narrative report cards. Qualitative assessment documents the growth of each student and supports and guides appropriate instruction based on their needs. Assessment interacts with instruction. Authentic assessment focuses on each child's successes rather than deficits and considers all areas of development, evaluating the child based on her own past achievements and potential, not by comparison to group standards. The child is able to see herself as a competent learner and individual.

PROFESSIONAL PARTNERSHIPS. The multiage classroom supports collaboration among colleagues in self-contained classes or among teachers in team-taught classes. It also recognizes parents as an integral part of the learning process. Parent-teacher partnerships are encouraged.

Organization and Philosophy of a Successful Multiage Classroom

Mixed ages

Three years with the same teacher

Family unit

Heterogeneous

Respect for the individual

Focus on success

Cross-age learning

Mentoring/ Leadership

Autonomous learners

Flexible groupings

No retention or promotion

No labeling

Child-centered

Authentic assessment

Professional partnerships

How Children Learn

A knowledge of how children learn is foundational to the multiage teacher's success in creating appropriate learning experiences and environment. The following are key concepts on how children learn. These concepts are based on present as well as past research and learning theories.

A CHILD LEARNS AS A WHOLE PERSON. Children develop and learn across all domains—physical, social, emotional, moral, aesthetic, and cognitive, each interacting with the others. One area cannot be separated out and addressed in a vacuum. For example, a child learning how to add numbers is developing a cognitive skill. If the child is excited to learn, she will probably pursue adding with keen intent. However, if a child does not feel she will be successful at adding, she will probably avoid the task whenever possible. In this case, cognition and affect (emotion) interact.

All domains of development are important. How a child interacts socially with peers is just as important as how well she can add. Because a child learns as a whole person, her education should nurture all areas of her development.

Multiage education develops the whole child, and the multiage classroom focuses on this development: intellectually, socially, emotionally, physically, and morally. Multiage teachers understand that all of these areas interact and that to educate only the intellect is naive. The multiage teacher places just as much importance on a child's social development as on her intellectual development.

A CHILD PROGRESSES THROUGH STAGES OF COGNITIVE DEVELOPMENT. The curriculum and environment of the multiage classroom are based on how children learn. Children between the ages of five and nine vary widely in their learning rates, styles, and personalities. All areas do not develop at the same rate even within the same child.

Psychologist Jean Piaget *(Piaget & Inhelder 1969)* suggests that children go through stages of cognitive development and at certain stages are capable of only certain types of intellectual endeavors. Piaget envisions four periods of development: Sensorimotor (typically two years and under); Preoperational (typically two to seven years); Concrete Operational (typically seven to eleven years); and Formal Operational (typically eleven to fifteen years). The primary multiage classroom stage is the Preoperational period when a child increases her mental ability to represent objects and events.

During the first period, Sensorimotor, a child relies on her senses to retrieve information about the environment. Now, in the Preoperational period, she begins to use symbols (mental images, words, gestures) to represent objects and events in her environment. But with this growth comes limitations. The child's view of the world is still strongly tied to perceptions. How something *looks* is how something *is* to the young child. She is unable to reverse her thought. This is why some children can write a sentence, using the sounds they know, but then are unable to read it back. Some can add but cannot reverse the operation and subtract. During this period, the child is also egocentric, that is, unable to assume another's viewpoint.

As the child develops and constructs her knowledge of the world through active engagement with the environment, she progresses through each stage of development. The ages for each stage are approximate and also vary with each child. However, it is important to be aware of Piaget's stages simply because they remind us that children are continually developing in their intellectual capabilities. Sometimes teachers will expect a child to accomplish tasks that are beyond her capabilities or current stage of cognitive development. This puts the child at extreme risk of failure. If the knowledgeable teacher patiently waits, the child soon will be able to understand and then successfully accomplish the task.

The multiage teacher makes himself aware of each child's cognitive development in order to be supportive and provide appropriate learning experiences.

In addition to stages of cognitive development are types of development. Gardner *(1983)* theorizes there are seven types of intelligences: Linguistic, Logical/Mathematical, Visual Spatial, Bodily Kinesthetic, Musical, Interpersonal, and Intrapersonal. Each intelligence develops at different rates in different children. Therefore to understand how a child learns, the multiage teacher must appreciate the variance in development in each of these areas, offer varied learning experiences, and use the stronger areas to develop the weaker areas. When we regard only one type of intelligence as being important, a large percentage of human potential goes unrecognized.

From *Creating the Multiage Classroom* published by GoodYear Books. Copyright © 1996 Sandra J. Stone.

A CHILD IS AN ACTIVE, NOT PASSIVE LEARNER. A child learns by becoming actively engaged with her environment and people around her. She must be an active participant in her own learning. The old adage, "A child learns by doing," is worthy of repetition.

In the multiage classroom, children actively engage the environment through centers, projects, and learning experiences with their peers. The teacher in the multiage classroom thus becomes the facilitator of learning. This role differs from the traditional role of giver of knowledge. It requires that the teacher allows and stimulates each child to learn by doing. As a facilitator, the teacher is responsible for creating a learning environment that actively engages children within a social context.

A CHILD CONSTRUCTS HER OWN KNOWLEDGE OF THE WORLD. As a child actively participates in her world, she constructs her own knowledge of it *(Piaget 1976)*. As she interacts with the environment and people, she constantly changes and reorganizes her knowledge, assimilating new experiences into her frame of reference. The teacher cannot "present" or "give" knowledge to a young child; the child must construct it for herself. Each child's construction of knowledge is personal and unique.

Consider Piaget: "[I]n order for a child to understand something, he must construct it himself. . . . Every time we teach a child something, we keep him from re-inventing it for himself . . . that which we allow him to discover by himself will remain with him visibly, . . . for the rest of his life" *(Piers 1972, 27)*.

Weikart *(1988, 65)* suggests that "teachers must be centrally committed to providing settings in which children actively learn through construction of their own knowledge. The child's knowledge comes from personal interaction with the surrounding world, from direct experience with real objects, from talking about experiences and ideas, and from the application of logical thinking to these events. . . ."

"[I]n order for a child to understand something, he must construct it himself. . . . Every time we teach a child something, we keep him from re-inventing it for himself . . . that which we allow him to discover by himself will remain with him visibly, . . . for the rest of his life"
—Jean Piaget

A CHILD'S LEARNING IS INDI-VIDUAL. Each child is unique in her progress; like snowflakes, no two children are exactly alike. Each child has her own "individual pattern and timing of growth, as well as individual personality, learning style, and family background" *(Bredekamp 1987)*. Therefore, children must have access to varied and open-ended experiences that allow for differences in their learning rates and styles. As they begin a learning experience, they proceed to build on what they already know. Children engage in problem-solving at their developmental levels, solving problems they recognize. Similarly, children will engage in reading at a level where they are successful.

Each growth step along the continuum must be celebrated with the child, so she sees herself as a worthwhile person. In the graded classroom, children who do not meet the grade expectations feel that something is wrong with them, and those who do not progress satisfactorily are assumed to have failed, rather than see that the system has failed to meet their needs *(Connell 1987, 33)*.

Children who excel oftentimes reduce their growth for fear of being different from the norm.

Multiage respects the individual. As *Connell (1987, 37)* notes, children in multiage classrooms see themselves as "fitting in" because "the differences are considered natural and normal." The diversity of the multiage group makes it impossible to view children as the same. The multiage classroom frees teachers to see children as individuals, which not only benefits each child, but also benefits the teacher. This freedom releases him from the traditional emphasis on teaching the curriculum and allows him to instead focus on teaching children.

The multiage classroom offers continuous learning and progress over at least a three-year period. During this time, each child has the opportunity to learn and progress continuously. No longer are children expected to learn all the kindergarten curriculum in kindergarten or the first-grade curriculum in first grade. Rather, the children are now taught and

assessed as individuals on their own continuum of learning. Without group expectations or norms, progress becomes a personal journey for each child.

The multiage teacher has the opportunity to encourage each child's natural learning rate with this gift of time. In a kindergarten through second-grade multiage classroom, the teacher knows that if a child does not read by the end of first grade, she has another year for her reading to develop. At the beginning of each year, the teacher knows where every child is on his or her continuums of learning, and where each needs to focus to reach the next level. No time is wasted each year getting to know the students' abilities from scratch. And, as each child begins to see the learning process as continuous in the multiage classroom, the notion of lifelong learning is instilled.

From *Creating the Multiage Classroom* published by GoodYear Books. Copyright © 1996 Sandra J. Stone.

A CHILD'S LEARNING IS A PROCESS. As children interact with their environment and other children, constructing knowledge is an ongoing process. How and when a child does this is not directly teachable. However, the teacher can support and encourage learning through active involvement in the learning process. For example, a child learns how to problem-solve by being personally engaged in solving a problem. A child learns to read by reading and to write by writing. To learn social skills, a child must interact with others. To learn to make decisions, she must be allowed to make decisions. Young children should learn in a setting where they can actively participate.

Multiage education uses the process approach to learning. In the multiage classroom, children learn skills in the process of becoming readers, writers, and problem-solvers. Children learn to read by reading and to write by writing. This approach acknowledges that each child constructs her knowledge of the world when she is actively and meaningfully engaged in learning how to learn. The process, then, is more important than the product.

A CHILD LEARNS BEST WHEN THE ACTIVITY IS MEANINGFUL AND RELEVANT. Research indicates that the more meaningful the activity is to the child, the more she understands, learns, and remembers *(Iran-Nejad, McKeachie, & Berliner 1990)*. For example, a writing activity is more meaningful and relevant to the child if she is writing a note to a classmate rather than copying sentences from a worksheet. A child is naturally curious and eager to learn and her interests serve to motivate her; if interested, she will explore, discover, and persevere until she successfully completes a task.

Multiage teachers choose their curricula based on interest and need. The traditional curriculum is usually determined by administrations and textbooks and does not meet the needs of multiage students. "Sequence of learning must be determined by each individual student and his or her teacher . . . no predetermined sequence is appropriate to all learners" *(Goodlad & Anderson 1989, xvii)*. The multiage curriculum respects the children's interests, abilities, learning rates, and styles. Children are involved in selecting topics in cooperation with the teacher. For some curriculum ideas for the multiage classroom, see Chapter 6.

A CHILD LEARNS THROUGH PLAY. Play is an important learning context for children. During play, children construct their knowledge of the world. Within this natural and intrinsically motivated context, "children use play to test ideas, discover relationships, abstract information, express their feelings and ideas, define themselves, and develop peer relationships" *(Stone 1993, 1)*. Bergen *(1988, 1)* suggests that "play has been undervalued as a curricular tool by educators and by parents because society has defined the goals of learning, especially school learning, very narrowly. . . . Play,

which allows children to choose their learning focus and which fosters a broad range of developmental goals, should be included as an essential learning element. . . ."

Wasserman *(1992, 135)* lists five benefits of play for children in the classroom: Children are able to

1. Generate (create) something new,
2. Take risks,
3. Avoid the fear of failure,
4. Be autonomous, and
5. Actively engage their minds and bodies.

In the primary multiage classroom, children have many opportunities to play and learn through play.

Specific centers are created in the classroom to accommodate their play, such as block centers, puzzle and game centers, the home center, life centers, thematic centers, interest centers, sociodramatic play centers, art centers, and music/movement centers (more on centers in Chapter 3). These centers allow young children in the multiage classroom the opportunity to construct their own knowledge of the world within the natural learning environment of play. Because play addresses the needs of the whole child, play in the multiage classroom is valued and promoted.

A CHILD LEARNS FROM SOCIAL INTERACTION. The process of constructing knowledge of the world is not done in isolation but rather within a social context. The child is a social being, and through social life she acquires a framework for interpreting experiences *(Bruner & Haste 1987)*.

Children learn from their differences. For example, as children collaborate on a problem, the discussion often results in a "cognitive conflict," or a difference in perspective. As the children discuss their differing viewpoints, they must explain themselves to each other. Growth occurs when they have to resolve their conflicting points of view.

In addition, children construct social skills in the context of social encounters. Working and playing together, they learn to share, help, nurture, negotiate, and cooperate. Social interaction is also important to a child's emotional development. As a child interacts with others, she has the opportunity to see that she is valued and accepted. This in turn contributes to high self-esteem and a healthy self-image.

In the multiage classroom, children learn from each other. A fundamental assumption in multiage classrooms is that children of mixed ages support one another's learning. By contrast, same-age classes, where the expectations are the same, encourage harmful comparison and create unhealthy competition among learners, rather than support and encouragement. Children in these classes are very aware of each other's development. For example, children know who is in the "high" reading group or the "low" reading group. They are compelled to know who has the best grades and who has the worst grades in the class as a way to validate who they are in the system.

In multiage classrooms, where differences are considered natural and normal, children cooperate rather than compete, and cooperation is vitally important if children are going to learn from each other.

The multiage teacher realizes that children learn from each other and uses social interaction in learning centers, cooperative groupings, play groups, and peer tutoring as the means to this end. Among mixed ages, children do not have to compete to meet the same expectations. Instead, they cooperate to help each other through the learning process.

A CHILD LEARNS BY IMITATION. While a child learns primarily as she interacts with the environment and people, she also learns by imitating. Children acquire many behaviors by observing—and imitating—a social model *(Bandura 1977)*. For example, if a child observes her dad reading the paper, she may then imitate him by pretending to read the paper.

The power of modeling is often overlooked in the classroom. A teacher can be an important model to a child. He may model how to read, write, and solve problems, as well as how to nurture, be kind, and show empathy. However, research shows that children are selective in whom they choose to imitate, usually preferring people who are warm and nurturing and/or who appear competent and powerful *(Shaffer 1988)*.

Children also imitate peers. Primary children prefer to imitate same-age classmates or older children. Lougee, et al. *(1977)* found that older models were imitated more than younger ones. Younger children may be more apt to imitate older children with greater social competence *(Mischel & Grusec 1966)*.

Multiage classrooms offer ample opportunities for modeling and imitation. Modeling is a powerful educational tool made more so when done by peers in mixed-age groups.

A CHILD'S AFFECT (EMOTIONS) IMPACTS HER LEARNING. A child's emotions and feelings interact with learning in a significant way. According to Piaget *(1976)*, emotion and cognition cannot be considered separately in the process of learning. Emotions direct us to relate to our environment and set off the learning process. Bearison and Zimiles *(1986, 3)* suggest that "without [emotion] there would be no interest, no need, no motivation; and consequently . . . there would be no intelligence." As we have seen, when children are interested in something, learning has more meaning and is more efficient *(Barbour & Seefeldt 1993)*.

One important feeling a teacher needs to support is the child's sense of autonomy. Autonomy means self-governed rather than other-governed. An autonomous child will develop responsibility for her own learning: directing her own process, making her own choices, and setting her own goals. Lack of autonomy can severely limit a child's desire to know. Autonomy also builds a child's confidence in herself. The self-confident child will pursue a problem; an apprehensive child will not.

Self-esteem also plays a significant role in the child's learning processes. The way a child feels about herself affects her achievements more than any other factor. "Children who feel good about their cognitive and social competencies tend to do better at school and have more friends than their classmates who feel socially or intellectually inadequate" *(Shaffer 1988, 190)*. Success is an important contributor to positive self-esteem. Therefore, facilitating success for every child in the classroom should be a priority.

Bloom *(1981, 108)* suggests that repeated success over a number of years increases the probability of a child developing a positive self-image and high self-esteem, and that "repeated success enables every child to withstand stress and anxiety more effectively, whereas repeated failure has the opposite effect." A child who successfully completes a challenging task gains confidence in herself. Success also motivates the child to continue learning and problem-solving. Fear of failure discourages the learning process.

Bloom goes on to suggest that the "failure of children to succeed with learning tasks should be regarded as a failure of curriculum and instruction rather than failure of the children."

Children also learn better in environments where they feel able to take risks. Risk-friendly environments invite children to explore, experiment, and solve problems without fearing failure.

How Children Learn

A child learns as a whole person.

A child progresses through stages of cognitive development.

A child is an active, not passive learner.

A child constructs her own knowledge of the world.

A child's learning is individual.

A child's learning is a process.

A child learns best when the activity is meaningful and relevant.

A child learns through play.

A child learns from social interaction.

A child learns by imitation.

A child's affect (emotion) impacts her learning.

Developmentally Appropriate Practices

Another key ingredient in a successful multiage classroom is the application of the principles of developmentally appropriate practice based on how children learn.

Unlike the curriculum-centered philosophy that predominates in graded schools today, developmentally appropriate practice suggests that curriculum should depend upon a child's level of mental ability and development in all areas. Multiage teachers must navigate both philosophies of education when implementing a multiage classroom, because they often work in schools that still give tests and grade children. However, multiage teachers should become advocates of developmentally appropriate practice, as the multiage classroom provides the perfect setting for applying its principles.

In a typical developmentally appropriate classroom, instructional strategies and the learning environment are designed to "fit the children" and their development. Children move about freely. They make choices at learning centers and work on projects. The teacher assumes the role of facilitator, planning the environment to support the children's learning. Children's desks are arranged in pods instead of rows. Sometimes learning tables replace desks.

The teacher takes opportunities to work with small groups or individuals based on need. The groupings are flexible. Children engage in active, hands-on learning and learn social skills in cooperative groups or play groups. The teacher supports this development by guiding each child when she needs it. In this classroom, social, emotional, and moral learning are just as important as learning how to read. Large-group instruction is minimal and usually takes place on a rug where the children sit around the teacher or another child. Portfolios document the child's progress by representing authentic work from meaningful projects. Each child's work is valued. The multiage classroom reflects purpose, activity, sharing, caring, and learning.

In the most traditional classroom, children sit quietly at desks doing worksheets and textbook-related activities. The children are encouraged to stay at their desks unless they have permission to get up. The class is quiet, never noisy. Children rarely socialize. The children learn by subject—a time for reading, math, social studies, and science. Most of the instruction is teacher directed and whole group. Small groups are usually established for reading or math rather than flexible groupings. Children are labeled by group—high, medium, low. A child's value is determined by how well she does in school, which is based on group norms such as "grade-level expectations," regardless of where the child is in the learning process. Grades are given for completed assignments and then averaged for the final report card grades. The classroom often reflects boredom, stress, discipline problems, and learning as "time on task."

The following list on pp. 20–22 distinguishes specific appropriate and inappropriate practices. It is based on NAEYC's position statement on *Developmentally Appropriate Practice in Early Childhood Programs Serving Children from Birth Through Age 8 (Bredekamp, ed. 1987)* as well as other established appropriate practices.

> **"The multiage classroom reflects purpose, activity, sharing, caring, and learning."**

From *Creating the Multiage Classroom* published by GoodYear Books. Copyright © 1996 Sandra J. Stone.

APPROPRIATE PRACTICE	INAPPROPRIATE PRACTICE
• Develop knowledge/skills in all areas and help children learn how to learn.	• Focus on discrete skills in primarily academic areas.
• Focus on children's successes.	• Focus on children's deficits.
• Have different expectations for different children.	• Have same expectations for children in same grade.
• Value every child, developing self-esteem and sense of competence.	• Evaluate children by group norms where some succeed and some do not.
• See every child as unique with her own rate of development and allow each child to move at her own pace.	• Expect every child to reach arbitrarily set goals, such as grade-level expectations, irrespective of an individual child's learning rate or previous knowledge.
• Provide integrated learning experiences through learning centers and projects.	• Divide curriculum into separate subjects with a certain amount of time allotted for each subject.
• Provide opportunities for children to learn by doing; skills are learned in meaningful contexts such as projects or centers; involvement is active.	• Engage in predominantly teacher-directed learning activities with whole group; pencil-and-paper activities; children working quietly at desks.
• Plan learning environments for the children.	• Plan lessons and correct papers.
• Support children working and playing individually or in small cooperative groups; promote social learning.	• Expect children to work alone, silently, at desks; discourage children from helping each other.

APPROPRIATE PRACTICE	INAPPROPRIATE PRACTICE
• Provide concrete, real, and relevant learning materials.	• Limit learning materials to primarily textbooks and workbooks.
• Provide opportunities for children to play both indoors and outdoors.	• Limit play opportunities so children have more time for academic tasks.
• Support pro-social behavior by providing opportunities for children to learn through actual social experiences in the classroom.	• Lecture on pro-social skills, but provide little opportunity for social interaction.
• Support a high level of moral development by providing opportunities for children to develop self-control, grow through mistakes, socially problem-solve, make choices, and take responsibility—all within meaningful social contexts and with positive guidance from a supportive teacher.	• Limit children's opportunities for a high level of moral development by imposing strict rules with rewards and punishments; make classroom control more important than children learning how to control themselves.
• Encourage intrinsic motivation: children learn because they see it as valuable and self-fulfilling.	• Reward learning with prizes or other forms of extrinsic motivation.
• Support all children as competent learners; never embarrass a child; value each child.	• Embarrass children, hold them up as examples of incompetent learners; devalue certain children.
• Model empathy, caring, passion for learning, enthusiasm, love for each child.	• Limit role as teacher to the dissemination of information.
• Allow children to achieve success as its own reward.	• Motivate children through giving grades.

APPROPRIATE PRACTICE

- Use authentic assessment such as portfolios.

- Report children's progress through narrative report cards or portfolios.

- Never resort to retention, which can seriously damage a child's self-esteem; support every child's learning; do not use grade-level expectations.

- Encourage parents and families to participate in the learning experiences of the child at school and at home.

- Provide at-home learning experiences that are relevant, enjoyable, and meaningful; realize that children also need time to play and enjoy their families.

INAPPROPRIATE PRACTICE

- Assess children through tests and worksheets.

- Report children's progress through graded report cards.

- Use retention or transition grades as a tool to get children on grade level.

- Limit parent involvement to conferences and open houses.

- Provide hours of homework with worksheets so children can practice discrete skills; academic skills are more important than personal and family recreation.

From *Creating the Multiage Classroom* published by GoodYear Books, Copyright © 1996 Sandra J. Stone.

SUMMARY LIST OF GOALS OF MULTIAGE CLASSROOMS

1. Create a family unit.
2. Establish one teacher for several years.
3. Develop self-directing, autonomous individuals.
4. Develop the whole child.
5. Build on each child's successes.
6. Enjoy learning now.
7. Develop individual potentialities to the maximum.
8. Use flexible groupings.
9. Encourage noncompetitive, cooperative social interaction.
10. Promote cross-age learning.
11. Use the process approach to learning.
12. Use varied instructional strategies within an integrated curriculum.
13. Support each child on his or her own continuum of learning.
14. Facilitate learning.
15. Use developmentally appropriate practices.
16. Choose the curriculum based on interest and need.
17. Use authentic assessment.
18. Evaluate each learner on his or her past achievements and own potential.
19. Respect and value children.
20. Promote professional parent partnerships.

CREATING YOUR OWN MULTIAGE PHILOSOPHY

It is important for you to develop your *own* statement of multiage philosophy grounded in research and appropriate practice. This philosophy will *guide* your practice and will be instrumental in *evaluating* your program. This part of the process is crucial to the development of an effective multiage program for the children and for you.

Use the following planning sheets to help you formulate your multiage philosophy. If you are working with a team of teachers, decide together what your beliefs are. Begin with the fundamental tenets of multiage education discussed in Chapter 1, but be sure to put them into your own words. Strengthen ideas that are particularly important to you. Your philosophy should reflect what you value. Claim ownership. Make the philosophy for your multiage classroom your own.

MULTIAGE PHILOSOPHY
Planning Sheet

1. How do young children develop?
(Consider the whole child: socially, emotionally, aesthetically, physically, intellectually.)

2. What motivates young children to learn?

3. What do young children need to learn?
(Consider the whole child: What would be a good curriculum for young children?)

4. What should be your role as the teacher of young children?

From *Creating the Multiage Classroom* published by GoodYear Books. Copyright © 1996 Sandra J. Stone.

5. What is the role of the environment in the development and education of young children?
(Consider physical, aesthetic, intellectual, social, and emotional environments.)

6. How can you appropriately assess young children's growth?

7. What is the role of the parent or guardian in the school?

8. What can a multiage classroom do to help you provide a good environment for young children to grow and learn?

Let your answers to these questions help you to decide on a philosophy for your multiage classroom. What implications does your philosophy have for your multiage classroom? First, develop general ideas and then select specific examples to demonstrate how your belief philosophy will affect the classroom. Use the planning sheet provided on p. 28 to record the results. Use your philosophy statement to guide your practice and evaluate your program.

MULTIAGE PHILOSOPHY
Planning Sheet

Philosophy	General Implications	Specific Examples

Sample Multiage Classroom Philosophy and Foundation Statements

The following are examples from various programs that have developed personal philosophies for their multiage classes. Each statement contains key elements that are common to good multiage programs.

Philosophy Statements

THE PRIMARY PROGRAM, MINISTRY OF EDUCATION, PROVINCE OF BRITISH COLUMBIA
The Primary Program nurtures the continuing growth of children's knowledge and understanding of themselves and their world. It provides a safe, caring, stimulating environment where learning flourishes.

The Program recognizes that children are individuals and every child is unique. The Program accommodates the broad range of children's needs, their learning rates and styles, and their knowledge, experiences, and interests to facilitate continuous learning. It achieves this through an integrated curriculum incorporating a variety of instructional models, strategies, and resources.

The Program honors the development of the whole child. It reflects an understanding that children learn through active involvement and play and that children represent their knowledge in a variety of ways. It recognizes the social nature of learning and the essential role of language in mediating thought, communication, and learning.

The Program views assessment and evaluation as integral components of the teaching-learning process. Assessment and evaluation support the child's learning; they assist the teacher in making appropriate educational decisions.

The Program values teachers and parents as partners in the child's education. Teachers and parents consult and collaborate to create for the child a climate of respect, success, and joy necessary for lifelong learning.
(Reproduced with permission of British Columbia Ministry of Education, Skills and Training.)

KENTUCKY'S PRIMARY SCHOOL PROGRAM

The Kentucky Primary School Program nurtures the continuing growth of children's knowledge and understanding of themselves and their world. This nurturing environment is characterized by developmentally appropriate practices, multiage, multiability classrooms, continuous progress, authentic assessment, qualitative reporting methods, professional teamwork, and positive parent involvement. We believe a program demonstrating these characteristics provides a safe, caring, stimulating environment where the child grows and learning flourishes.

The Primary Program recognizes that children grow and develop as a whole, not one dimension at a time or at the same rate in each dimension. Therefore, the program reflects an understanding that children learn through active involvement using instructional practices that address the social, emotional, physical, aesthetic, and cognitive needs of children.

The Primary Program provides a classroom climate that is noncompetitive and encourages children to learn from one another as well as from their teachers. Diversity of skills and knowledge is accepted and accommodated by grouping and regrouping children for an effective instructional program.

The Primary Program flows naturally from the preschool program and exhibits developmentally appropriate practices. These practices allow for the broad range of children's needs, learning styles, knowledge, experiences, and interests. Children can experience success while progressing according to their unique learning needs. Continuous learning is enhanced through a coordinated and integrated curriculum incorporating a variety of instructional strategies and resources including play.

The Primary Program views authentic assessment and qualitative reporting methods as integral components of the teaching-learning process. This continuous assessment supports a child's learning and assists the teacher in making appropriate educational decisions.

The Primary Program values teachers and parents as partners in a child's education. Teachers regularly collaborate, plan, consult, and involve parents to create for children a climate of respect, success, and joy necessary for lifelong learning.

"In every task the most important thing is the beginning . . . especially when you deal with anything young and tender."
—Plato, *The Republic.*

(Kentucky's Primary School: The Wonder Years, undated p. 7)

SCALES PROFESSIONAL DEVELOPMENT SCHOOL, TEMPE, ARIZONA

We believe Scales multiage program promotes a noncompetitive, cooperative, caring atmosphere, where children grow at their own developmental rate utilizing learning styles and areas of high interest in an integrated curriculum. Children (ages 5, 6, and 7) have the same teacher for three years. This component helps to ensure success in the early years of school by allowing time for a strong family unit and a nurturing relationship with the teacher. In the multiage program, we strive to celebrate learning through an active, hands-on approach, cooperative groupings, self-direction, peer tutoring, and developmentally appropriate practices. The curriculum promotes an integrated language approach that includes the following:

1. Reading and writing across the curriculum;
2. The teacher as facilitator of learning, providing an environment where each child's potential can be fully developed;
3. Children working at different developmental levels;
4. Flexible, instructional groupings based on needs;
5. Assessment based on the individual child's stage of development; and
6. Opportunities for children to be leaders and mentors.

(Scales Professional Development School Brochure, Tempe, Arizona)

Foundation Statement

After the overarching philosophy statement has been crafted, a foundation, or mission, statement can be distilled from it for publication or presentation. This statement should express in a paragraph the beliefs and direction of your multiage classroom. Note how the Scales Professional Development School philosophy statement has been condensed into the succinct mission statement that follows.

SCALES PROFESSIONAL DEVELOPMENT SCHOOL, TEMPE, ARIZONA

Mission Statement: We believe Scales Multiage Program promotes a noncompetitive, cooperative, caring atmosphere, where children grow at their own developmental rate utilizing learning styles and areas of high interest in an integrated literate environment. *(Scales Professional Development School Multiage Brochure, Tempe Elementary School District #3)*

AVOIDING THE PITFALLS

Multiage teachers may stumble over these common pitfalls if they are new to the process. Making good decisions regarding your multiage program is critical to its success.

TEACHING CURRICULUM, NOT CHILDREN. For a multiage classroom to succeed, it must focus on teaching children and not teaching curriculum. Some teachers try to use a different curriculum for each grade level in the multiage classroom. This never succeeds, and it puts undue stress on the teacher. A multiage classroom is not three separate grade levels in one class; it is one class of multiage learners. The teacher who uses a first-grade reader for the first graders, a second-grade reader for the second graders, a third-grade reader for the third graders, and so on, is doomed to fail. The multiage teacher must see her children as one class of mixed-age learners who are in the process of learning, each one at a different stage. She simply cannot teach three different curricula and survive.

SELECTING AN INAPPROPRIATE MIX OF CHILDREN. Teachers sometimes err in the selection of children for their multiage classrooms. Some interpret the mixing of ages as an opportunity to put all the children who are of lower abilities across several grade levels into one multiage classroom. This is a serious mistake! Such a class becomes emotionally draining.

Other teachers select children based on whom they perceive will be compatible with multiage learning, often the high achievers. Some schools maintain waiting lists for their multiage classrooms. When parents see how beneficial the multiage classroom is for children, they want to enroll their children in these classes. Oftentimes these are parents who have high expectations for their children, and the children tend to be high achievers. Selecting only above-average children for multiage classrooms is also a serious mistake! Such a class provides a closed-ended curriculum instead of an environment that inspires and promotes individual growth.

Another problematic combination is putting together all the top first-grade students and the low second-grade students. This type of aggregation is disastrous for both the children and the teacher. This competition is not productive or healthy for many children.

The multiage classroom works best as a heterogeneous group of learners. For each age level of children, there should be a representation of high-, average-, and low-learners. Balancing the class with a variety of learning rates creates the most beneficial learning and teaching climate. This balance encourages both teacher and children to see each student as an individual on his own continuum of learning. Without the balance, it is tempting for the teacher to group by ability across grade lines, thus counteracting the many benefits of mixed-age learning.

NOT ADEQUATELY ADDRESSING THE NEEDS OF THE OLDER CHILD. Many parents and teachers who are new to multiage classrooms wonder about the older child in the multiage classroom. Will this child be challenged enough in a group of younger children? It is imperative that the multiage teacher keep the older child's needs in focus. Enter each year with the goal of taking each child as far as his potential will allow. An observant teacher will keep her focus on the needs of every child.

One of the great benefits of the multiage classroom is that each child can grow to his potential. In same-age classes, the curriculum dictates how far a child can go. In the multiage classroom, the curriculum is open-ended for all children. Even though the older child may be the age of most third graders, he might be reading on a fifth-grade level or solving problems at a fourth-grade level. There is no ceiling on the progress a child can make in a multiage classroom.

NOT CONSIDERING PARENTS, ADMINISTRATORS, AND COLLEAGUES. A successful multiage will involve parents, colleagues, and administrators right from the beginning. New multiage teachers frequently complain that the parents just don't understand what the teachers are doing.

Parent education at the onset is critical. Parents need to feel comfortable with the process before they can ever become advocates of multiage classrooms.

Meet with parents before implementing a multiage classroom. If presented well, most parents quickly see how beneficial the multiage classroom will be for their children. However, respect a parent's decision not to allow his or her child to participate in multiage classrooms.

Administrators and colleagues also need to understand the philosophy and goals of the multiage classroom. Educating administrators and colleagues will defuse many a future misunderstanding.

Multiage teachers in schools with traditional grades must not be critical of other teachers who do not choose to establish multiage classrooms. Keep in mind that change is slow. Alienating people by criticizing their instructional strategies will never encourage the sharing of ideas. Respect all colleagues.

From Creating the Multiage Classroom published by GoodYear Books. Copyright © 1996 Sandra J. Stone.

DESIGNING THE PHYSICAL ENVIRONMENT

Designing an appropriate physical environment for a multiage classroom is of critical importance. The environment must be conducive to the philosophy and goals of the multiage classroom. It should provide for choice, movement, "hands-on" experiences, noncompetitive and cooperative social interaction, enjoyment, flexible groupings, and autonomous learning.

DESIGN MODELS. The following three design models will help you visualize a quality multiage learning environment. Notice that individual desks are limited or removed from the classroom, allowing space for learning centers, projects, and small-group work. Remember that in the multiage classroom, children spend most of their time in learning centers or small, cooperative groups.

Multiage Environment 1

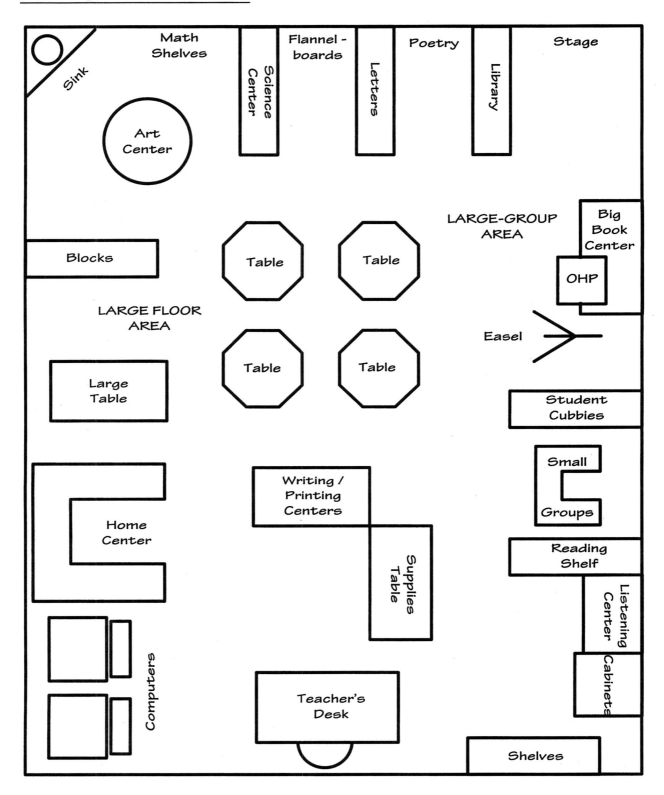

Let's walk through **Multiage Classroom Environment 1** on p. 36 for a better understanding of how the environment "works" for the teacher and children.

Starting at the upper right-hand side, walk around the classroom clockwise past the **Big Book Center,** the **OHP** (overhead projector), **the Easel,** and a **Large-Group Area,** used during large-group instruction. Such instruction takes place as the children sit on a carpeted floor area, allowing for community and intimacy between you and the children as well as among the children. This is preferable to children sitting at desks. Teachers conduct Shared Book, Modeled Writing, Writer's Workshop, Read-Alouds, and various other group experiences in the large-group area. Children also use this area during center time to read Big Books, read stories, or solve math problems on the overhead projector, and read books from the library.

Children may place their individual belongings in the **Student Cubbies.** Since the classroom does not have individual desks, it is important that each child has a private place to put her own things. A child's cubby is accessible at all times to the child. Notes, letters, reminders, and student work are delivered directly to the cubbies.

At the **Small-Group Table,** small, flexible groupings can gather, usually with the teacher while other children are engaged in centers or projects. A horseshoe-shaped table works well. Here, the teacher may work with children on Guided Reading, Literature Circles, math instruction, editing, and conferencing. The **Reading Shelf** contains multiple copies of literature for Guided Reading and Literature Circles.

The **Listening Center** consists of several tape recorders with two earphones for each recorder so that a pair of children may listen to a story from one recorder. The Listening Center accommodates four to six children at a time. Books and tapes hang on the wall in plastic bags or are filed in plastic bags in a container. Children choose their own stories and tapes from the selection provided and read the stories as they listen to them on tape. Sometimes an activity accompanies a book.

Metal **Cabinets** provide storage for the teacher and can be used for magnetic letters. Here, children write messages or practice making words and word families. The **Shelves** are more storage for the teacher, and the **Teacher's Desk** provides a place for the teacher to plan.

Computers function as a center for the children, who monitor their own use of the computers and teach each other how to use them. A printer helps for story writing.

The **Home Center** becomes a sociodramatic play area during center time. It contains a stove, refrigerator, sink, phone, table, and chairs, and includes a rocking chair. Dolls and a doll crib as well as grocery items from the children's homes are displayed. Books about making birthday cakes and patterned books are good additions to the center. Paper and pencils are available.

Children use the **Large Table** for table block constructions and to create projects. On the **Large Floor Area,** children use floor blocks, Lego®, floor puzzles, or they meet in small groups for discussion and planning.

The **Art Center** consists of a round table, sink, supplies on shelves, and an easel for painting. Children complete specific projects or create their own here.

Math Shelves at the **Math Center** contain bins with manipulatives to be used as portable centers on the open table areas. The **Science Center** also contains equipment that may be used for specific science investigations. Children may work at the science center desk, or at the open tables.

At the **Flannelboards,** children retell stories and invent their own. Flannelgraph numbers are also available for play and computation. The **Letters Center** includes letter games, letter puzzles, and letter sand trays to encourage children to play and use letters. A Letters Center is especially useful for younger children.

The **Poetry Center** includes a hanging rack with poetry posters used in class during Shared Poem. At the Poetry Center, children read the familiar poems and then create their own poetry books.

A **Library** is a necessity in the multiage classroom. It should include a good selection of literature that children use during centers as well as for independent reading. Be sure to provide a variety of reading genres as well as reading levels.

The **Stage** area is simply a wall dressed with colorful paper and hanging sheets (to frame the stage). Here, children act out stories and poems and conduct Readers Theater. A puppet theater stands near the stage.

In the center of the classroom are several **Tables.** These tables are used for many purposes. Children might write in their journals here after a large-group Modeled Writing. Small groups can work at the tables, and they are good for portable centers. Overflow from centers in the classroom can be accommodated by the tables.

Children make books and write stories in the **Writing Center.** Book models, felt pens, paper, and dictionaries supply this table.

The **Printing Center** contains wooden printing letters and print pads for children to play with and print messages. They can also make thumbprint creatures and write stories about them.

The **Supplies Table** contains various classroom supplies, open and available for the children to use. Children's portfolios and center folders are also housed on this large table.

This multiage environment allows children to move freely from center to center. Children have opportunities to work in small, cooperative groups; large groups; or simply by themselves. The classroom has large areas, small areas, and even little nooks and crannies. This environment encourages active learning.

Multiage Environments 2 and 3 on pp. 39–40 provide additional ideas for designing your environment. Use them to help develop your own design on the planning sheet provided for you on p. 41.

Multiage Environment 2

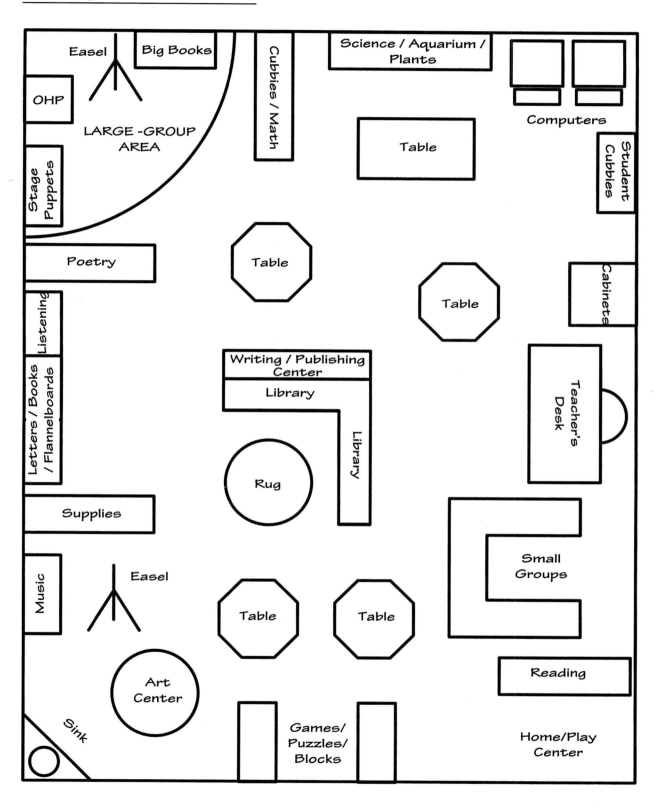

Easel

Big Books

OHP

Cubbies / Math

Science / Aquarium / Plants

Computers

LARGE-GROUP AREA

Stage Puppets

Table

Student Cubbies

Poetry

Table

Table

Cabinets

Listening

Writing / Publishing Center

Library

Letters / Books / Flannelboards

Library

Teacher's Desk

Rug

Supplies

Music

Easel

Table

Table

Small Groups

Art Center

Reading

Sink

Games/ Puzzles/ Blocks

Home/Play Center

Multiage Environment 3

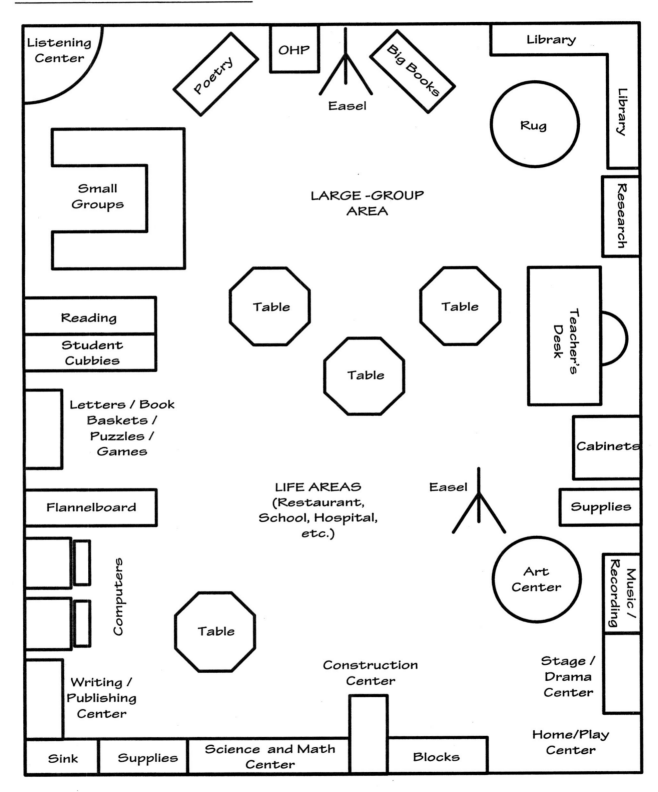

Your Multiage Environment Planning Sheet

ALL ABOUT CREATING LEARNING CENTERS

A learning center can be defined as a place where a child or a small group of children go to engage actively in some activity such as retelling a story, reading a Big Book, solving a problem, investigating a topic, listening to a story, or even painting a picture.

Learning centers provide children with opportunities for hands-on learning, cooperative learning, social interaction, real-life problem solving, autonomous learning, and most of the other goals of a multiage classroom. The teacher facilitates learning during large- and small-group learning times, but at the centers, children practice their skills, invent, create, and explore. Using the analogy of swimming, the teacher works with each child to move her along in her "swimming" skills within the context of real and meaningful experiences, "the water." At the centers, children explore these skills without the teacher, playing in the "water" and practicing their skills. Centers present opportunities for personal growth at one's own pace.

From *Creating the Multiage Classroom* published by GoodYear Books. Copyright © 1996 Sandra J. Stone.

Characteristics of Centers

CHOICE. Choosing the centers at which they wish to work is important because it allows the children the opportunity to make decisions for themselves. Some teachers use a chart indicating where each child goes for the day. Each day the names on the chart rotate, making sure children go to the appropriate centers. However, in this model, decisions are made for the children. Managing the chart also takes time from the learning process. In the multiage classroom it is important to *trust* children to make their own decisions. If one wants children to learn how to makes choices, think for themselves, and assume responsibility for their own learning, then one must provide those opportunities. Making center decisions for children denies them the opportunity to direct their own learning. Choice is self-motivating, and children enjoy their learning experiences.

FLEXIBILITY OF TIME. Flexibility of time spent at centers is a companion to choice. Children need to decide how long they stay at each center. Some teachers ring a bell every 10 to 15 minutes to move children from center to center. But this diminishes the children's opportunities to choose and make decisions, and it interferes with the learning processes. One child engaged in writing a story may want to stay at the Writing Center for 30 minutes. Another child who is just beginning to write may stay 10 minutes. Someone may be in the middle of an important discovery or an exciting story when the bell rings. Children need time to fulfill their learning needs.

SELF-DIRECTED LEARNING. Centers are not teacher-directed activities; instead they provide children with opportunities for self-directed and self-motivated learning and to become responsible for their own learning. After making initial choices as to which center or centers to engage, a child must also decide what to write, what to listen to, what book to read, and how to solve a problem. Learning becomes a personal adventure for each child rather than a mandate from the teacher. Self-directed learning forms the foundation for lifelong learning.

OPEN-ENDED ACTIVITIES. Open-ended activities are important in a multiage classroom because of the variety of learning rates. Such activities allow each child to engage *successfully* in an activity at her own skill level. For example, at the Writing Center, the children are making monster books. After creating their monster covers, each child writes a monster story. This open-ended activity allows the older child to write a story with a beginning, middle, and end. She writes in complete sentences and paragraphs. The younger child engages the same center, but her story comprises a simple sentence and illustration. Her sentence reflects her stage of writing as she begins to write letters for sounds and uses one letter for the first consonant sound in a word. Both children complete the same open-ended activity at their current skill levels. In a narrowly defined center, not all children can engage in the activity successfully.

HANDS-ON ACTIVITIES.

Learning centers should encourage active learning and not function as work stations filled with worksheets. Each center should provide opportunities for children to construct their own knowledge by doing, exploring, discovering, inventing, playing, or practicing their skills. Remember that skills are not only academic. Children are also learning the social skill of how to take turns, the emotional satisfaction of completing a painting, and small-motor coordination as they manipulate puzzle pieces.

Hands-on learning also engages children to think for themselves. At the Science Center, children must reason why some objects float and some sink as they actually place the objects in the water. At the Block Center, children must think how to organize the blocks so they can accomplish their goal. At the Art Center, children must decide the best way to attach wood pieces into a sculpture that stays together.

INTEGRATED THEMATIC CENTERS.

Teachers often integrate learning centers into the current thematic unit. For example, if the theme is Bears, the centers reflect this theme. At the Writing Center, the children write fictional stories about bears based on the Shared Book reading of *Goldilocks and the Three Bears*. At the Science Center, the children examine animal tracks and place them into categories. At the Art Center, the children make bear tracks to decorate the border of a class Big Book they have written.

GENERIC CENTERS.

It is advantageous for the teacher to have generic learning centers such as a Listening Center, Writing Center, Science Center, and so forth. Generic centers are easier for the teacher to manage. The centers themselves don't change every few weeks, only the content of the centers. For example, a Writing Center is generic. Children always write at the Writing Center. However, if the theme is Bears, the children write about bears. When the theme changes to Monsters, the children write about monsters. Some teachers try to plan novel centers for each thematic unit. Novel centers are narrowly based on the theme. As the theme changes, so do the centers. Novel centers require the teacher to create new activities for each theme rather than create new experiences within each generic center (i.e., writing, listening, play). Creating novel centers is very difficult for the teacher. You may plan a few novel centers, but all in all, generic centers provide for active learning and also meet the time management constraints of the teacher.

PLANNING CENTERS WITH CHILDREN. Planning centers with your children is also important. Ownership of the classroom motivates learning. Engage your children in planning thematic studies and accompanying centers. Decide together what options may be available at learning centers. Of course, you will have ideas you wish to explore. Your ownership role is important too. But keep in mind that children have wonderful ideas and by implementing them, their enthusiasm for the centers will increase enormously.

Children should also feel comfortable adding centers of their own creation. They may bring things from home or take a trip to the library to acquire learning materials for the centers. Planning together increases everyone's ownership of the learning processes.

ORGANIZED CENTERS. All learning centers should be organized and purposeful. Children should know what to expect at each learning center and know which ones are available, or open, for center time. During large-group community time, the teacher can give instructions for learning center activities.

CENTER CARE. During the first few weeks of class, children should learn how to take care of the centers. Caring for centers increases the children's opportunities for responsibility and ownership. For example, children should know how to rewind tapes at the Listening Center and how to put away the materials so the center is ready for the next person to use. If the teacher cleans up the centers every day, he denies the children this important responsibility.

VISUAL ACCESS. Centers should always be placed so the teacher can see the children at the centers. The teacher should know at all times what children are doing. This is important for safety as well as management.

CENTER SPACE. Centers should vary in the amount of space they take up. Some centers should be large enough to allow small groups of children maximum room to explore and create. Other centers might be sized for just one or two children at most. Place the centers wisely. The Block Center does not work well near a quiet Reading Center, but next to the Home Center, it may encourage creative interactions.

As you create your learning centers, be flexible and observant. Consider the goals of the multiage classroom. See what is working well and what is not. Don't be afraid to make changes and to experiment.

Ideas for Classroom Centers

The following is a listing of generic centers for multiage classrooms. Many of the centers include literacy elements that create a literate environment.

From *Creating the Multiage Classroom* published by GoodYear Books. Copyright © 1996 Sandra J. Stone.

BIG BOOK CENTER. This center contains all the Big Books used for Shared Reading. The Big Book Center also contains overheads of poems or short literature pieces, which are used with older children during Shared Reading. Class-made Big Books are also kept at the Big Book Center. At this center, two or three children choose a Big Book or Shared Reading piece and read it together. Younger children should use a pointer to help everyone follow along at the same speed.

OVERHEAD PROJECTOR CENTER. This center contains the overhead projector and materials for individuals or small groups to read or use. Children may read overhead stories created in small reading groups, or they may manipulate shapes or figures to solve math problems.

The sun came out.

LISTENING CENTER. This center contains books and tapes for individual reading enjoyment. Here, children choose the books they want to read or listen to. Providing several headphones for each recorder maximizes the number of children who can use the center at once. Place books and their accompanying tapes in plastic bags and hang them on the wall or keep them in a box. Books on tape could be coordinated with the current thematic unit, while representing a variety of reading levels. Books can be recorded for the Listening Center by the teacher and/or parents. If parents record, send a book and tape recorder home with a child. As the parent reads the book into the recorder, the child uses a bell or noisemaker to indicate when to turn the pages. This involves children *and* parents in reading and the ownership of centers.

Occasionally, the teacher may wish to provide an open-ended activity for the children to complete at the Listening Center. Perhaps they write or illustrate their favorite part of a story, write a new dialogue for several characters, or focus on story elements such as the setting or main characters.

LIBRARY CENTER. The Library Center should offer literature at various reading levels. If possible, display the books so the children can see the covers. Furnish the Library Center to invite children to sit and read books. A rocker and beanbag chairs are good additions, along with a floor rug where children can sit and read. Rotate the selection of books on a regular basis to add interest. Collect books from the school, community, or personal libraries. Invite children to bring favorite books from home as well.

BOOK BASKETS CENTER. Book baskets contain familiar books used during Guided Reading or Literature Circles. Invite children to read the books over and over again and to share them with others.

LETTERS CENTER. This center benefits younger children in the multiage classroom who need exposure to letters to learn to recognize them. The Letter Center might include letter puzzles, magnetic letters on trays, sandpaper letters, alphabet books, and flannelboards and letters. Place a flip book of letters in a plastic shoe box filled with a small amount of sand so that children can trace letters from the book in the sand. Provide a spray bottle of water so children may occasionally trace letters in wet sand.

POETRY CENTER. This center contains the poster poems, a selection of poems written on poster boards, which are used in Shared Poem (part of Shared Reading). Poster poems may be placed in a box or hung from a chart holder so that pairs of children can select favorite poems to read together. Each child keeps an individual poetry book at the Poetry Center. Every week copies of the Shared Poem are added to the books for the children to read and illustrate. The children take their poetry books home periodically so they can read them to family members. At the end of the year, each child has a wonderful collection of poems she and the class have enjoyed together.

READ THE WALLS CENTER. The walls, in a literate environment, display books children have made, Big Books the class has created, language experience charts, posters, projects, and creative writing. Cover chalkboards with butcher paper to create display areas. During center time, several children walk around the room and "read the walls." Some teachers provide fun sunglasses (with the glass removed) and colorful pointers to enliven the adventure. Reading the walls gives younger children the opportunity to practice reading familiar material.

WRITING CENTER. The Writing Center should be an enjoyable place to create books; make sure it is supplied with pencils, felt pens, paper, and dictionaries. In addition to writing stories, children can actually create the book covers and design unique books. If you are studying Trees, children might design a tree book from a pattern or their imagination before actually writing the story. During a study of worms, children could cut out worm shapes from construction paper to be used as the cover and pages of their books. Story starters are great for a Writing Center. Story starters give children a topic to begin writing about. Pictures from magazines make great story starters.

DRAMA CENTER. A stage and a puppet theater define the Drama Center. Hang large sheets of colorful butcher paper on a wall and then drape decorative sheets on either side to define the stage area. Provide children with simple props or encourage them to bring props from home so that they can act out familiar stories and poems or create their own plays. Acting out stories gives children the opportunity to employ more elaborate vocabulary, gain a sense of story, negotiate roles, and engage planning skills. The puppet stage also gives children the opportunity to act out stories.

FLANNELBOARD CENTER. Keep a collection of flannel figures from familiar stories at the Flannelboard Center. Several children at a time can use the flannel figures to retell the stories. Also furnish generic flannel figures and encourage children to create their own stories. The Flannelboard Center should also include flannel letters, numbers, and shapes with which children can make words, solve problems, or invent designs. Keep portable flannelboards on hand so that more children can use this center together. Portable flannelboards may be made from cardboard covered with flannel.

MUSIC CENTER. On record and tape players in the Music Center, children may enjoy favorite recordings. To encourage literacy, display words from songs on posterboard.

ART CENTER. The Art Center contains various art supplies and smocks as well as an easel or two. Here children paint, sculpt with clay, and create with construction paper. They should know how to access the supplies, how to use them, and how to put them away.

Occasionally, ask children to write stories or descriptions of their artwork. Turn the walls of the Art Center into a gallery of children's creative work.

CONSTRUCTION CENTER. The Construction Center is furnished with floor blocks, table blocks, Lego®, and Lincoln Logs®. It should be big enough for children to build and create with these materials. The Construction Center gives children the opportunity to explore dimensional materials and to learn to get along with others as they create together and share.

MATH CENTER. The Math Center offers a variety of manipulatives including geoboards, tangrams, and Unifix® cubes. It is also a good place to gear activities to the class theme. If the class is studying Trees, for example, children might measure leaves at the Math Center.

SOCIAL STUDIES CENTER. This center contains materials related to the class theme. At the Social Studies Center, children may create a map for "monster land," research transportation in pioneer days, or graph votes in a class election.

SCIENCE CENTER. Materials at the Science Center usually include items that are specific to the class theme. If the class is studying Marine Life, the Science Center might provide a number of shells for classification. A thermometer and barometer might complement a study of environments. Choose activities at the Science Center to encourage investigation and exploration.

HOME CENTER. The Home Center includes items such as a stove, sink, cupboards, kitchen supplies, table, and chairs. This is a good place to encourage literacy by stocking it with books that have to do with cooking or the home, note cards, paper and pencils, envelopes, and so on. When literacy materials are made available in a center, children are more likely to engage in literacy-related play.

Remember that children learn through play. In the Home Center, children play, interact socially, invent stories, read to each other, use language, and enjoy themselves and as such, the Home Center is a valuable addition to a primary classroom. The goals of the multiage classroom include social and emotional development in addition to intellectual development. Play in the Home Center addresses all three of these areas.

PLAY CENTERS. Invent Play Centers to go along with units of study. If you are studying Dinosaurs, create a dinosaur land. If you are studying Space, design a spaceship. Giving children the opportunity to play within the thematic unit increases their opportunities to use related vocabulary, solve pertinent problems, and create associated stories, all in a meaningful context.

WORK CENTERS. Work Centers take occupations as their theme and give children the chance to play in a variety of settings: grocery store, office, school, doctor's office, restaurant, gas station, airport, and so on.

PUZZLES AND GAMES CENTER. This center includes games such as Boggle®, Scrabble®, Lotto® card games, puzzles, and the like. Choose games that encourage word usage or problem solving and promote the use of higher-order thinking skills. Children also learn social skills while playing games.

RECORDING CENTER. In the Recording Center, children record stories they can read, original story creations, or group chants of stories. Each child should have her own recording tape. These tapes may become part of the Listening Center and are also included in portfolios.

COMPUTER CENTER. A variety of software should be available at the Computer Center for reading, computing, or solving mysteries. With the addition of a printer, the Computer Center becomes an excellent companion to the Writing Center as children write and edit their work on the computer and then publish their own stories.

RESEARCH CENTER. The Research Center offers resources to help children seek out information. Encyclopedias, nonfiction books, maps, and a globe, all make good components of this center. Usually these materials relate to the class's current unit of study.

CURRENT EVENTS CENTER. Stock this center with newspapers and magazines that children may read or use for research. Children can report on what they learn at the Current Events Center to the large group at a later time.

MAILBOX CENTER. Children use this center to write notes or letters to each other or to the teacher. Its design may vary. Try marking out a large area on the wall where children post notes with adhesive putty or sticky notes. The center contains a writing desk, paper, and pencils. Teachers sometimes create individual mailboxes from coffee cans or milk cartons to place at this center.

NOVEL CENTERS. Centers can be created at any time to fit what is going on in the classroom. If the children discover a number of ladybugs outside, they may choose to make a ladybug center. Maybe you are reading books about food and decide to make a "cooking" center where children read simple recipes to make noncooked edible treats.

Plan Your Own Centers

Two center planning sheets are provided on pp. 55–56, one listing generic centers and the other blank for your own ideas. Another sheet is provided on p. 57 for planning either centers or projects in an integrated curriculum. Fill in a planning sheet with your ideas and the materials needed. For example, under Listening Center, list the books and activities the children will engage in. Usually your center planning will reflect your theme. Keep in mind that not all centers have to be open at the same time.

From *Creating the Multiage Classroom* published by GoodYear Books. Copyright © 1996 Sandra J. Stone.

Generic Centers

Big Book	Listening
Library	OHP
Poetry	Writing
Drama	Play
Science	Social Studies
Art	Math
Research	Home
Flannelboard	Computer

Your Ideas for Centers

_____	_____
_____	_____
_____	_____
_____	_____
_____	_____
_____	_____
_____	_____
_____	_____

Centers/Projects in an Integrated Curriculum Planning Sheet

Managing Centers

Remember that centers provide children with opportunities for self-directed, autonomous learning. Children should be able to choose the centers they visit and determine the length of time they stay. Most children will make wise choices; some will need positive monitoring. While most of the children are at centers, the teacher will be working with a small group of children (i.e., Guided Reading). The children must be responsible for their own learning at the centers, so the teacher is free to concentrate on the needs of children in cooperative learning groups.

There are several ways to manage centers that involve children in the process.

CENTER POCKET FOLDER. Give each child a pocket folder. Stapled to the top of the pocket folder is a center record-keeping chart with pictures to illustrate each center.

PICTURE CHART. The picture chart is a visual way for young children to choose to keep track of their center activities. As a child completes a center, she colors in the appropriate image and places her work in the folder. The chart may be coordinated with the thematic unit. For example, if a child goes to the Writing Center, she will color in the writing picture and then place her story in the folder. If a child has painted a picture at the Art Center, she will color in the picture on the chart and include a note as to what she did at the Art Center. If you are studying monsters, use a monster graphic. The picture chart is attached to the pocket folder. A monster picture chart is provided on p. 60.

If pocket folders are color coordinated, children can easily retrieve them from a box or file on their way to centers. When center time concludes, they return the folders to the box or file. This way, the management of the centers is largely under the control of the children. The teacher may look quickly at each chart to see how well each child is doing in negotiating the centers and determine who may need additional monitoring or help. A chart is used for the length of the thematic unit, usually two or three weeks. Children may repeat centers during this time and circle previously colored images.

DAILY PLAN CHART. The Daily Plan Chart is another way for children to choose and keep track of their center activities. On a list of available centers, each child keeps track of her daily participation. The planning chart may also be attached to a pocket folder. A blank daily planning chart is provided for you on p. 61.

Centers

Week of: **September 30**   Theme: **Monsters**

Name _____

Daily Plan Chart

Name _____   Theme _____

Centers	Mon.	Tues.	Wed.	Thurs.	Fri.

The Project Approach—An Alternative to Centers

Within the multiage classroom, children will not only work at centers, they can also undertake projects that allow them to work in small groups toward a common goal. A project is "an extended study of a topic usually undertaken by a group of children, sometimes by a whole class, and occasionally by an individual child." *(Katz & Chard 1989, 209)*

Projects integrate the learning processes and curriculum, providing opportunities for mixed-age interaction and an in-depth understanding of the topic. The teacher and children decide on and plan the project together. However, the teacher acts more as facilitator or consultant; projects should be directed by the personal interests of the children. They might take a few days or several weeks, depending on the scope.

For example, a project might be based on the children's observation of worms on a rainy day. The children will explore worms—how they eat, where they live, what value they are to people. Perhaps they'll create a worm terrarium. First, the children ask questions, plan what and how they will investigate, find answers to their questions, and finally plan how they will report or display their findings.

The worm project can involve children in reading about worms, writing down information, drawing pictures and charts, graphing information, designing a terrarium, building the terrarium, creating a healthy environment for the worms, caring for the worms, dissecting worms, analyzing worm compost, advertising worms to sell, creating a price list, etc.

The project approach offers an alternative to centers. Children will work in small groups to accomplish different components of the project. During project time, the teacher needs to be more available to facilitate than she does with centers.

INSTRUCTIONAL STRATEGIES

Instructional strategies in the multiage classroom are varied, although most are geared to small groups of children. Large-group instructional strategies will be addressed in Chapter 5. Within the multiage environment, most of the instructional strategies are for small groups of children working at centers and projects. Three effective small-group strategies are

1) Discovery Learning
2) Cooperative Learning
3) Questioning

DISCOVERY LEARNING. The opposite of expository learning, discovery learning takes place in a planned environment and involves active learning. In expository learning or lecture, the teacher presents or gives information to the children. In discovery learning, the children discover relationships, concepts, and principles for themselves and through projects. This is a more meaningful process for children because they are constructing their own knowledge. The teacher can promote discovery learning by planning a classroom environment where children examine purposefully chosen materials at centers and through projects. After examining materials, children will uncover relationships, find solutions, and make generalizations. Of course, not all children's discoveries are planned, nor should they be. Discovery learning should be open-ended as well as purposeful. Children should have the freedom to go beyond the goals or objectives of the teacher.

COOPERATIVE LEARNING. In the primary multiage classroom, cooperative learning occurs primarily at centers, in projects, and in small learning groups. Cooperative learning, a small-group learning strategy, is an *informal* process for young children in the primary multiage class. Cooperative learning strategies for intermediate grades use competition between groups, rewards, and grading, but this is not appropriate for primary children. Motivation for cooperative learning is intrinsic rather than extrinsic.

Children benefit from informal cooperative learning groups because they have the opportunity to learn from each other. Older children scaffold learning for younger children, which supports younger children in accomplishing tasks beyond their current capabilities. Children of mixed ages also engage in "cognitive conflict." A child who sees something from one perspective asks another child to justify her perspective, resulting in cognitive growth for both children.

QUESTIONING. Questioning is an important instructional strategy for the teacher to use as a facilitator in centers, with projects, and in small-group instruction. Questioning, modeled by the teacher, also continues in self-directed learning.

Teachers can use two kinds of questioning strategies. The first is called *convergent questioning*, which calls for only one correct answer. Questions of this type ask children to recall specific information. The second type of questioning is called *divergent questioning*, which can elicit many answers.

Divergent questioning is preferred over convergent questioning because it encourages children to use higher-order thinking skills such as analysis, synthesis, evaluation, comprehension, generalization, inference, and application. The following simple questions can be used to direct children's learning in centers, project work, or small-group instruction.

1. What did you notice? (Observing)
2. How are these alike/different? (Finding patterns)
3. Can you give an example? (Generalizing)
4. Why is this an example? Why does this relationship exist? (Inferring)
5. What would happen if? (Hypothesizing)

(Jacobsen, Eggen, & Kauchak 1989, 188)

Questioning in the multiage classroom should promote children's critical thinking skills. Critical thinking is the *process* of thinking through. Questions should move children to observe, conclude, generalize, evaluate, and so forth.

From Creating the Multiage Classroom published by GoodYear Books. Copyright © 1996 Sandra J. Stone.

Grouping in the Multiage Classroom

Grouping in multiage classrooms takes many forms: individual, small and large, formal and informal. Groupings are always varied and flexible.

LARGE GROUP. In the multiage classroom, you are a "family" of learners. Don't minimize the importance of building this "community." Use large-group times for sharing and enjoying each other as well as learning together.

SMALL GROUP. Small groups may be informal or formal cooperative learning groups. Sometimes the groups are teacher-selected and sometimes student-selected. Small groups are not the traditionally formed static groups of high, medium, and low students, who are grouped based only on ability. While some ability grouping may occur, the group is called together based on need and disbanded when the need is met.

INDIVIDUAL. Children should have the opportunity to work alone at a center or on a project. The teacher may also work one-to-one with a child.

Let's work together on this project.

Informal Groupings.
Children may be grouped informally for cooperative learning. The following are some ways to group children:

Centers. At centers, groupings are usually self-selected and flexible. Two or more children informally engage in a center together. The learning is open-ended.

Projects. Grouping for projects may be student-selected or teacher-selected. Children may choose to work together on a topic of interest to all in the group. The children pursue a common goal or accomplish a specific task. In project work, the cooperative group stays together until completion of the project.

Problem-solving group. This group may be formed by students or teacher to solve a particular problem. Perhaps it is a predetermined math problem, or it could be one that has developed from a class discussion.

Needs group. The teacher usually selects this cooperative group based on the needs of certain students in the class. A needs group works together on a particular concept or skill.

Interest group. Students can form this type of cooperative group, which convenes based on common interest. For example, a group of four children might decide to do a Literature Circle on a favorite book, or research a topic they all enjoy.

Learning-style group. The children in this teacher-selected cooperative grouping share common learning styles.

Friends group. To make up this group, children select other children with whom they enjoy working. Friends groups may occur informally at centers or formally in project work.

Peer tutor. Peer tutoring involves teacher-selected or student-selected pairs of children, one of whom assumes the role of tutor to help the other child with individualized instruction.

Learning pairs. Children work together in learning pairs to reach a common goal. Learning pairs, or buddies, may read a book together, share opinions, or discuss an idea. Teacher or students may select learning pairs.

Support group. Members of this cooperative group come together to support and help each other. Children in a support group might read each other's portfolios and offer supportive comments, or help each other edit or solve a social problem.

From *Creating the Multiage Classroom* published by GoodYear Books. Copyright © 1996 Sandra J. Stone.

Formal Groupings.

Formal cooperative groups usually occur during project work. A formal group establishes roles and conducts project and group social skills evaluations. In determining roles, the group must decide who will be responsible for what. Roles may include the *coach* (the person who makes sure everyone participates), the *organizer* (the person who makes sure all the supplies are available), the *facilitator* (the person who reads directions and makes assignments), and the *evaluator* (the person who conducts the evaluations). The needs of the group may require other roles.

A formal group establishes a goal (what the members would like to accomplish) and social goals (what social skills they would like to practice). At the end of the project, the group or individual members evaluate the project:

1. What did we (I) do well?
2. What would we (I) do the same/differently next time?
3. What did we (I) learn?

Social skills are also evaluated:

1. Did we (I) help each other? How? (get materials, show how to do something)
2. Did we (I) encourage each other? How? (praise, listen, respect opinions)
3. Did we (I) cooperate? (take turns, share, work together)

Role of the teacher.

In both formal and informal cooperative learning groups, the role of the teacher is as facilitator of learning and manager of the learning environment.

A Word About Managing the Classroom

Developing Autonomous Learners

The teacher who assumes the role of "always in charge" leaves little room for children to achieve the multiage goal of becoming self-directing, autonomous individuals. If allowed, children learn to be dependent on the teacher for nearly everything. This is not only a problem for the children, it puts a strain on the teacher and on classroom management. The multiage teacher, on the other hand, is always looking for ways to "turn over" the classroom to the children, to facilitate them "taking responsibility" for their learning exploration. Consider the following:

Teacher in Charge	vs.	Responsible Children
Cleans up centers		Clean up centers
Delivers notes for home		Deliver notes for home
Settles all disputes		Settle own disputes
Makes all learning choices for children		Make own learning choices
Evaluates all work		Evaluate own work

In the multiage classroom, where the children are allowed to be responsible for the class and their learning, children quickly learn to think for themselves and make decisions, without always going to the teacher to ask, "What do I do next? May I do this? May I get paper from the shelf?" Obviously, the teacher must assume some roles, particularly where the safety of the children is concerned. But many roles can be released to the children, and class management becomes intrinsic; the classroom runs itself. Consequently, the teacher has more time to work with the children and their educational needs.

Involving the children in the management of the classroom demands *trust* and *risk-taking*. The teacher must trust children to make decisions and give them the freedom to take risks that may result in occasional failure. In return, children who feel trusted and free to take risks become competent, responsible individuals.

Teachers in active, child-managed classrooms notice that discipline problems are minimal. The children keep busy making choices, solving problems, helping each other, exploring, and inventing.

Creating the Pro-social Classroom

Positive management is much easier in a pro-social classroom. In a pro-social classroom, children and teacher nurture, support, and encourage one another. Pro-social behaviors "can best be enhanced in a setting that emphasizes and exemplifies commitment to shared values, mutual respect and concern, and a sense of community" (Solomon, Watson, Delucchi, Schaps & Battistich 1988, 530). Pro-social behaviors thrive in the multiage community. Consider the following characteristics of the pro-social classroom.

RELATIONSHIP WITH TEACHER. According to Solomon, et al., *(1988, 528)* children are more likely to "acquire positive attitudes and behaviors when they experience warm and affectionate relationships with teachers." Teachers who are warm and accepting toward their students, rather than "businesslike," are more likely to foster classrooms with positive and friendly intergroup interaction *(Solomon 1979).* The first step in creating the pro-social classroom is to establish an atmosphere of love, warmth, caring, trust, humor, and respect for each child. When a teacher respects and supports a child, he will receive tenfold that respect and support in return.

TEACHER AS MODEL. Teachers who model pro-social behaviors add a powerful component to the pro-social classroom. The teacher should model how to be empathetic, helpful, kind, cooperative, encouraging, and consoling. Children will imitate these behaviors.

CHILDREN AS MODELS. The cooperative atmosphere of the multiage classroom tends to promote pro-social behavior. Mixed ages allow older children the opportunity to mentor and model for younger children. Older children take the responsibility to "look after" the younger ones—consoling younger children who have been hurt; assisting younger children who need help doing something; interceding in play groups to help children take turns. As children mature in the multiage class, each one has the opportunity to be the "older" child, to be the model and the mentor.

OPPORTUNITY FOR INTERACTION. Children with the opportunity to interact with each other socially learn how to get along. Cooperative learning activities enhance children's understanding and valuing of fairness, responsibility, helpfulness, and mutual respect.

DEVELOPMENTAL DISCIPLINE. In the multiage classroom, teachers understand that children are not only developing their literacy and math skills, but also their social skills.

69

With this understanding, teachers take time to teach and facilitate social learning and responsibility. This is critical for children in the primary years. Instead of removing a child to a "time out," the teacher takes the time to help the child learn how to show empathy and make restitution, facilitating the child's development of self-control and interpersonal skills.

Teachers hoping to create a pro-social atmosphere should not resort to assertive discipline, as reward and punishment do not encourage higher moral development and self-control. In the pro-social classroom, teachers should provide a positive environment that cultivates a child's inner desire to be accepted and valued.

BE POSITIVE. A positive teacher will see pro-social behaviors in the classroom. If a teacher focuses on children's negative behaviors, they quickly return with more negative behavior. If the teacher focuses on positive attributes, the children quickly become positive people. Focusing on the positive must be a conscious effort that is diligently pursued. Children soak up positive support; everyone likes to be shown he or she is valued. Positive comments encourage children to continue helpful behaviors and to see themselves as cooperative individuals. Negative comments accomplish the opposite. Place the focus not on doing things to please the teacher, but rather on attributes the child is demonstrating. For example, a teacher should say, "*You* are so helpful," instead of, "*I like* how you help."

The multiage teacher communicates with parents regarding their children's pro-social behaviors. Frequent cards home can inform parents of a child's kind word, good deed, or wise choice.

PRO-SOCIAL ACTIVITIES. The opportunities that a multiage classroom provides for children to take responsibility and help others are the "hands-on" learning experiences needed to develop pro-social behaviors. Pro-social activities are just as important as academic activities.

Managing a multiage classroom can be extremely enjoyable. Develop a partnership with your children by allowing them the freedom to be responsible, self-directed learners. Create a pro-social environment. You will find that you have time to enjoy the adventure and be the teacher who can support each child in the classroom in a positive way.

From *Creating the Multiage Classroom* published by GoodYear Books. Copyright © 1996 Sandra J. Stone.

CHAPTER FOUR

PLANNING THE MULTIAGE CURRICULUM

GOALS OF THE CURRICULUM

Educating the Whole Child

The first priority of the multiage curriculum is to educate the whole child. While the traditional curriculum focuses primarily on academics—reading, writing, math, science, and social studies—in the multiage classroom, teaching academics is just one of the educational goals. Multiage teachers also concentrate on social, emotional, and physical goals because they know that children are more than just minds; they are whole beings. Children integrate all these areas in their approach to learning.

Focus Goals

The multiage classroom focuses on teaching the children and not on teaching an arbitrary curriculum. In the past, the teacher planned lessons based on pre-established goals for a grade level that were usually prescribed by a textbook. This approach assumes that all children are at the same place at the same time and does not accommodate their different learning rates and styles. The goals of this curriculum are primarily academic.

In the multiage classroom, the teacher establishes broad focus goals that take into account the whole child. Each goal represents a developmental process of learning: each child learns to read, write, solve problems, think critically, socialize, and grow emotionally and physically on his own continuum.

Let's take a look at the focus goals and examine how a multiage teacher addresses them in her classroom.

FOCUS GOAL: READ. Children in the multiage classroom are in the process of becoming readers. The multiage teacher prepares the environment so that all the children in the class can "learn to read by reading." To do so, the teacher creates a literate environment through centers, Shared Reading, Modeled Writing, Independent Reading, language experience, and reading in the content areas. Now, all the children can engage in the act of reading even though they will be at different levels of development. For example, during [large group] Shared Reading of the Big Book *The Carrot Seed*, a younger child will "read" the story by memorizing the text and using the picture clues. An older child will actually read the text. All the children can successfully engage the text whatever their developmental level.

At centers, all the children can be involved in the open-ended reading activities. From a variety of books and tapes at the Listening Center, for instance, each child makes his own choice about what he wishes to "read" and enjoy. At the Big Book Center, children choose books to read together from a variety of Big Books at different reading levels. Familiarity with the texts from Shared Reading enables every child to "read" or "tell" the story.

During Guided Reading or Literature Circles, the teacher selects a group of children at similar developmental levels to work on a particular text. Such small-group work enables the teacher to teach skills based on individual reading needs. She can then assess each child's reading needs and make appropriate instructional decisions based on those assessments.

During Independent Reading or at the Library Center, children again choose books that are appropriate for their abilities. Children will self-select those books with which they know they will be successful. The teacher informally monitors these selections. Detailed strategies for facilitating reading will be addressed in Chapter 5.

FOCUS GOAL: WRITE.
Children in the multiage classroom are in the process of becoming writers at different levels of development. The classroom environment enables them to "learn to write by writing." At the Writing Center, all children can engage in open-ended writing activities. Perhaps the younger children write stories about monsters after hearing *Where the Wild Things Are* by Maurice Sendak. They may use beginning sounds and no spacing: *MMZS.* (My monster is scary.) Another child may write: *I LK GD MNSRS.* (I like good monsters.) An older child may write a descriptive paragraph: *One day a monstr came to my hous. He crawled under my bed and draged a toy anmal with him.* Each child engages the writing process at his developmental level.

At the Science Center, the children write down their discoveries. Each child records at his developmental level what he discovers. All the children can participate in this open-ended writing activity.

During Modeled Writing, the teacher demonstrates broad-based skills for all the children. The children write in their learning journals, again at their own levels. The teacher frequently conferences with each child, helping him to the next stage of development.

Just like the focus goal of reading, the teacher provides an environment and activities that engage children in meaningful writing. The teacher works with each child individually or in small editing groups on specific skill needs. See Chapter 5 for detailed ways to achieve the writing goal.

FOCUS GOAL: SOLVE PROBLEMS. Accomplishing this goal depends on providing multiple opportunities for children to solve problems in the course of classroom "work" and encouraging them to make the necessary decisions to solve those problems. Problem solving can be learned in many contexts including mathematics, science, and social studies. For example, at a Science Center, a group of mixed age children try to find a way to get water from one area to another without carrying it in a container. At a Math Center, children may ponder how they can purchase the items they need at the store and still have enough change left over for a treat. At a Social Studies Center, the children may be solving the problem of how to share a limited number of materials. In all the centers, the children are learning to solve problems by actually solving problems within a meaningful context.

Projects also offer an excellent forum for problem-solving. Children working on projects solve problems that occur in the process of getting materials, cooperating with each other, planning what and how to investigate the topic, and reporting or demonstrating the findings.

FOCUS GOAL: THINK CRITICALLY. Children "learn to think by thinking," so the multiage teacher must create the opportunities for children to think. She guides the thinking of the children in her class by asking high-level questions that require more than factual answers. Such questions encourage the children to reach beyond the simple recall of information, requiring the children to practice critical thinking skills such as comprehension, application, analysis, synthesis, and evaluation. These questions may begin with "Why do you suppose . . .," "Can you give me an example?" "What do you notice?" "How are these similar/different?" The multiage teacher uses such questions in the context of centers, projects, and small- and large-group discussions.

FOCUS GOAL: SOCIALIZE. Realizing that young children, particularly, are in the process of becoming social, the multiage teacher creates an environment where they can interact frequently and practice social skills. In the Play Center, children learn how to take turns and negotiate roles. In the Writing Center, children learn how to respect another's point of view, enjoy social learning, and help one another. During project work, children learn how to support each other and share responsibilities.

FOCUS GOAL: EMOTIONAL WELL-BEING. The multiage teacher knows how important it is for young children to feel secure and loved. Self-esteem significantly influences a child's learning and sense of well-being. If a child feels incompetent, he may not engage in solving problems because he fears failure. A child with positive self-esteem is more likely to take risks in his own learning processes. An insecure child may act out aggressively or be painfully shy. A secure child experiences the joy of learning and living.

The multiage teacher seeks to establish a classroom community that values and accepts each child. Concentrating on success in learning rather than failure helps each child see himself as a competent person.

FOCUS GOAL: PHYSICAL WELL-BEING. The mixed-age children in the multiage classroom are growing and developing physically at different rates. The focus goal of physical well-being honors each child's developmental stage. The multiage teacher knows that a young child may not have the physical dexterity to write on lines, yet an older child has mastered that skill. Thus, physical expectations should match each child's physical abilities.

The multiage teacher also knows that young children tire easily. In a mixed-age classroom, some of the children may need periods of rest when others do not. As active learners, young children cannot sit for long periods of time. The multiage teacher must provide for freedom of movement in the classroom, as a child's physical well-being affects the child's learning.

"A child with positive self-esteem is more likely to take risks in his own learning processes."

INTEGRATING THE CURRICULUM

What Is an Integrated Curriculum?

Traditional methods separate the curriculum into distinct segments throughout the instructional day. For example, reading is taught from eight to nine o'clock, math from nine to ten, and social studies from two to three. An integrated curriculum takes a more holistic approach, breaking down the curricular walls and integrating the learning process. The teacher chooses a topic or theme to focus on for a week, several weeks, a month, or even the entire year. Integrating the focus goals with the theme, the children engage in the process of learning, reading, writing, solving problems, thinking critically, and socializing. If the theme for a two-week period of time is Bears, the children will read about bears, write about bears, and solve problems about bears, learning to use skills within a meaningful context rather than practicing them in isolation. An integrated curriculum focuses on the processes of learning rather than on memorizing the content of the curriculum.

How Do I Plan An Integrated Curriculum?

For the teacher, planning an integrated curriculum should be much more than merely following prescribed plans. Creating an integrated curriculum also endows the teacher (and children) with ownership of the classroom and the learning processes.

To plan an integrated curriculum, complete a curriculum web. (See the Integrated Curriculum Web Planning Form on page 77.) Choose a theme and place it in the center of the web. Write the content areas you would like to address in the surrounding boxes. Then brainstorm content topics and experiences that would integrate your content areas into the theme. See page 78 for a Completed Curriculum Web on the theme of Bears. From the brainstorm list, decide on which ideas would work well in centers, projects, and small- or large-group learning experiences. Place the ideas within your instructional day.

INTEGRATED CURRICULUM
WEB PLANNING FORM

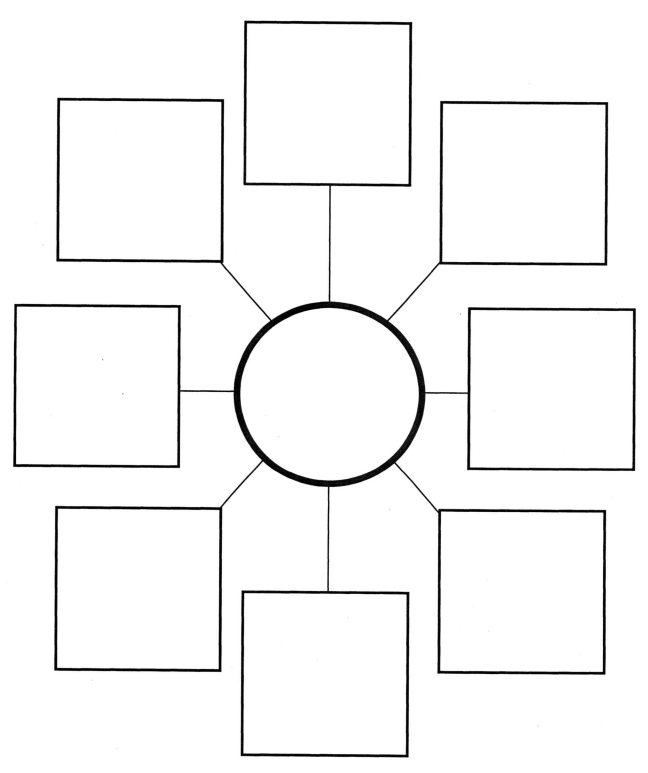

COMPLETED CURRICULUM WEB

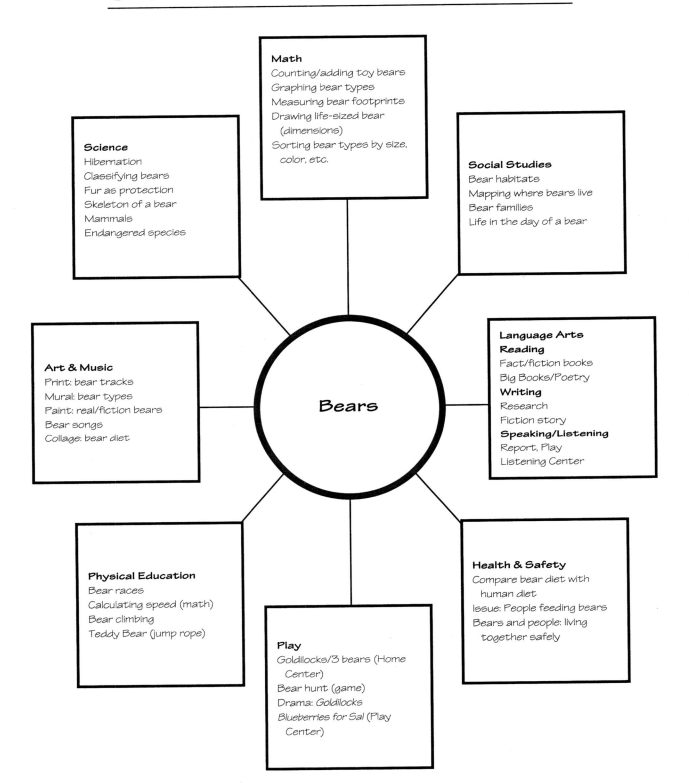

Math
Counting/adding toy bears
Graphing bear types
Measuring bear footprints
Drawing life-sized bear
  (dimensions)
Sorting bear types by size,
  color, etc.

Science
Hibernation
Classifying bears
Fur as protection
Skeleton of a bear
Mammals
Endangered species

Social Studies
Bear habitats
Mapping where bears live
Bear families
Life in the day of a bear

Art & Music
Print: bear tracks
Mural: bear types
Paint: real/fiction bears
Bear songs
Collage: bear diet

Bears

Language Arts
Reading
Fact/fiction books
Big Books/Poetry
Writing
Research
Fiction story
Speaking/Listening
Report, Play
Listening Center

Physical Education
Bear races
Calculating speed (math)
Bear climbing
Teddy Bear (jump rope)

Play
Goldilocks/3 bears (Home
  Center)
Bear hunt (game)
Drama: *Goldilocks*
Blueberries for Sal (Play
  Center)

Health & Safety
Compare bear diet with
  human diet
Issue: People feeding bears
Bears and people: living
  together safely

From *Creating the Multiage Classroom* published by GoodYear Books. Copyright © 1996 Sandra J. Stone.

Designing Open-Ended Activities for Mixed Ages

As you plan your integrated curriculum, it is important to design open-ended activities for centers and projects. *Open-ended* means that there is more than one way to do the activity. Every child, no matter what his developmental level, should be able to engage in the activity. Observe the differences between the following closed and open-ended activities at centers.

Closed Activities	Open-Ended Activities
• Complete a worksheet on verbs.	• Write a story with action words (verbs). Use a brainstorm list if you wish.
• Read *Blueberries for Sal* by Robert McCloskey.	• Select a book of your choice about bears from your book basket or class library.
• Follow directions on a worksheet and provide the correct answers on bear prints.	• Write what you discovered from your investigation of bear prints.
• Use a yardstick to measure the height of a life-sized drawing of the bear.	• Measure the life-sized drawing of a bear using a ruler, yardstick, or blocks. (Older children measure to the quarter inch or inch, and younger children measure how many ruler lengths or block lengths.)
• After listening to a taped story, write a descriptive paragraph about the setting.	• Listen to a story. Draw or write about the setting.
• Complete addition problems.	• Count bears by color. Create your own problems. Share them with a friend.

Remember, if the center or project is overly prescriptive or strictly defined, not all your children will be able to engage in the activity successfully. At centers or with projects, children should be able to work independently or with a group with minimal assistance from the teacher. You can accomplish prescribed activities and defined objectives with small groups or with individual children, thus meeting their specific needs.

THE INSTRUCTIONAL DAY

After you brainstorm topics and experiences for your theme, you'll need to place the ideas within your instructional day. Four different plans are provided to help you design your own daily schedule. All the models can be used for the kindergarten through first grade, kindergarten through second grade, kindergarten through third grade, and first through third grade multiage classrooms. The first, based on the New Zealand model, focuses on extensive literacy engagement. Models 2 and 3 offer variations on a typical integrated curriculum day. Chapter 6 discusses implementation of each curricular piece of models 1, 2, and 3.

INSTRUCTIONAL DAY
MODEL 1

(Based on New Zealand Literacy Model Approach)

A.M.

_ **Opening (large group)**
Calendar, news from home, shared book/poem

_ **Guided Reading Groups/Centers**
Small Guided Reading groups meet with teacher while the rest of the class works at centers that focus on literacy.

Centers: Big Book, Listening, Writing, Letters, Notes, Printing, Flannelboard, Drama, Home, Play, Science, Social Studies, OHP (Overhead Projector), Art, Music, Computer, Poetry, Library, Read-the-Walls

_ **Recess**

_ **Modeled Writing (large group)**
Journals and conferencing

P.M.

_ **Read to Children (large group)**

_ **Independent Reading**
Children read books from the library or book baskets. Reading may be individual or social. Social reading occurs in pairs and small groups.

_ **Guided Math/Centers**
Teacher meets with small groups of children based on need while the rest of the class works at centers with a focus on math, science, and social studies.

Centers: Geoboards, tangrams, puzzles, blocks, Lego®, math games, flannelboard, manipulatives, and open-ended math, science, and social studies activities

_ **Sharing Time**
Closing activities

INSTRUCTIONAL DAY
MODEL 2

A.M.

— **Opening (large group)**
Daily news, shared book/poem, community time

— **Independent Reading/Centers**
Children monitor own progress with Reading Logs. After children complete reading, they choose literacy-based centers. Teacher works with individuals or small groups based on need.

— **Literature Circles (small groups)**
Children work in small groups. Teacher may direct one group a day.

— **Recess**

— **Writers' Workshop/Modeled Writing (large group)**

P.M.

— **Read to Children (large group)**

— **Guided Math/Centers**
Teacher meets with small groups of students based on need while the rest of the class works at math, science, and social studies centers.

— **Project Time**
Children plan and implement project plans based on topic or theme.

— **Sharing Time**
Author's chair, Readers Theater, project presentations

INSTRUCTIONAL DAY
MODEL 3

A.M.

__ **Opening (large group)**
Daily news, shared book/poem, community time

__ **Project Time**
Children plan projects based on topic or theme, usually focused on science, social studies, or literature. Children are involved in all aspects of the curriculum during project time (e.g., reading, researching, computing, solving problems, designing, drawing, playing within topic, writing, composing). Most projects are accomplished through small, cooperative groups.

__ **Recess**

__ **Literature Circles/Guided Reading Groups/Centers**
Children work in small groups. Teacher may direct several groups a day. Children also engage at literacy-based centers.

P.M.

__ **Read to Children (large group)**

__ **Writers' Workshop/Modeled Writing**
Journals and conferencing

__ **Guided Math/Centers**
Teacher meets with small groups of students based on need while the rest of the class works at math, science, and social studies centers.

__ **Sharing Time**
Project presentations, author's chair, Readers Theater

INSTRUCTIONAL DAY
MODEL 1 WITH BEAR THEME

Let's take a look at the Bear theme as it might apply to Instructional Day, Model 1.

A.M.

— **Opening (large group)**
Calendar, news from home
Shared Big Book:
> *Goldilocks and the Three Bears* (James Marshall). Focus on fact versus fiction, key vocabulary, and skills (question marks, quotation marks, blends).

Shared Poem
> "Fuzzy Wuzzy Was a Bear." Focus on rhyming words, irregular spellings, and contractions. Read or act out shared poems from previous weeks.

— **Guided Reading Groups/Centers**
Small Guided Reading Groups: Select books appropriate for each group. Choose extended activities to tie in with the theme, if possible. For example, one group may read *The Zoo* (Andrea Butler). After reading the book during Guided Reading, the children will innovate the book to "The Bear." Children will make a group book and illustrate it. Another Guided Reading group may read the book, *There's a Nightmare in My Closet* (Mercer Mayer) and make an overhead projector story called "There's a Bear in My Bedroom!" A third Guided Reading group may practice writing *B*s and then use the magnetic letters to make *B* words.

Centers
Big Book: Children read *Goldilocks and the Three Bears* in pairs.
Listening: Children choose to listen from a selection of books that represent fact and fiction about bears: *Brown Bear, Brown Bear, What Do You See?* (Bill Martin, Jr.), *The Biggest Bear* (Lynd Ward), and *Blueberries for Sal* (Robert McCloskey). Children may also listen to a true story about Smoky the Bear.
Writing: Children will choose to write a fact or fiction book about bears. They will first design a bear book cover from materials at the Writing Center.
Letters: Children will manipulate letters at the Letter Center.
Notes: Children will write notes to Smoky the Bear.
Printing: Children will make thumbprint forest animals, including a bear, and then write about their creation. Children may also use stamp printing letters to label the animals.

Flannelboard: Children will retell the story, *Goldilocks and the Three Bears*, using flannelboard story figures.

Drama: In the stage area, children will act out the story *Blueberries for Sal*.

Home: Children may role-play the story *Goldilocks and the Three Bears*. Simple props will be added to the center.

Play: Children may play with bear masks created at the Art Center.

Science: Children will sort and graph various types of bears based on descriptions.

Social Studies: Based on previous class discussion, children will match bear types to regions on a map. Older children will research information on one bear type of their choice, focusing on the bear's habitat.

OHP: Children will read overhead stories created by classmates during Guided Reading.

Art: Children will make bear masks to use at the Play Center. Children may also choose a bear type to paint at the art easel. Paintings will be added to a class mural on bear types. Children may also create a poster on fire safety using Smoky the Bear.

Music: Children will create a new song to be used with a Smoky the Bear poster created at the Art Center.

Computer: Children will use available software. If a printer is available, children may type the stories they created at the Writing Center.

Poetry: Children will read the poem card for the week, "Fuzzy Wuzzy Was a Bear." Children will then illustrate their own copies of the poem and add it to their own poetry books.

Library: Children may choose from a variety of books to read. Some of the books reflect the Bear theme, both fact and fiction. Children may use the library books to research the social studies topic.

Read-the-walls: Children walk around the room with a friend, reading the wall print in the literacy-rich classroom.

_   **Recess**
Children may play "Teddy Bear, Teddy Bear" with jump ropes. Some children may wish to act out one of the stories read at the Listening Center such as *The Biggest Bear*. Simple outdoor props may be provided.

_   **Modeled Writing (large group)**
Teacher will discuss content on bears each day. During journal writing, children will use the content to write a fact or fiction story in their journals. The teacher will conference individually with children as they complete their journal entries.

P.M.

_   **Read to Children (large group)**
The teacher will read both fact and fiction bear-related books as well as favorite stories. Children will participate as guest readers during this time, reading to the group a favorite book and/or a book from Guided Reading.

Independent Reading

Children read books from the library or book baskets. Children may choose from a variety of books, which also include fact and fiction bear books. Reading may be individual or social. Social reading occurs in pairs and small groups.

Guided Math/Centers

Teacher meets with small groups of children based on need while the rest of the class is at centers with a focus on math, science, and social studies.

General Centers:

Geoboards, tangrams, puzzles, blocks, Lego®, math games, flannelboard, manipulatives

Theme Centers:

Research—Children will research the size of various bear types and then use rulers to create life-sized bear murals.

Measuring—Children will measure life-sized bear murals created at the Research Center. Children will also measure bear prints and organize the prints from largest to smallest.

Weighing—Children will place rocks in a milk carton until the cartons weigh approximately one pound. Children will then look at a chart of bear types and their weights to find the lightest and heaviest bear type.

Counting—Younger children will count bears by type and then graph them. Older children will also add different categories of bears together to find out how many there are.

Estimation—Children may estimate how many bears they think live in various regions of the world as indicated on a large map. (How many bears do you think live in the polar regions?) Estimations are written on paper and posted on the map (with child's name). At the end of the week, reference books are checked by older children to find the approximate number for each region.

Sharing Time

Children will share items they completed at centers.

Themes provide endless possibilities for engaging children in the processes of learning how to read, write, solve problems, and think. Working at centers and projects involves children in real and meaningful activities instead of isolated drills and practice.

PLANNING THE CURRICULUM *WITH* CHILDREN

Planning the curriculum with your children means ownership of the learning processes for all of you. Here are some ideas to help you plan together. Hold planning sessions weekly, monthly, quarterly, and/or yearly.

WEBBING is an excellent way to generate theme ideas based on children's interests and then to generate topics about your chosen theme. Have in mind themes you would like to address during the year, quarter, or month. As you generate ideas from the children, also add your own so that you can quickly assess the children's interest in the ideas you would like to explore. Be flexible as well as realistic. You are the final authority on what will work based on available resources. Be honest with the children if you must decide to go in a direction that is not their first choice. Remember that not all areas of the curriculum need to be generated collaboratively with the children. Let's first look below at a webbing of general themes you and the children would like to explore.

Desert

Weather

Dinosaurs

Water Cycle

Mammals

Transportation

Friends

Families

Seasons

Space

Habitats

Topics We Would Like to Explore

Monsters

Fantasy

Literature Themes

Ecology

The West

Geology

Famous People

Pilgrims

Explorers

Ocean

Insects

After you choose the theme, make another web to identify appropriate topics and experiences. Some teachers devise a preliminary web independently and then invite the children to add their ideas. Other teachers use a preliminary web only as a personal guideline as they plan themes with the children. The web below is based on the literature selection *Millions of Cats* by Wanda Gag.

From this general webbing of topics based on the theme Millions of Cats, select specific ideas to fit your topics into content areas such as was done for the Bears theme. Suggestions can then be made for centers, projects, and learning experiences. Centers may include categorizing cat types, writing cartoon scripts for cartoon cats, drawing cats, and reading about cats. Projects could include putting on a pet show with stuffed animals; making a Big Book to illustrate the phrase, "Cats here, Cats

there, Cats and kittens everywhere, Hundreds of cats, Thousands of cats, Millions and billions and trillions of cats"; creating a cat musical; and researching historical cats and their importance to particular cultures. Learning experiences could include a trip to the local humane society, a classroom visit from an animal groomer, and choosing and caring for a classroom pet.

Lifespan of a Cat		Pet Care
Types of Cats	Wild Cats	Mammals
Cats in History		Cats as Friends
What is a Million?	**Millions of Cats**	Fictional Cats
Pets	Health/Diet	Beauty	Loneliness
Pet Show	Cartoon Cats	Domestic Cats
Cats in Art	Humane Society	

K-W-L Chart. The K-W-L Chart (*Ogle 1986; Carr and Ogle 1987*) is an easy way to address a specific theme with a group of children, particularly when planning projects. Using the theme of Cats, make a chart with a column for **K** (What do I know?), **W** (What would I like to know?), and **L** (What have I learned?). List things the children know about cats under **K** and then ask what they would like to know. From the **W** category, the children will explore how they will find out the information and plan accompanying projects. Some teachers

add an **H** (How will I find out?) category to the chart, so children can specifically note how they will find the information.

Hang the K-W-L Chart in a prominent place in the classroom so children can add questions as they explore the theme. At the end of the study, children will complete the last section, **L** (What have I learned?). Children will use their experiential knowledge from centers and projects to answer their own questions.

Planning Sheets. You can also plan topics with children by completing planning sheets on an overhead projector. Ask the children what they would like to explore at centers, as projects, and as learning experiences (small and large group). Use the center, project, and learning experience planning sheets provided in Chapter 3, pp. 55–57, and Chapter 4, p. 77.

Long-Term Curriculum Planning

Good long-term planning is critical in the multiage classroom since you will teach the same children for several consecutive years rather than a different group each year. How does one plan for this type of instructional commitment?

Before you begin, remember several important foundations for planning the multiage curriculum. The goals of the multiage classroom focus on process learning. The content, while important, is not as important as the process of children learning how to learn. Some teachers feel it necessary to plan three completely different years so the children will not be engaged with the same content from one year to the next. This presents an issue for discussion. If the focus is on process, then content is only the medium for the process.

Besides, there is nothing wrong with children engaging the same content for an additional year. We don't just read a book once and never return to it. Think about how many times you have read the same book to children throughout a year or years of teaching. Children ask for favorite books again and again. New insights and understandings unfold from multiple readings. Repeating content areas offers other opportunities to engage the topic, possibly from a different perspective. After an additional year(s), children will engage the topic from a more mature perspective with different abilities.

Based on these foundations, a multiage teacher can proceed to plan several years of curriculum, using some content areas an additional year and adding new ones intermittently throughout the three-year period. For example, in a kindergarten through second-grade multiage classroom, the class may study Deserts the first year and again the third year. During the third year, the original first and second graders have moved on to another class. The original kindergartners are now second graders, and they will engage the Desert study in an entirely different way. Use the form on page 94 to make your long-term plans.

Here are several options to consider when doing long-range planning.

OPTION 1. Plan three years of curriculum based on various themes. Each year will consist of approximately one-third new teacher-selected themes, one-third child-selected themes, and one-third repeated themes.

OPTION 2. Plan with teams of teachers. Share ideas and exchange themes. For example, during the first year, Teacher A will study Bears, Nursery Rhymes, Habitats, Monsters, and Oceans. Teacher B will study Cats, Fairy Tales, Space, Insects, and Families. Teacher C will study Deserts, Amphibians, Friends, Geology, and Author Eric Carle. These three teachers will then exchange themes with each other, providing ideas and materials for centers and projects.

OPTION 3. Plan a general theme for each year. Plan topics related to the theme with the children. For example, year one may have the general theme of Habitats. From this theme, the children and teacher will pursue related topics on Animal, Insect, Ocean, and People habitats. Year two may have the general theme of Travel. The class will pursue topics in Transportation, Travel in Colonial Days, Travel in the Space Age, Travel Inventions, City Planning, and Travel Resorts. These topics may be recycled for another three years or three new general topics may be selected.

OPTION 4. Create a thematic unit center within the school where teachers can contribute resources on each thematic unit. These units can then be shared across the school community. Some units may be designated primary or upper-level units.

Short-Term Planning

With themes selected for the year, begin to plan each unit by deciding on the length of your exploration. Some themes may demand only one week of study, whereas others may engage the children for several weeks.

Be flexible in your planning. You and the children may wish to take occasional detours. Perhaps a flood in your community prompts you to explore this topic, or you decide to investigate a national concern that has made headline news. Maybe a selected theme is of particular interest to the children, so you extend the study for a week or more. Good planning allows for flexibility according to the needs and interests of the children. Short-Term Planning Forms are provided on pp. 95–96. You can also use the webbing and K-W-L Chart techniques as you make general plans. Specific weekly and daily planning techniques are addressed and provided in Chapter 5.

TEACHING SKILLS WITHIN THE THEMATIC CONTEXT. As you make long-term and short-term plans, you will also plan how to teach skills according to the children's cultural needs within the thematic context. Broad-based skills are addressed during large-group instructional times. Specific skill instruction is addressed individually and in small groups, based on the needs of the children. For example, during large-group

Shared Book, you might focus on fact vs. fiction, quotation marks, and letter identification. During Guided Reading, you might cover reading strategies, retelling, and compound words. To tailor your skill lessons to the actual needs of the children, base the lessons on authentic assessment (portfolios) and not on a prescribed curriculum. Examples of skill lessons in context are provided in Chapter 5.

LONG-TERM PLANNING
FORM

Year One	Year Two	Year Three
Topics/Themes:	Topics/Themes:	Topics/Themes:

From *Creating the Multiage Classroom* published by GoodYear Books. Copyright © 1996 Sandra J. Stone.

SHORT-TERM
PLANNING

Theme/Topic:

Approximate Length of Time:

Shared Reading:

Shared Poem:

Related Books/Resources:

A.M. Centers/Projects:

P.M. Centers/Projects:

Learning Experiences:

SHORT-TERM PLANNING FORM

Centers	Projects	Learning Experiences

CHAPTER FIVE

STRATEGIES FOR TEACHING CONTENT

Teaching content to a mixed-age group of children requires instructional strategies that differ from traditional approaches. In traditional, same-age classrooms, teachers present content areas sequentially based on the prescribed curriculum in the adopted texts. For example, first graders learn to read moving through the sequenced skills as presented in a series of progressively difficult readers and worksheets. In math, children work through a text that sequences the concepts by increasing difficulty.

In keeping with multiage philosophy, the multiage teacher must help each child develop her skills and understand concepts within the content areas along her own developmental continuum using the process approach to learning. To do this, the multiage teacher presents broad-based skills in large-group instruction and concentrates on *specific* children's needs during small-group and individual instructional times.

During large-group instructional times, the curriculum is opened up through broad-based skills (skills ranging from simple to complex to address needs of mixed-age learners) so children may fit into the instruction based on where they are in the developmental process. Broad-based skill instruction allows children to refine skills that might traditionally be below their grade level and challenges them to engage skills that might traditionally be above their grade level.

During small-group and individual instruction, the teacher focuses on the skills individual children need to advance on their personal continuums. Grade level should not define small-group and individual instruction; instead, create groups based on children's needs. Groups usually include children of mixed ages and are flexible. Children do not remain in a group for the entire year. Each group disbands when it meets its need.

Multiage teachers must regard instruction in the content areas from a perspective different than teaching children the curriculum. If teaching the curriculum, it would be easy for the multiage teacher to group children by grade level within the classroom and teach the appropriate curriculum to each grade-level group. However, this approach to content instruction is disadvantageous for both teacher and children and doomed to fail. Some multiage teachers address content curriculum by grouping children across grade level or ability lines within a multiple-teacher context. For example, Teacher A instructs the beginning readers and Teacher B the fluent readers; or Teacher A teaches first grade math skills while Teacher B covers second grade math skills. Note, however, these teachers are still teaching the curriculum rather than the children.

Without separating children out along grade levels to teach them a sequence of content area skills, how does the multiage teacher instruct children in the content areas? This chapter will give you effective guidelines and techniques. Even though here the content areas are addressed individually for clarity, remember that in the multiage classroom they should be integrated for more holistic learning.

From Creating the Multiage Classroom published by GoodYear Books. Copyright © 1996 Sandra J. Stone.

Grouped by Age   **Better: Grouped Randomly**

Creating a Literate Environment

As we have seen, to accomplish the focus goals of reading and writing, the multiage teacher must create a literate classroom environment. In the primary years, children develop rapidly in their literacy skills, and a literate environment facilitates this development. When surrounded by opportunities to engage in meaningful literacy activities, children mature in their understanding of literacy and their own ability to read and write.

A literate classroom combines environmental and instructional elements to support literacy growth. The literacy-based centers and instructional strategies of the multiage approach create such a classroom. Literacy-based centers are covered in Chapter 3. Let's now examine multiage instructional strategies designed to promote literacy.

Listening

Art

Drama

Letters

Read-the-Walls

Computer

Science

Blocks

Big Books

OHP

Independent Reading

Literature Circles

Reading to Children

Readers Theater

Shared Reading

Centers

A Literate Environment

Strategies

Math

Poetry

Book Baskets

Games and Puzzles

Library

Writing

Play

Health

Social Studies

Flannelboard

Publishing

Guided Reading

Modeled Writing

Writers' Workshop

Language Experience

Independent Writing

New Zealand, with the highest literacy rate in the world, is a strong exponent of multiage education in the primary grades. Because they are highly effective with mixed-age learners, we will focus on New Zealand's literacy strategies: Shared Reading, Guided Reading, and Modeled Writing.

Shared Reading

Shared Reading is a teacher-directed, large-group reading strategy (*Holdaway 1979*). Typically, in the primary classroom, the teacher uses a Big Book during the Shared Reading time. Shared Reading is a *daily* event where the Big Book is used as an instructional tool to promote reading enjoyment, support children's reading at all levels of development, and teach broad-based skills.

Indeed, Shared Reading lends itself well to teaching skills in context to the entire class of mixed-age learners. The multiage teacher chooses broad-based skills for Shared Reading. Broad-based skills are skills that range from the very simple to the complex, thus reaching the wide variety of needs of mixed-age learners. Through portfolio assessment (addressed in Chapter 7) and small-group instruction, the multiage teacher should be well aware of the specific needs of the children in his class. During Shared Reading, the teacher focuses on the skills he knows the children need. These *skills* range from concepts of print and word structure to reading strategies and comprehension skills. If younger children need reinforcement on the simple skills of letter identification, the teacher chooses a letter to emphasize throughout the book. If older children are beginning to understand the more complex concept of compound words, the teacher selects this to focus on throughout the book. Shared Reading texts provide a real context for focusing on any number of skills.

Teaching broad-based skills opens up the curriculum for all learners so that each child can embrace skills based on her current understanding. Skills are revisited throughout the year providing needed repetition.

The Shared Reading Planning Form (see p. 102) may be used to organize your focus skills. An example of a completed form is also provided (see p. 103).

101

YOUR SHARED READING
PLANNING FORM

Day 1	Day 2	Day 3	Day 4	Day 5
Big Book/Text	Big Book/Text	Big Book/Text	Big Book/Text	Big Book/Text
Skills	Skills	Skills	Skills	Skills
Poem	Poem	Poem	Poem	Poem
Skills	Skills	Skills	Skills	Skills
Other Poems	Other Poems	Other Poems	Other Poems	Other Poems
				Extended Activity

From *Creating the Multiage Classroom* published by GoodYear Books. Copyright © 1996 Sandra J. Stone.

COMPLETED SHARED
READING PLANNING FORM

Day 1	Day 2	Day 3	Day 4	Day 5
Big Book/Text Read *The Very Hungry Caterpillar* (Carle)	**Big Book/Text** Reread book chorally with children.	**Big Book/Text** Reread book chorally with children.	**Big Book/Text** Reread book chorally with children.	**Big Book/Text** Reread book chorally with children.
Skills Discuss key vocabulary: *Swiss cheese, salami, stomach-ache, cocoon.* Predict.	**Skills** Introduce period.	**Skills** Review period. Introduce capital S.	**Skills** Review period, S, and introduce commas in a series.	**Skills** Review previous skills; introduce dedication page.
Poem Read "Caterpillar" for enjoyment	**Poem** Reread "Caterpillar" chorally with children.	**Poem** Reread "Caterpillar" chorally with children.	**Poem** Reread "Caterpillar" chorally with children.	**Poem** Reread "Caterpillar" chorally with children.
Skills Discuss vocabulary: *wriggled, stretched.*	**Skills** Introduce double consonants.	**Skills** Review double consonants; Introduce rhyming words.	**Skills** Review double consonants, rhyming words; Introduce *ed* endings.	**Skills** Review double consonants, rhyming words, *ed* endings.
Other Poems "Hickory, Dickory Dock"	**Other Poems** "The Moon"	**Other Poems** "The Snail"	**Other Poems** "Twinkle, Twinkle Little Star"	**Other Poems** "Fuzzy Wuzzy"
				Extended Activity Make watercolor butterflies; write group poem.

Shared Reading takes approximately 15 to 20 minutes a day. The teacher places a Big Book on an easel around which the entire class sits on a floor rug. The teacher uses a pointer as he reads the story with the children. A sample follows of what goes on over a series of days while the class reads a Big Book during Shared Reading.

DAY 1. The teacher enthusiastically introduces the Big Book and reads the book to the children for enjoyment. As the teacher reads, he discusses any vocabulary that might be new, talks about the pictures, and encourages the children to predict what will happen next. The teacher models what reading sounds like. The first reading of the book is very similar to discussing and enjoying a good "read-aloud" book.

DAY 2. The teacher rereads the Big Book, inviting the children to join in the reading. Children who are fluent readers will read along. Emerging readers may simply repeat familiar phrases in the text. All children are encouraged to join in. As the teacher rereads the text with the children, he stops periodically to focus on one skill within the context of the story. For example, in reading the Big Book *The Carrot Seed* (Ruth Krauss), the teacher may stop to ask the children to find a capital and a lowercase *C*. Or, he may pause and ask the children to find quotation marks. After the teacher reads a page chorally with the children, he may say, "Oh, look! I think we may have a lowercase and capital *C* on this page. Can you find them?" The teacher waits for all the children to look, sometimes asking them to raise their hands or show how many lowercase *C*s they

found. He then selects one child to come to the easel and use the pointer to locate the appropriate items. The teacher should praise the child. Of course, never embarrass a child if the skill is located incorrectly. Perhaps say, "Good try! You are so close. Let's look in this line. Do you see it? Good job!" As the reading progresses, children continue to locate the focus skill of capital and lowercase *C*s, which may occur on pages 3, 7, and 12, for instance. On the second day with a Big Book, the teacher should focus on just one skill, being careful not to interrupt the flow of the story.

From Creating the Multiage Classroom published by GoodYear Books. Copyright © 1996 Sandra J. Stone.

DAY 3. On the third day, the teacher rereads the story again, inviting the children to participate orally. As the teacher reads, he focuses on yesterday's skill and introduces a new one, asking children to find the skills within the text and to use the pointer to locate the focus skill. Again, the teacher focuses on the two skills without chopping up the text.

DAY 4. The teacher rereads the story chorally with the children, focusing on previous skills and adding a new one.

DAY 5. The teacher rereads the story chorally with the children, focusing on skills from previous days and adding one more. After reading the story, the teacher invites the children to participate in an extended activity based on the story. The children may do an innovation or retell of the story, creating a new Big Book with their own illustrations. An innovation is made with the children by their changing the words of the story but keeping the same pattern. For example *The Carrot Seed* could be changed to "The Watermelon Seed." The characters are also changed. The children may act out the story as a play, do an art-related project, or write their own stories on the topic.

The original Big Book is then placed in the Big Book Center where it can be read by both emerging and fluent readers over and over again along with other Big Books from previous weeks. A tape and small copy of the book may be placed in the Listening Center.

"If younger children need reinforcement on the simple skills of letter identification, the teacher chooses a letter to emphasize throughout the book. If older children are beginning to understand the more complex concept of compound words, the teacher selects this to focus on throughout the book."

SHARED READING DAILY GUIDELINE

Day 1:   Read the Big Book to the children for enjoyment. Focus on unfamiliar vocabulary, discuss pictures, and predict outcome.

Day 2:   Reread the Big Book, inviting the children to read along. Introduce one focus skill.

Day 3:   Reread the Big Book chorally with the children. Review Day 1 focus skill. Introduce a new skill.

Day 4:   Reread the Big Book chorally with the children. Review focus skills from Days 1 and 2. Introduce a new skill.

Day 5:   Reread the Big Book chorally with the children. Review focus skills from Days 1, 2, and 3. Introduce a new skill.

Enjoy an extended activity with the children: innovate or retell the story, dramatize the story, complete an art-related project, conduct a science-related or social studies–related learning experience, design a wall mural, create a theme-related Play Center, write a song or poem to go along with the story, or write individual stories related to the book's theme.

Not just a Big Book event, Shared Reading may also utilize the text of a selected piece of literature. Choose a book to share with the class. For example, you may select *Sylvester and the Magic Pebble* (William Steig). Following the Big Book Shared Reading format, simply read the text to the children on the first day. Enjoy the book, discuss key vocabulary, and do some predicting. On the following days, make overheads of selected pages from the text. Using an overhead projector, chorally read one or more pages each day with the children. Focus on specific skills. In the following passage, you could focus on broad-based skills such as using commas in a series of sentences, the words *ceased* and *vanished, -ed* word endings, syllables, long vowel sounds in double vowel words, and the author's word selection.

To his great surprise the rain stopped. It didn't stop gradually as rains usually do. It CEASED. The drops vanished on the way down, the clouds disappeared, everything was dry, and the sun was shining as if rain had never existed. (*Sylvester and the Magic Pebble*, Steig, 1989, p. 5)

At the end of the week, enjoy the entire story again. The book may also be discussed during small-group Literature Circles to promote comprehension.

SHARED POEM. After the children enjoy a Shared Book experience with a Big Book or literature text, introduce a poetry selection that complements the Big Book or literature text. For example, if you are reading a Big Book on frogs, the poem should also be about frogs.

Write the poem in large print on poster board so the children can read the text. Share the poem in the same manner as you did the books. On the first day, introduce the poem, reading it to the children for enjoyment. On the following day invite the children to read the poem with you. Use a pointer as you read. Choose one skill or teaching point to focus on for the day. You may want to look at rhyming words, beginning sounds, blends, key vocabulary, or imagery. Chorally read the poem with the children every day during the week, adding new skills or teaching points. Poems from previous weeks may be enjoyed each day as well. At the end of the week, you may do a culminating activity on the Big Book, literature text, or poem selection. Children may dramatize the poem, write stories about the poem, create a new poem using the same pattern, or complete an art or craft project using ideas from the poem.

The poem can then be added to your Poetry Center collection of Shared Poems so that during center time the children can read their favorite poems over and over again. Create a poetry book of Shared Poems for each child in the class to keep at the Poetry Center and illustrate each week during center time.

Guided Reading

Guided Reading is a small-group instructional strategy, during which the teacher supports each child's specific reading development. While the teacher conducts Guided Reading with small groups of children, the rest of the class participates in literacy-based centers.

In the multiage classroom, Guided Reading is a selective strategy that groups children by reading level: emergent, developing, and fluent. However, the groupings are flexible and cross age distinctions. Emerging readers may be the oldest or youngest, as may developing or fluent readers. Groups are not labeled. (Guided Reading time can be interchanged with Literature Circles during which different groups of mixed ages and mixed abilities enjoy a literature selection.)

Teachers can use Little Books such as those by Celebration Press, an imprint of ScottForesman. These Little Books present individual, high-interest stories that increase in reading difficulty. They encourage children to read for meaning, rather than to simply decode. Children learn to use the three cueing systems (meaning, grammar, phonics) that good readers use.

For Guided Reading, the teacher selects a book based on Running Records (a reading assessment method addressed in Chapter 7), that he knows is appropriate for the children in the group. A copy of the book is given to each child. For emergent or developing readers, the teacher follows the Guided Reading plan outlined on pp. 109–110. For fluent readers, follow the Guided Reading plan on p.111.

Guided Reading Plan for Emergent or Developing Readers

1) INTRODUCE THE BOOK. Before reading the story, the teacher sets the children up for a successful first read by doing a "book introduction" (*Clay 1989*). Discussing the cover and the pictures in the book with the children, the teacher frames the story as he goes through the book page by page, drawing out or using key vocabulary or phrases and discussing cues to help the children remember certain words. He gives a detailed, supportive introduction or a minimal introduction based on the children's instructional needs.

2) CHILDREN READ THE STORY ALONE. The teacher next asks the children to read the story to themselves. This allows the children to practice their own reading strategies while the teacher observes. (Beginning readers may read the story aloud to themselves.)

3) CHILDREN READ THE STORY CHORALLY. Next, the children read the story chorally, following the teacher who models fluency and expression. The teacher also observes as the children read to see if each child is successfully negotiating the text.

4) CHILDREN PARTNER READ. Next, each child partners with the child sitting next to her. The partners take turns reading the story to each other, being sure to compliment each other upon completion of the reading. During the partner read, the teacher selects one child to read to him in order to take a Running Record on the child's oral reading of the story. This enables the teacher to assess whether the story is appropriate for the child's emerging literacy skills. If it is not, the teacher will select a more appropriate text for the child. The teacher also asks the child to retell the story in order to evaluate the child's comprehension of the story. The teacher adds the Running Record and Story Retell analysis to the child's portfolio.

5) EXTENDED ACTIVITY OR SKILL INSTRUCTION. After reading the text, the teacher may select a skill on which to focus, for example, beginning sounds of words as cues. The teacher directs the children to use the skill to find beginning sounds in the story. Children then practice the skill by writing the letters with those sounds or matching them to certain words within the story. Then they reread the story to find the letters again.

The children may also engage in an extended activity. For example, perhaps they innovate the story and make a group book or individual books. The book *The Zoo* (Andrea Butler) might be innovated to "The Farm." The children may retell or innovate the story and put their story and illustrations on overheads. Then, at the Overhead Projector Center, they can read the stories during center time.

Or perhaps, the children create a group poster or mural using key words from the story. The children may "play" with letters at the Letters or Printing centers. The extended activity engages the children in meaningful activities with the focus skills addressed during Guided Reading.

6) CHILDREN TAKE THE BOOK HOME FOR ADDITIONAL READINGS.
The children take the Little Books home and read the story to an adult or older sibling. This strategy supports them as they learn to read by reading. The children return their books the following day along with a Record of Reading that has been initialed by the listener.

7) CHILDREN REREAD THE STORY.
During Guided Reading, the children reread the text chorally before beginning a new text. The book is then placed in a book basket that contains other Little Books the children have successfully read. These Little Books may be read over and over again during Independent Reading or center time.

For fluent readers, Guided Reading follows a different process that supports these readers by building on their independent reading skills. Here are guidelines for using Guided Reading strategies with fluent readers.

From *Creating the Multiage Classroom* published by GoodYear Books. Copyright © 1996 Sandra J. Stone.

Little Red Riding Hood

Basket

Guided Reading Plan for Fluent Readers

1) **INTRODUCE THE STORY OR SELECTED PAGES OF THE STORY.** Introduce the whole book if it is short, or selected pages if it is a long story. This introduction helps children, even fluent readers, have a successful first read. During an introduction for fluent readers, the teacher focuses on key vocabulary. The children find the words in the text and discuss their meanings. When the children engage the text independently, the children will know how each word sounds and be able to read it with meaning.

2) **CHILDREN READ THE STORY OR PASSAGE TO THEMSELVES.** After the introduction, the children silently read the story or passage while the teacher observes how they negotiate the text.

3) **CHILDREN AND TEACHER DISCUSS THE PASSAGE.** After the silent reading, the teacher may ask questions that help the children to think critically about the passage. The teacher then repeats the Guided Reading process for each passage until the entire story is read. The teacher may have the children chorally read certain passages to model fluency and expression.

4) **EXTENDED ACTIVITY OR SKILL INSTRUCTION.** After reading the story, the teacher may focus on a particular skill from the story context and/or engage the children in an extended activity. For skills, the children may focus on compound words, syllables, or synonyms. As extended activities, the children may write a new ending to the story, create a play, make a mural, write a group book, or do research on a topic introduced by the story.

5) **TEACHER COMPLETES RUNNING RECORD.** While the children are engaged in an extended activity, the teacher asks one child to read a passage from the story. To assess the child's reading strategies and determine whether the book is appropriate for the child, the teacher completes a Running Record and adds it to the child's portfolio.

Guided Reading is a specific strategy that enables the teacher to come alongside each child in the reading process and support her individual reading skills. Using Running Records and knowledge of the cue systems, the teacher can effectively support each child's successful reading development. However, it is important to remember that Guided Reading should not be used to group children by grade level to move them through a prescribed curriculum such as a basal reading series. In the multiage classroom, children comfortably progress in reading at their own rates and do not compete with each other, but rather encourage each other.

A Sample Guided Reading Planning Form is provided on p. 112 along with a blank form on p. 113.

SAMPLE GUIDED
READING PLANNING FORM

Day	Group 1	Group 2	Group 3	Group 4
1	**Book:** *The Zoo* **Skill:** Beginning sounds **Activity:** Play with letters at Center.	**Book:** *Climbing* **Skill:** Words: *I, go, up* **Activity:** Retell and illustrate story on overheads.	**Book:** *Sleepy Bear* **Skill:** Compound words: *into, tiptoe* **Activity:** Make puppets and retell the story.	**Book:** *Waiting* **Skill:** -ing endings **Activity:** Illustrate -ing words.
2	**Book:** *The Farm* **Skill:** Beginning sounds **Activity:** Write letters T, B, and L on chalkboards.	**Book:** *Where Is Nancy?* **Skill:** Question marks **Activity:** Act out the story.	**Book:** (Literature Circles) **Skill:** **Activity:**	**Book:** (Literature Circles) **Skill:** **Activity:**
3	**Book:** *I Like* **Skill:** Beginning sound (*l*), sight word *like* **Activity:** Make "I like" books.	**Book:** *Have You Seen?* **Skill:** Question marks **Activity:** Write group story with question marks.	**Book:** *What Is a Bat?* **Skill:** Question marks; contractions **Activity:** Research facts about bats.	**Book:** *Philippa and the Dragon* **Skill:** Contractions; compound words **Activity:** Create a zigzag dragon storybook.
4	**Book:** *Our Baby* **Skill:** Beginning sounds: T, B, L; *likes* **Activity:** Poster "Baby Likes"	**Book:** *Ants Love Picnics, Too* **Skill:** Words: *do, too* **Activity:** "I love" food poster	**Book:** (Literature Circles) **Skill:** **Activity:**	**Book:** (Literature Circles) **Skill:** **Activity:**
5	**Book:** (Literature Circles) **Skill:** **Activity:**	**Book:** (Literature Circles) **Skill:** **Activity:**	**Book:** *Just Like Grandpa* **Skill:** Same and different **Activity:** Innovate story to "Just Like Grandma."	**Book:** *Dad Didn't Mind at All* **Skill:** Contractions **Activity:** Make a contractions game.

YOUR GUIDED
READING PLANNING FORM

Day	Group 1	Group 2	Group 3	Group 4
1	Book: Skill: Activity:	Book: Skill: Activity:	Book: Skill: Activity:	Book: Skill: Activity:
2	Book: Skill: Activity:	Book: Skill: Activity:	Book: Skill: Activity:	Book: Skill: Activity:
3	Book: Skill: Activity:	Book: Skill: Activity:	Book: Skill: Activity:	Book: Skill: Activity:
4	Book: Skill: Activity:	Book: Skill: Activity:	Book: Skill: Activity:	Book: Skill: Activity:
5	Book: Skill: Activity:	Book: Skill: Activity:	Book: Skill: Activity:	Book: Skill: Activity:

Literature Circles

Literature Circles, another effective strategy for multiage classrooms, can be interchanged with Guided Reading. (Some multiage teachers conduct both Guided Reading and Literature Circles during the instructional day.) Literature Circles are an excellent way to engage mixed-age and mixed-ability learners in an interactive literature-based learning group.

A simple definition of a Literature Circle is a small group of children who come together to discuss the same book as a way of reflecting on their reading and deepening their understanding of literature. The group ranges in size from four to six children and usually forms around the students' choice of book. For example, the teacher may introduce three literature books. The children then select the one they would like to read for discussion in a Literature Circle. After the children have read the book (or either have had the book read to them or have listened to the book at the Listening Center), they meet to share and discuss the book.

Depending on the length of the book, the children may meet for approximately twenty minutes one to four times a week. The teacher may attend all, some, or at least one of the sessions.

When literature circles are first introduced, the teacher models how to discuss the book as well as how to take turns and respect the opinions of others. Circles should be interactive. Every child should be a valued participant in the book discussion.

As the children become more independent in the discussion process, the teacher allows them to direct the group. The group selects a leader and decides on the number of pages or chapters that are to be read for each discussion session if the book is lengthy. The group also determines the topic or topics to be discussed. The teacher may add to the topic discussion list. Discussion of the book may also involve the children in organizing the text using a graphic organizer such as a comparison chart, story web, or character analysis chart.

As older children first read the book independently, they may write responses to selected questions in their own Literature Response Journals. For example, children may write about "What is my favorite part?"or "What did I like or dislike about the main characters?" They can also write about other personal responses to the book before attending the Literature Circle. Writing in response journals helps to prepare children for the group discussion. Younger children may simply think about specific questions as they read or listen to the book. If the reading of the book is done at home, parents may help their children think about specific discussion questions before they join the Literature Circle at school the next day.

As you plan discussion questions, be sure that the questions are relevant to the text and that they involve the children in the text and discussion. Don't plan too many questions. A listing of possible Literature Circle discussion questions follows on p. 115. A Literature Group Planning Form is on p. 116.

From Creating the Multiage Classroom published by GoodYear Books. Copyright © 1996 Sandra J. Stone.

Literature Circle Discussion Questions

Below are examples of questions you may use. Choose questions that fit the story or create your own questions.

Why did you choose this book?

Does the book tell a good story?

Could this story really have happened?

Who are the characters? Who did you like/dislike?

What was your favorite/least favorite part of the book?

Where did the story take place?

Who tells the story?

What do you think is the theme/moral of the story?

What type of story is this?

How did this story make you feel?

Did this story make you think about something you have not thought about before?

Was there a lesson to be learned in this book?

Did you like the way the author wrote the story?

What is the mood of the story?

Are there words or phrases that help you feel or understand the characters/story?

Literature Circle Group Planning Form

Date:

Book:

Group Members:

Discussion Questions:

Reflections:

Goal for Next Meeting:

Read Alouds

Reading aloud to children in the primary multiage classroom should be a daily event. During Read-Aloud time, children enjoy listening to stories that capture their minds and hearts. Teachers model what reading sounds like and the joy of reading a book. In the multiage classroom, a variety of Read-Aloud picture books should be available. Short chapter books may also be utilized.

The teacher is the primary reader, but he also encourages "guest readers" to share favorite books. Guest readers range from emergent to fluent readers. In the multiage classroom, all levels of reading are accepted and supported by the children. Children often select books that are read aloud for their Independent Reading time.

Independent Reading

Independent Reading should be an integral daily part of the primary multiage program. However, "independent" does not imply reading alone. Independent Reading is not a form of Sustained Silent Reading (SSR) where children read quietly with no social interaction and little choice about what is read. Independent Reading in the multiage classroom takes advantage of the benefits of the social interaction between mixed-age learners.

During Independent Reading, children choose books from the classroom library or book baskets to read individually, with partners, or in social groupings. Some children select books and find a quiet place to read alone. Other children pair up with friends and enjoy reading a favorite book together. Small groups of children gather together, and one child becomes the teacher and reads to the group. Emergent readers read to fluent readers. Fluent readers model reading skills for emergent readers. Independent Reading is a social time for enjoying reading together. During this time, children also enjoy reading to the teacher, who can use the opportunity to observe children's reading progress.

Reading Across the Curriculum

Reading in the multiage classroom is integrated across the curriculum. If children are studying about bears, they are reading about bears. If they are studying fairy tales, they are reading fairy tales. Reading does not occur only during reading time, rather reading is a tool for unlocking all areas of the integrated curriculum.

Most of the content-integrated literacy centers focus on reading. Children read books and poems, read directions, read to get things done, and read for information. Projects also offer opportunities for reading across the content areas. If children are pursuing a project on geology, they will read for information, read to get things done, read what group members write, and read for enjoyment.

Again, the focus for reading in the multiage classroom is to "learn to read by reading." Thus, children develop their reading skills in a meaningful and functional environment within an integrated curriculum.

Modeled Writing

This New Zealand instructional strategy works well with mixed-age learners. Every day the teacher models the writing process and then the children write in "learning" journals. The teacher conferences with every child frequently throughout the week, addressing each one's specific needs and goals.

Modeled Writing should be integrated across the curriculum. If the class is studying birds, then Modeled Writing offers an opportunity to write about birds. If the class is enjoying a selection of literature on fictional space creatures, then during Modeled Writing, the children learn how to write letters to these extraterrestrial beings.

Like Shared Reading, Modeled Writing provides a strategy for teaching broad-based skills within the context of a whole-class learning experience. Through Modeled Writing, children learn both reading and writing skills, as well as punctuation, composition, spelling, grammar, editing skills, and writing in different genres. The teacher may focus on skills that range from simple beginning sounds and periods at the end of a sentence to more complex skills such as using commas with introductory clauses and using descriptive words. In one Modeled Writing lesson, the teacher may address letter recognition for emergent readers and writers as well as quotation marks for fluent writers. Opening up the writing process invites the children to enter into it at their own level of understanding. Many children pick up skills that would normally not be taught at their grade level, while others review skills that secure their competency. As all the children engage in the process of writing, the teacher focuses on individual successes and needs during conferencing.

From Creating the Multiage Classroom published by GoodYear Books. Copyright © 1996 Sandra J. Stone.

The following is a *daily guideline* for conducting Modeled Writing with mixed-age learners:

INTRODUCE THE WRITING CONTEXT. The teacher introduces the context (content) to give the children something to write about. Here are examples of various writing contexts:

Read a literature or poetry piece. The story or poem selection may be foundational to your theme. For example, the theme for the week or several weeks may focus on *Clifford, the Big Red Dog* stories by Norman Bridwell. First, the teacher reads the story, *Clifford, the Small Red Puppy*, enjoying it with the children and discussing it. The teacher asks, "If you had your choice of a dog, what kind of dog would you have?" and then model writes a few sentences about the kind of dog he would choose. Or, the teacher might choose a poetry selection from Shared Poem and have the children innovate or create similar poems on the topic. Stories and poems make excellent introductions for a writing context.

Introduce a topic. The topic is usually based on the current classroom theme. For example, if the children are studying birds, the teacher may discuss the different types of birds around the world. The children briefly focus on one or two birds. Do these birds fly? What do they eat? Where do they live? The teacher may show the children a poster of these birds and their similarities and differences and then model write several sentences describing these birds.

Topics could be content-oriented (science, social studies, or health, for instance), open-ended, or experience-related. The teacher may engage the children in a discussion of the types of houses people live in, their favorite television shows, or the class trip to the bakery before model writing about the topic.

Introduce a genre. The teacher may use Modeled Writing to introduce writing genres such as the personal narrative, poetry, letter writing, retelling, or factual or imaginative writing. The teacher reviews examples of the genre and then models writing in that genre.

MODEL WRITE, USING ONE OF THREE STRATEGIES. After introducing the writing context, the teacher model writes on chart paper or in a large class journal while the children watch. Throughout the week of writing, the teacher varies these three strategies:

Strategy One: Compose with the children. This strategy is especially valuable for emerging writers. The teacher verbally models how to think about what he will write, articulates the sentence(s), and then begins writing in front of the children, inviting them to suggest letters for sounds, spacing, and punctuation. For example, the teacher says, "I think I will write about having a very small dog. I will write, 'My dog is little. He fits in my pocket.'" The following dialogue might develop between the teacher and children as the teacher writes on the chart or journal:

Teacher: *My . . . what letter starts My . . . m m m m . . . ?*

Children: M.

Teacher: *Capital M or lowercase M?*

Children: Capital.

Teacher: *Why?*

Children: It's the beginning of a sentence. (*Teacher writes* M.)

Teacher: *My. What is the next letter?*

Children: It sounds like *i* but it's *y.* (*Teacher writes* y.)

Teacher: *What do I do before I start the next word?*

Children: Finger space. (*Teacher shows how to insert a finger space.*)

Teacher: *Dog. What letter starts dog . . . d d d d . . . ?*

The teacher proceeds through all the sentences as the children tell him what to write.

This process may also be used with fluent writers. Instead of asking for sounds and spacing, the teacher focuses on composing, spelling, and punctuation skills. For example, the teacher may ask the children to think of appropriate adjectives to describe the dog, what to do before writing the next paragraph (indent), or where to put the commas when writing a list.

From *Creating the Multiage Classroom* published by GoodYear Books. Copyright © 1996 Sandra J. Stone.

Strategy Two: Write with errors. In this model, the teacher verbalizes thinking through "What shall I write?" and then writes several sentences with errors as the children silently read along. For example, the teacher may write the sentences, "My dog is little. He fits in my pocket," like this: *mi dgiz litl he fitz in mi pkit.* The teacher then reads the sentences with the children. Next, he invites the children to find the errors. One child at a time uses a felt pen to correct one error until all the errors are corrected.

Strategy Three: Write the correct model; focus on skills. In this strategy, the teacher first verbalizes the thought process for writing. He then writes several sentences (correct model) as the children read the sentences silently. Next he invites the children to read the sentences chorally. The teacher focuses on several skills within the sentences such as punctuation, blends, compound words, spelling rules, capitalization, and so forth. The teacher asks the children to find each focus skill. One child at a time locates the skill and circles it with the felt pen. For example, in the sentences, "My dog is little. He fits in my pocket," the teacher may ask the children to find a capital letter. A child finds the capital *M* and circles it. The teacher may then ask the children to find a word with two syllables. A child finds *pocket*, circles it, and then divides the syllables.

CHILDREN WRITE IN LEARNING JOURNALS. After the teacher has modeled the writing process for the children and has focused on specific skills, she invites them to write in their learning journals. Each child writes within the context (literature piece, poem, topic, genres), choosing how she wishes to address it. Children may also select another topic if they so desire. (If it has been presented well, most children enjoy writing within the introduced context. However, if a child just returned from an exciting trip with her family, she may want to choose to write about it. Always allow children the opportunity to choose.)

The open-ended Modeled Writing strategy encourages all learners in mixed-age classes to write within their own developmental abilities. For example, an emergent writer may write, *I L M D.* ("I like my dog.") A fluent writer may compose several paragraphs describing her dog.

Conferencing with each child as she finishes writing, the teacher can usually talk with at least half the class in one day. Each conference is individualized. If a child needs to begin using spacing, the teacher helps the child focus on that need. If a child needs help in paragraphing, the teacher focuses the child on that need. In each case, the teacher helps the child reflect on her own writing, and then nurtures the child to the next level of development. (See the Writing Development Chart in Chapter 7.) Samples from the children's learning journals are placed in their portfolios to document growth.

On p. 122 is an outline of the modeled writing strategies. On pp. 123–124 is an example of how to plan a week of daily Modeled Writing, along with a blank form for your own planning purposes.

MODELED WRITING STRATEGIES

Strategy 1

Compose Together

1. Teacher verbalizes thought process for writing.

2. Teacher writes sentences as children choose letters for sounds, spacing, punctuation, or compose sentences and paragraphs.

3. Teacher and children read sentences chorally.

4. Children write in journals.

Strategy 2

Write with Errors

1. Teacher verbalizes thought process for writing.

2. Teacher writes sentences with errors as children read silently.

3. Teacher and children read sentences chorally.

4. Children correct errors.

5. Children write in journals.

Strategy 3

Write Correct Model

1. Teacher verbalizes thought process for writing.

2. Teacher writes sentences using correct model as children read silently.

3. Teacher and children read sentences chorally.

4. Children circle focus skills.

5. Children write in journals.

From *Creating the Multiage Classroom* published by GoodYear Books. Copyright © 1996 Sandra J. Stone.

MODELED WRITING PLANNING FORM

Day 1	Day 2	Day 3	Day 4	Day 5
Writing Context	**Writing Context**	**Writing Context**	**Writing Context**	**Writing Context**
Read *Where the Wild Things Are* (Sendak). Discuss monsters, in general.	Discuss *Where the Wild Things Are* (Sendak). If you were Max, where would you go? Would there be monsters there? If not, what would be in your magical land?	Discuss *Where the Wild Things Are* (Sendak). Choose a monster from the book. Describe the monster.	Read *There's a Nightmare in My Closet* (Mayer). Discuss the boy's feelings. Write about your feelings if you had a monster in your closet.	Discuss *There's a Nightmare in My Closet* (Mayer). Discuss the monster's feelings. Where did the monster come from? Does he have a family?
Strategy	**Strategy**	**Strategy**	**Strategy**	**Strategy**
Write with errors.	Write correct model.	Compose with children.	Write with errors.	Write correct model.
Story/Sentences	**Story/Sentences**	**Story/Sentences**	**Story/Sentences**	**Story/Sentences**
"Some monsters are scary. Some monsters are not." Sm monstrs r skry sm r not	"I would go into my land through a mirror. Inside the mirror would be friendly creatures."	"The scary monster is big with black horns and an ugly face like an angry bull. It has a large beak like an eagle."	I would be afraid if a monster lived in my closet. I would move!" i wd be afrad if a monster livd in miclosset i wd mov	"The monster is a child even though he is big. He is afraid of being alone!"
Skills	**Skills**	**Skills**	**Skills**	**Skills**
Spelling *some* and *are*; periods; spaces.	Compound words; *would*; beginning sounds *w* and *m*; syllables.	Describing words; *has, like; ea* words	*Would*; capitals; exclamation point; spellings; spaces	Syllables; exclamation point; spaces; capitals; periods.

YOUR MODELED WRITING
PLANNING FORM

Day 1	Day 2	Day 3	Day 4	Day 5
Writing Context	Writing Context	Writing Context	Writing Context	Writing Context
Strategy	Strategy	Strategy	Strategy	Strategy
Story/Sentences	Story/Sentences	Story/Sentences	Story/Sentences	Story/Sentences
Skills	Skills	Skills	Skills	Skills

Writers' Workshop

Another strategy for modeling the writing process is called Writers' Workshop. In Writers' Workshop, the teacher demonstrates how to web a story, use word banks, or create story maps. The children are divided into three groups: writing, editing, and publishing. While one group works on composing stories, the editing group meets to read and edit their stories with the teacher or partners. After the stories are edited, they are printed in book format, often on a computer. The publishing group illustrates and binds their printed stories. Writers share their published stories during an event called an author's tea or author's chair. All stories become part of the classroom library. Writers' Workshop successfully supports mixed-age and mixed-ability writers. Younger children may write stories five or six lines in length, while older children may compose five or six paragraphs. No matter what a child's stage of writing development, she can participate in writing stories. As the teacher edits with each child, he nurtures the child's development to the next stage of writing. Children also learn how to edit their own work.

It is recommended that a teacher use either Modeled Writing or Writers' Workshop since using both in the same day exhausts young writers. Many multiage teachers use Modeled Writing daily for several weeks and then switch to Writers' Workshop for several weeks.

Writing Across the Curriculum

Children are encouraged not only to read but also to write across the curriculum. Independent writing occurs at both centers and in projects. For example, when children are studying about fables, they write fables. When they are studying about sea creatures, they research and write about sea creatures. They compose their own stories at the Writing Center, record the results from an investigation at the Science Center, address notes to classmates at the Mail Box Center, and write and illustrate poems at the Poetry Center. The children learn to write by writing in a meaningful and functional environment through many open-ended experiences.

MATH

Teaching mixed-age children in the content area of mathematics is similar to facilitating their reading and writing. Because of the multiage focus on teaching children rather than curriculum, grade-level expectations do not drive math instruction. Rather, each child engages at her own pace in *experiential* math through centers, projects, and small-group instruction based on need. Math in the multiage classroom is also integrated into the whole curriculum. Bredekamp (1987, 71) suggests that the goal of a mathematics program is to "enable children to use math through exploration, discovery, and solving meaningful problems. Math activities are integrated with other relevant projects, such as science and social studies. Math skills are acquired through spontaneous play, projects, and situations of daily living."

Developmental Math

Developmental math is a term that reflects the philosophy that children are developing in their construction of mathematical concepts. Each child personally engages in constructing her own knowledge. According to Piaget *(1976)*, children pass through stages of intellectual development. All children pass through these stages in the same sequence, but at different rates. Understandings explored in previous stages are the foundation for later stages. Children are in constant transition from one stage to the next and often demonstrate thinking characteristic of more than one stage *(Labinowicz, 1985).*

From *Creating the Multiage Classroom* published by GoodYear Books. Copyright © 1996 Sandra J. Stone.

Piaget categorizes four major stages of intellectual development. The stages with approximate ages are:

1. Sensorimotor
   (birth to two years)

2. Preoperational
   (two to seven years)

3. Concrete operational
   (seven to 11 years)

4. Formal operational
   (11 and older)

In the primary multiage classroom, children are usually in the preoperational stage, transitioning to the concrete operational, or already in the concrete operational. Children, ages five through eight, move from the preoperational to the concrete operational stage of thinking. As Kamii *(1982)* suggests, children actively construct math schema based on experiences that incorporate concrete to abstract thinking.

However, the importance of the sensorimotor stage should not be overlooked. In this stage, the children explore the world by "making comparisons in space and discriminating between three-dimensional objects. These abilities are prerequisite to classifying and grouping objects and events. Without these abilities, a true understanding of many mathematical concepts would be very difficult, if not impossible" *(Schultz, Colarusso & Strawderman, 1989, p. 5)*

In the preoperational stage, children are guided by sensorial experiences and perception, rather than logic. Children attend to specific attributes and cannot process multiple comparisons, or conserve quantity *(Schultz, Colarusso & Strawderman, 1989)*. In this stage, children cannot reverse their thought processes. For example, subtraction, a reverse of addition, is often difficult for young children.

Preoperational children do have the ability to represent action through thought and language. They can classify objects that are similar or have common characteristics. They develop one-to-one correspondence, which makes it possible for children to learn how to count, add, and subtract. During this stage, children can order objects by size, texture, taste, or color in ascending or descending order. Seriation skills are essential for understanding the meaning and order of numbers *(Schultz, Colarusso & Strawderman, 1989)*.

During the concrete operational stage, children begin to reason logically and question their perceptions. They are now able to manipulate their environment through mental pictures rather than just through concrete experiences. Even though concrete operational children begin to think logically, they are still limited to physical reality and the need is still great for manipulatives at this developmental stage *(Schultz, Colarusso & Strawderman, 1989; Labinowicz, 1985)*. During this stage, children acquire reversibility of thought and conservation.

A developmentally appropriate mathematics program for children five through eight years old would include the following components:

- Number and Numeration
- Operations of Whole Numbers
- Rational Numbers
- Measurement
- Geometry
- Problem-Solving/Math Reasoning

For a complete listing, see *Early Childhood Curriculum: Developmental Bases for Learning and Teaching* by S. C. Wortham (Merrill, 1994) pp. 391–393.

As noted by Wortham *(1994),* the components of a mathematics program for children ages five to eight is *only* a guide not a prescriptive sequence. She notes that children in multiage classrooms can work on "the same objective at different age and ability levels through cooperative learning groups or paired student interactions" *(p. 394).*

Experiential Math

It is critically important for young children to have real and meaningful mathematical experiences to prepare them for the transition into the concrete operational stage of logical thinking. However, even children who are beginning to reason are still limited by physical reality and need manipulative experiences.

Five- to eight-year-olds should be given multiple opportunities to engage in concrete mathematical experiences: classifying, comparing, ordering, patterning, counting, exploring shape and space, measuring (time, money, temperature), exploring simple fractions, and developing a vocabulary that reflects mathematical concepts. Providing mixed-age learners with these experiences can be accomplished through an integrated curriculum that involves centers and projects as well as real-life situations.

Open-Ended Math Centers

Centers provide excellent opportunities for children to engage mathematical concepts at their own levels of understanding. Centers also allow children time to explore and manipulate materials. At open-ended math centers, each child develops concepts of number and constructs relationships, which no one can do for her. The center activities that follow focus on providing these types of experiences through the use of manipulatives:

From *Creating the Multiage Classroom* published by GoodYear Books. Copyright © 1996 Sandra J. Stone.

COUNTING EXPERIENCES. Centers with *counting* activities encourage children to develop their rote counting and understand one-to-one correspondence. Have them count with beads, beans, buttons, small toys, shells, seeds, and so forth. While older children may count to make a graph, younger ones count as they match different items in one-to-one correspondence. Children may count out four shells to place on an ocean floor or six leaves on a tree for an art activity. When studying *The Very Hungry Caterpillar* (Eric Carle), children may match pom-pom caterpillars to plastic fruits. Is there an equal match? Or are there more caterpillars or more fruit?

CLASSIFYING EXPERIENCES. *Classifying* involves grouping like things together. Children may sort objects by one attribute such as use, color, shape, or size. Or they may sort objects by several attributes such as color and shape. At a Science Center, children may sort shells by size and type when studying the sea, or sort rocks by type or weight when studying geology. Perhaps they classify magnetic and non-magnetic materials while using a magnet.

COMPARING EXPERIENCES. *Comparing* is the process of establishing a relationship between two objects. This involves defining specific attributes with descriptive vocabulary like *smaller, bigger, longer, longest, heavier, thicker, lightest, softer, louder, fastest.*

Children may compare size, shape, distance, weight, color, sound, or taste. At centers, children may compare plants by size, rocks by weight, or worms by length. Which of two ice cubes melts first? Does the heart beat faster after sitting or running for two minutes? At a Flannelboard Center, where the open-ended objective is to compare the characters of two stories in as many ways as possible, younger children might compare by size, whereas older children might contrast the characters dispositions.

ORDERING EXPERIENCES.

Comparing forms the foundation for *ordering* and measuring. Ordering is the process of arranging objects based on specific attributes. At centers, children may order the life-cycle of a butterfly, or order rocks by weight, from the lightest to the heaviest. Perhaps they arrange plants from shortest to tallest, order a story from beginning to end, or order the cereal boxes by size at the Home Center.

PATTERNING EXPERIENCES.

Recognizing patterns from the simple to the complex is also an important mathematical concept. Activities should allow the children to engage in pattern recognition and creation at their own levels of understanding, whether they are making patterns with pattern blocks, creating patterns at the Art Center, or experimenting with auditory patterns at the Music Center. As children design necklaces from colored macaroni, one child may devise a complex pattern while another child creates a simple pattern, yet the activity engages both children. Have children identify patterns in butterfly wings, snake colorings, or playground equipment.

SHAPE AND SPACE EXPERIENCES.

Children explore *shape and space* as they move, build, compare, and observe within their environment. Have them investigate shapes and spaces at Block, Play, Flannelboard, and Art Centers and while using math manipulatives such as geoboards or pegboards. Centers should engage children in measuring, constructing large and small projects, and using shapes and space in art activities.

MEASURING EXPERIENCES.

Measurement includes time and money as well as linear and liquid measurement.

Young children still developing a sense of measurement should not be prematurely expected to understand it in the abstract. Some teachers expect children to tell time at six years of age when they may not conceptually understand time until eight.

Children's experiences with measurement should be concrete and range from simple to complex. At centers, for example, while younger children count the number of coins, older children can determine their value. Younger children may decide which box is longer, whereas older children may measure the boxes with a ruler. As younger children "play" with measuring cups at a sand table, older children determine how many cups of sand will fill a certain container. Open-ended measuring at centers allows each child to engage the process at her own level of understanding.

FRACTION EXPERIENCES. At centers, children can experience wholes and parts from the simple to the complex. Remember that young children have difficulty understanding the concept of equal pieces and need time to practice with sizes that are the same and different. Children may take a whole graham cracker and break it into parts. Are they the same (equal)? A whole circle or rectangle may be cut into equal parts to accomplish an art activity. Playhouse pizza may be divided into equal parts for a pizza party at the Home Center.

Again, the activities should be open-ended, as children will come to them with different levels of understanding. For example, at a Recipe Center, younger children may split a piece of bread in half, whereas older children may divide the bread into fourths as they make a peanut butter snack.

NUMBER EXPERIENCES. Centers may also provide children with opportunities to use abstract symbols (numbers) with and without associating them with concrete objects depending on the child's development. For example, to find out how many objects will fill each of two containers and then how many objects in all will fill both, younger children might count all the objects from both containers, while older ones count the objects in each container and then add using number symbols. At a Store Center, younger children may count dimes by tens to get $1 for the price of a toy. Older children might choose several toys and then add numerically to see if they have enough money for their total purchase.

Open-ended centers that promote math experiences integrate easily into the curriculum. Counting, comparing, ordering, and measuring can be done within the context of a thematic study. Other centers may focus only on mathematical concepts without integration into the curriculum.

Math Games

Math games can provide math experiences during center time or in cooperative groups and allow children to use number concepts in the context of play. Kamii (1985) suggests choosing appropriate games that are neither too difficult nor too easy. However, she also recommends not worrying too much about the appropriateness of a game because children will naturally gravitate to the games they like to play and at which they succeed. Kamii suggests putting each game in a box to make them easily accessible for the children. She also suggests introducing a new game first to a few children. Then they can teach a group of children and so on.

Appropriate card games include War, Go Fish, and Concentration. Popular board games include tick-tack-toe, Number Bingo, Dominoes, Double Parcheesi®, and Sorry®. Dice games and shape games are also suitable. Encourage children to create their own versions of games to integrate with a thematic study.

Daily Living Math

Children in multiage classrooms should experience the practical role math plays in our daily lives. To provide such opportunities, teachers allow children to engage and direct various activities in the classroom, such as distributing snacks, taking attendance, voting, collecting money, and putting away materials. As multiage teachers promote autonomy in their classrooms, they find many more ways for children to use mathematics every day.

Use the form on p. 135 to plan Math Centers, Math Games, and Daily Living Math activities.

Projects

Projects can also provide practical math experiences for young children. Nelson and Worth *(1983)* suggest that problem situations should involve real objects or simulations of real objects; capture the interest of the children; engage the children in moving, transforming, or modifying the materials; and offer opportunities for different levels of solution. Some children should be able to solve the problem using simple strategies, while others employ more sophisticated means.

A thematic study of habitats might stimulate many activities involving math: surveying the school and graphing those who live in apartments, homes, and townhomes; measuring and building a playhouse habitat; comparing and contrasting animal habitats; creating a scale map of a home; comparing rural and urban populations and types of habitats; using place value in writing population numbers; adding and subtracting the price of homes in a given area for comparison; comparing the size of land measurements; and so forth.

Guided Math

While children are engaged in centers, the multiage teacher works with small groups of children on specific math skills based on their needs. During Guided Math, children may use manipulatives to count or add, learn place value, estimate, make predictions, work with prime numbers, subtract, multiply, and divide. The teacher leads each flexible grouping based on the participants' need to explore concrete or abstract concepts, expecting no more from each child than the child understands. A Guided Math Planning Form can be found on p. 136.

Math in the Instructional Day

As we know, center and projects integrate math into the curriculum. If the current thematic study is caterpillars, the children may write caterpillar story problems at the Writing Center, graph the food eaten by *The Very Hungry Caterpillar* (Eric Carle) at the Math Center, create caterpillars using circles at the Art Center, and order the life-cycle of a butterfly at the Science Center.

Some multiage teachers use the morning center time to focus on literacy-related activities and the afternoon to concentrate on science and math. For example, during a study of dinosaurs, the class may write and read about dinosaurs in the morning and then visit open-ended math-related dinosaur centers in the afternoon. Perhaps they weigh toy dinosaurs (younger children to the pound and older children to the quarter pound) at one center. At another, they measure toy dinosaurs. (Younger children decide which is longer using blocks or colored string, and older children may measure by the inch or quarter inch using a ruler.) A dinosaur store allows children to use money to buy dinosaurs by making transactions based on their own knowledge base. Another center may have children comparing and contrasting the size and weight of extinct dinosaurs. Younger children may compare by ordering dinosaurs by size and weight, older children actually compute the mathematical differences in size and weight.

If you are using the project approach, the children engage in solving dinosaur-related problems. As children work in small cooperative groups throughout the day, the teacher may also work with small math groups based on need.

The Importance of Social Interaction

Piaget *(1976)* and others suggest that social interaction is necessary for children to learn how to think logically. Social interaction facilitates how children construct number concepts. Multiage classrooms provide a rich opportunity for children to learn from each other. Interacting at centers, during projects, and in small cooperative groupings helps children to construct logico-mathematical knowledge.

MATH CENTERS

MATH GAMES

DAILY LIVING MATH

GUIDED MATH
PLANNING FORM

Day	Group 1	Group 2	Group 3	Group 4
1	Skill: Manipulatives:	Skill: Manipulatives:	Skill: Manipulatives:	Skill: Manipulatives:
2	Skill: Manipulatives:	Skill: Manipulatives:	Skill: Manipulatives:	Skill: Manipulatives:
3	Skill: Manipulatives:	Skill: Manipulatives:	Skill: Manipulatives:	Skill: Manipulatives:
4	Skill: Manipulatives:	Skill: Manipulatives:	Skill: Manipulatives:	Skill: Manipulatives:
5	Skill: Manipulatives:	Skill: Manipulatives:	Skill: Manipulatives:	Skill: Manipulatives:

From *Creating the Multiage Classroom* published by GoodYear Books. Copyright © 1996 Sandra J. Stone.

SCIENCE

Science as a Process

Like reading, writing, and solving problems, science in the primary multiage classroom is viewed as a process. It consists of two main areas: investigation and knowledge (Mayesky 1995). Mayesky (1995, 339) suggests that "science is a thing; sciencing is an action." Although the process of learning "how to find answers is considered more important than the answers themselves," both are valued. The process of *sciencing* engages everyone in the multiage classroom as they investigate to discover knowledge. Unlike sequenced content learning by grade level, sciencing is an active experience with the focus on *doing*—observing, investigating, and discovering. Children in multiage classrooms particularly benefit from the social interaction and collaborative learning that takes place as they pursue sciencing together. Each child progresses at her own rate of understanding from "concrete learnings (facts) through conceptual images (concepts) to more abstract generalizations" (Leeper, Witherspoon, and Day 1984, 338). Wortham (1994, 414) notes that as young children "make the transition from preoperational to concrete operational thinking, they can move from totally active experiences to activities where they can use thought processes to understand concepts." These transitions take place within the sciencing process.

Discovery Science

To promote the process of sciencing, multiage teachers practice *discovery science* with their students by creating an environment where children can observe, compare, explore, and investigate. Discovery science encourages children to use higher-order thinking skills while engaging in sciencing. The following open-ended questions target the science process skills:

OBSERVING
What did you notice?

COMPARING
How are these alike or different?

CLASSIFYING
In what ways can these objects be grouped or sorted?

MEASURING
How can we measure what is happening?

DISCUSSING/REPORTING
How can we communicate our discoveries so others will understand?

PREDICTING
What do you think will happen?

From *Creating the Multiage Classroom* published by GoodYear Books. Copyright © 1996 Sandra J. Stone.

Consider these open-ended questions as well:

How many different kinds of properties can you find?

(floats, sinks, soft, hard, heavy, light, blue, rough, round)

How can you change a property?

(How can you make this liquid a solid? How can you make the color darker? How can you make the object float?)

What will happen if you change the conditions?

(What will happen if you put the plant in a dark closet? What will happen if you place a dried apple in water?)

What could you do to change the property?

(What could you do to make this object that floats sink? What could you do to this celery stick to change its color? What could you do to this sand to make it like clay?)

In what ways could you change the conditions so the property is better?

(In what ways could you help this plant grow faster? In what ways could you change this soil so it is better for plants to grow in?)

What conditions are best for the property?

(What conditions are best for plants to grow? What conditions are best for food to stay fresh? What conditions are best for frogs to reproduce?)

Open-ended questions direct children in the process and can be used for investigation and discovery at centers as well as during projects.

Using Science Themes

In the multiage classroom, science makes an excellent focus for the integrated curriculum. Use the webbing approach to plan your science themes and topics across the content areas. As an example, review a web with the science topic Plants at its center on p. 141.

Open-Ended Science Centers

You can now design centers to reflect the science theme across the curricular areas. For example, children could listen to stories such as *The Carrot Seed* (Ruth Krauss) at the Listening Center and

write fictional stories about magical seeds at the Writing Center. At the Drama Center, they might dramatize the story *Jack and the Beanstalk*. At the Science Center, children may record plant growth in their observational logs. Of course, these open-ended experiences allow all children of mixed ages and abilities to participate.

Science centers can also be tailored to specific scientific investigations. Furnish these centers with the appropriate materials for exploration, investigation, and experimentation: observation logs, a magnifying glass or microscope, scales, a thermometer, a stethoscope, batteries, a funnel, a compass, a

gyroscope, a prism, convex and concave lenses, a stopwatch, magnets, science reference books, materials for experimentation and observation, plants, terrariums, aquariums, and classroom pets. Other resources might include a collection of interesting items such as shells, lichens, seeds, sandpaper, cork, and rocks.

Heller and Turner *(1988)* suggest creating Science Centers around basic areas of study: Reptile Center (snakes, turtles, iguanas), Arthropod Center (insects), Water Communities Center (freshwater pond animals and vegetation). Other specific centers could focus on geology (rocks and fossils), matter and energy (magnets, electricity, balloons), living things (plants and animals), earth and universe (astronomy), and so forth.

INTEGRATED CURRICULUM WEBBING

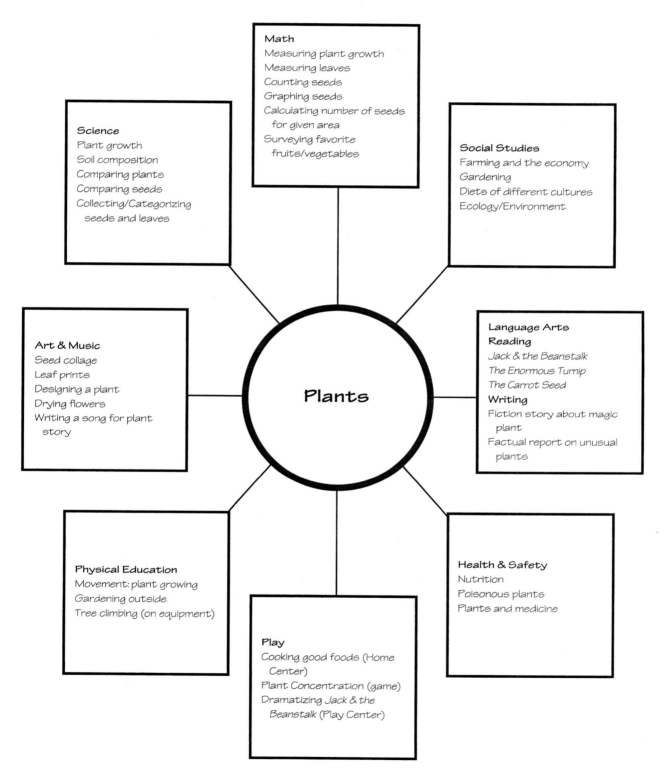

Math
Measuring plant growth
Measuring leaves
Counting seeds
Graphing seeds
Calculating number of seeds
  for given area
Surveying favorite
  fruits/vegetables

Science
Plant growth
Soil composition
Comparing plants
Comparing seeds
Collecting/Categorizing
  seeds and leaves

Social Studies
Farming and the economy
Gardening
Diets of different cultures
Ecology/Environment

Art & Music
Seed collage
Leaf prints
Designing a plant
Drying flowers
Writing a song for plant
  story

Plants

Language Arts
Reading
Jack & the Beanstalk
The Enormous Turnip
The Carrot Seed
Writing
Fiction story about magic
  plant
Factual report on unusual
  plants

Physical Education
Movement: plant growing
Gardening outside.
Tree climbing (on equipment)

Play
Cooking good foods (Home
  Center)
Plant Concentration (game)
Dramatizing *Jack & the
  Beanstalk* (Play Center)

Health & Safety
Nutrition
Poisonous plants
Plants and medicine

Science Projects

Projects make an exciting way to approach a science theme. After the children choose a topic based on personal interest or a community concern, the class decides how to investigate it. The K-W-L Chart approach covered in Chapter 4 *(Ogle, 1986; Carr & Ogle 1987)* can help in focusing on questions for investigation. Topics may be broad (change, energy, ecology) or specific (life-cycle of a frog, plant growth). Small cooperative groups may investigate one area of a broad topic, or each group might conduct its own investigation of one specific class topic. Consider the following examples:

PROJECT TOPIC: "Change"
Group 1: Change in plants
Group 2: Change in weather
Group 3: Change in space
Group 4: Change in matter

PROJECT TOPIC: "Life-cycle of a Frog"
Groups 1, 2, 3, 4: Set up a frog hatchery tank, record observations, make predictions, illustrate the life-cycle of a frog, measure tadpoles.

Another way to investigate specific topics with small cooperative groups is to have your children generate the topic of interest, ask a question about the topic, and then formulate a hypothesis. For example, perhaps for the topic "soil," the question is "Does water soak into some types of soil faster than others?" The hypothesis is "Water soaks into sand faster than clay." The group now plans its experiment to see if the hypothesis is correct.

How projects develop will depend on your class and the interests of your children. Keep in mind that even though the children are working with science projects, they are reading, writing, and solving problems; the curriculum is integrated within the science theme. The following planning sheets will help you plan both Science Centers and projects.

SCIENCE CENTERS

Observing, Comparing, Classifying, Measuring,
Discussing/Reporting, Predicting,

Materials:
Process(es):
Question(s):

Observing, Comparing, Classifying, Measuring,
Discussing/Reporting, Predicting,

Materials:
Process(es):
Question(s):

Observing, Comparing, Classifying, Measuring,
Discussing/Reporting, Predicting,

Materials:
Process(es):
Question(s):

Observing, Comparing, Classifying, Measuring,
Discussing/Reporting, Predicting,

Materials:
Process(es):
Question(s):

SCIENCE PROJECTS

Group Members:

Topic:

Group Members:

Topic:

Group Members:

Topic:

Group Members:

Topic:

PLANNING AN EXPERIMENT

Group Members:

Topic:

Question(s):

Hypothesis:

Procedure:

Findings:

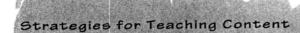

SOCIAL STUDIES

Social Studies as a Process

Young children are developing in their social knowledge, skills, and attitudes. Just like science, reading, and writing, social studies is viewed as a process in the multiage classroom that supplies a rich environment for supporting it.

In the multiage classroom, social studies encompasses two primary processes: *becoming social beings* and *learning about the world in which we live*. According to Leeper, Witherspoon, and Day *(1984, 292)*, it is important to help young children "grow beyond concern for themselves alone toward a concern for others and a knowledge of the social world in which they live." Mayesky *(1995, 434)* defines social studies as "the study of human beings in their environment and of the concepts, skills, and attitudes that are needed in order to become social beings." For young children, social studies must address the process of becoming social. Social development includes attitude and value learning as well.

The second process focuses on learning about the world in which we live through studies in values, civics, history, geography, economics, sociology, anthropology, ecology, and current issues. The processes to learn include locating information, organizing information (classifying, comparing/contrasting, summarizing, graphing), and interpreting and reflecting on information.

Focusing on the Social in Social Studies

The first goal of social studies in the multiage classroom is to support children as they become social beings. As Wortham *(1994, 422)* suggests, "social development . . . in primary classrooms is nurtured through the daily process of living, playing, learning, and working together." The multiage teacher encourages this development by creating many opportunities to involve children socially. Children of various ages work together at centers and on projects; they play together at indoor play centers and in outdoor play groups. Mixed-age children also share in daily living as they eat lunch together, plan together, share ideas with one another, and help each other. Children learn social skills within the meaningful context of socialization. They learn to cooperate, negotiate, share, take turns, see another's perspective, respect each other, care about one another, and help one another. They learn to take responsibility for their actions and to settle their own problems. The children also learn about themselves, gaining a sense of belonging and self-worth. They see that others value them. Spending three years together supports the children's sense of belonging; mentoring and nurturing by older children promotes their self-esteem.

The lack of competition among the children in the multiage classroom empowers the socialization process. Different expectations for different children, frees them to support and encourage one another. Modeling of social skills by older children also promotes socialization. Older children model sharing, helping, caring, negotiating, and taking turns. They engage younger children in these social processes and scaffold behaviors for them.

The teacher acts as facilitator, creating a social environment, modeling social behaviors, and coming alongside each child to help her develop socially. Teachers realize that young children are egocentric, that they believe the world revolves around them. Young children have difficulty seeing another's point of view or sharing their possessions. The multiage teacher supports each child's development in these areas, resisting anger and frustration when a child does not share or fights over who is first. The teacher realizes that developing social skills is a process, like developing skills in reading, writing, and mathematics. While helping children to resolve their problems, the teacher uses the opportunity to teach social skills. The teacher takes the time to help children learn how to share and be kind because social growth is just as important as academic growth.

Social Studies as a Content Area

The second aspect of social studies involves content areas such as history, geography, and social sciences. Multiage study in these content areas focuses more on concepts, processes, and values than on facts. Children construct their own concepts and values as they engage in meaningful activities. Seefeldt *(1993, 101–102)* notes that "concepts cannot be taught; they can only be constructed by each individual. Teachers can, however, nurture children's embryonic concepts by providing a rich environment and conditions that will foster the development of fully formed, accurate, and complete concepts of social studies." Consider the areas and concepts on p. 149.

Using Social Studies Themes

Like science, social studies makes an excellent focus study for the integrated curriculum. Use the webbing approach to plan your social studies themes and topics across the content areas. As an example, review the web on p. 150 with a social studies theme and "Habitats" at its center.

Open-Ended Social Studies Centers

Centers may be created to reflect the social studies theme across the curricular areas. For example, using the Habitats theme, children would play house at the Home Center, act out *The Three Little Pigs* at the Drama Center, and listen to stories about the habitats of *Amos and Boris* (William Steig) and the adventure of *The Little House* (Virginia Lee Burton). At the Science Center, children could research safe environments for safe habitats and graph a survey of the different types of homes of children in the school. They might read about various habitats and write stories about their own habitats.

From *Creating the Multiage Classroom* published by GoodYear Books. Copyright © 1996 Sandra J. Stone.

Social Studies Area	Concepts
Values	Everyone has worth and dignity.
Civics	Rules can help us live together successfully.
History	We live with change and the passage of time.
Economics	People work; people buy and sell goods.
Geography	Earth is where we live; we can find places, travel to places; places differ in location and climate.
Anthropology	People live by certain values and traditions. People are both the same and different.
Sociology	People live in families and communities. Families and communities are both the same and different.
Ecology	People are responsible for caring for the Earth.
International Understandings	People live in other countries.
Current Issues	We live in a changing world

Source: Leeper, Sarah, Ralph Witherspoon, and Barbara Day. *Good Schools for Good Children.* New York, NY: Macmillan, 1984, pp. 299–300.

INTEGRATED CURRICULUM WEBBING

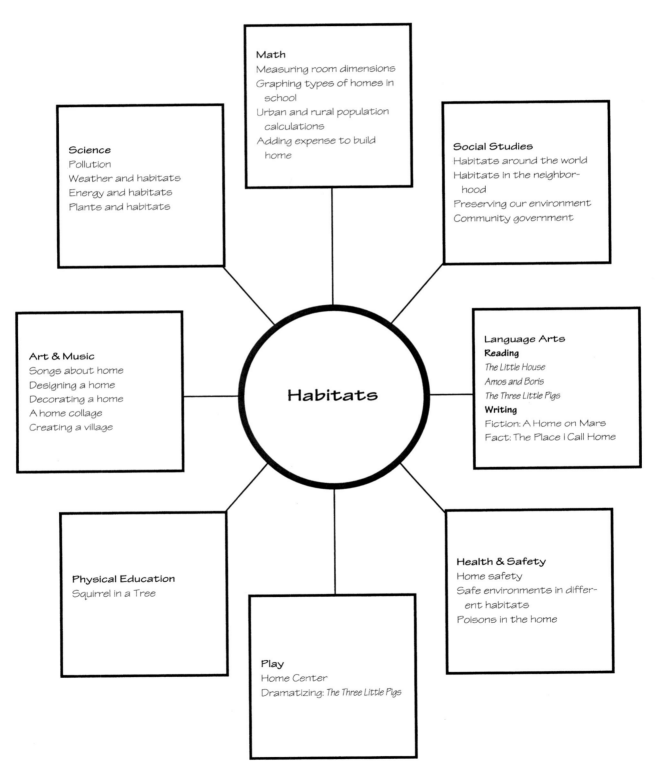

Math
Measuring room dimensions
Graphing types of homes in
  school
Urban and rural population
  calculations
Adding expense to build
  home

Science
Pollution
Weather and habitats
Energy and habitats
Plants and habitats

Social Studies
Habitats around the world
Habitats in the neighbor-
  hood
Preserving our environment
Community government

Art & Music
Songs about home
Designing a home
Decorating a home
A home collage
Creating a village

Habitats

Language Arts
Reading
The Little House
Amos and Boris
The Three Little Pigs
Writing
Fiction: A Home on Mars
Fact: The Place I Call Home

Physical Education
Squirrel in a Tree

Play
Home Center
Dramatizing: *The Three Little Pigs*

Health & Safety
Home safety
Safe environments in differ-
  ent habitats
Poisons in the home

Generic centers in the classroom can support social studies concept development in the following ways:

PLAY CENTERS. Life Play Centers in the classroom support both social skill development and social studies concept development. For example, children who play post office, gas station, grocery story, doctor's office, movie theater, bank, and toy shop learn about their community. The post office lends itself to learning about mail and different parts of the country and world, and road maps can be made available at the gas station. A cash register and money promote the concepts of supply and demand at the grocery store. Concepts about economics underlie the Bank Center.

BLOCK CENTER. At the Block Center, children learn mapping skills by building communities and designing neighborhoods.

SAND AND WATER CENTER. As they construct roads, tunnels, bridges, valleys, and mountains at the Sand and Water Center, children get hands-on experiences with geography.

HOME CENTER. The Home Center is an ideal place to practice social skills. Children play out different family roles, learn to negotiate roles, and practice life social skills.

ART CENTER. At the Art Center, children examine and replicate art such as pottery, paintings, and weavings from different cultures and historical periods.

MUSIC CENTER. The Music Center offers cultural, historical, and contemporary music and dance.

WRITING CENTER. Children may describe political views, experiment with different genres of writing, compose historical pieces, and design travel brochures.

LIBRARY CENTER. The Library Center should contain books that reflect all aspects of the social studies.

POETRY CENTER. The poems at the Poetry Center may be interpreted from different social studies perspectives such as cultural awareness, social issues, geography, and history.

Some centers may be specifically set up for focusing on social studies. For example, a Geography Center may offer a globe and maps as well as books about places on our Earth. Artifacts from the past and pictures of different time periods might furnish a History Center. An Anthropology Center could focus on different cultures and traditions. Centers can also focus on values and self-concept development. Like all centers in a multiage classroom, those with a social studies theme should be open-ended so all children can participate and should also encourage cross-age learning.

Social Studies Projects

Social studies lends itself to creative projects. The topics may come from the children's personal interests or a current global or local issue. After the children choose the topic, they decide on how to proceed. Project topics can be broad like government or pollution, or specific like school government or the history of travel. Small cooperative groups may investigate one area of the broad topic or each group may study a certain area of a specific topic. For example:

PROJECT TOPIC: "Pollution"
Group 1: Human-Made Air Pollution
Group 2: Natural Air Pollution (volcanoes, forest fires)
Group 3: Freshwater Pollution
Group 4: Saltwater Pollution

PROJECT TOPIC: "History of Travel"
Group 1: Travel Long Ago`
Group 2: Travel Now
Group 3: Travel in the Future

PROJECT TOPIC: "The Class Election"
Group 1: Campaign Managers
Group 2: Election Officials
Group 3: Publicity (TV, Newspaper)

The topics chosen for social studies projects will depend on your class. Whatever the topic, the children will be reading, writing, and solving problems, and the curriculum will be integrated within the social studies theme. The following planning sheets will be helpful in planning social studies centers and projects.

From *Creating the Multiage Classroom* published by GoodYear Books. Copyright © 1996 Sandra J. Stone.

SOCIAL STUDIES
CENTERS

Values
Civics
History
Economics
Geography
Anthropology
Sociology
Ecology
International Understandings
Current Issues

SOCIAL STUDIES PROJECTS

Group Members:

Topic:

Group Members:

Topic:

Group Members:

Topic:

Group Members:

Topic:

From Creating the Multiage Classroom published by GoodYear Books. Copyright © 1996 Sandra J. Stone.

ART, MUSIC, PLAY, AND MOVEMENT

Providing for Creative Expression

Creative expression is an important part of a young child's learning experiences in the multiage classroom. Mayesky (1995, 4) defines creativity as "a way of thinking and acting or making something that is original for the individual and valued by that person or others." A child exercises her creativity as she finds a new way to solve a problem or creates a new product such as a picture, a song, a poem, or an invention. As with all learning, creative expression involves both a process of *discovering*, which depends on the imagination, playing with ideas, and exploring, as well as *proving*, which involves using skills to evaluate ideas, analyze results, and test solutions. Mayesky (1995, 10) also suggests that when "children can go at their own pace and figure out their own way of doing things in a relaxed learning situation, they are likely to become more creative." In the multiage classroom, children should encounter many opportunities for creative expression. Leeper, Witherspoon, and Day (1984, 381) note that "the creative being does not emerge suddenly. The creative person develops gradually and grows by meeting problems and situations, recognizing them, and being able to solve or face them successfully. Experiences in art, music, movement, and other activities in children's centers can contribute to the development of a creative person."

Creative Centers

One effective way to provide opportunities for children to engage in creative expression is to incorporate such opportunities into your centers. Creative centers should *always* be available during center time, not just occasionally.

ART CENTER. Furnish the Art Center with supplies that children can access themselves, such as crayons, markers, paper, glue, paint, chalk, and clay. If possible, painting easels should be permanent fixtures. The art activities may be open-ended, giving children the chance to choose what to create. The activities at the center may also reflect the current theme. For example, if you are reading about *Clifford, the Big Red Dog* (Norman Bridwell), children may create large portraits of Clifford at the painting easels. If you are studying monsters, children could make paper-bag masks at the center. During a study of plants, the children may make leaf rubbing designs.

MUSIC CENTER. At the music center, children can choose to listen to a variety of favorite music and songs, read song books or printed lyrics, or sing along with their favorite pieces. The center may also offer instruments on which the children can create their own music. Perhaps they will record their own songs and music on tapes. The Music Center might tie into the current theme. The children may create their own musical chant to go along with the Big Book *The Hobyahs* (retold by Brenda Parkes and Judith Smith), or listen to music that reflects the theme of friendships, or songs that depict the weather.

PLAY. Play Centers provide children with many creative opportunities. Play Centers may range from a Home Center, thematic Play Centers, Life Centers (grocery store, bank, shoe store), Building Centers (blocks, Lego®, Lincoln Logs®), and Puzzles and Games centers. At Play Centers, children grow cognitively, socially, emotionally, and physically.

The creative process of play is intrinsically rewarding for children and extremely valuable for their development. Primary multiage teachers should not overlook the importance of play and should make sure to provide for play on a daily basis.

MOVEMENT CENTERS. Centers that allow for creative movement may also be tied to Play, Music, Poetry, and Drama centers. Children should be encouraged to move to music, create their own dances, engage in finger plays, dramatize poetry, act out stories, and play games with movement. For example, they could interpret water dripping, flooding, melting, or spilling at a Movement Center when studying a water unit. Perhaps they can exercise parts of the body as they recite a poem during a study of human anatomy. The children may also pantomime sadness, happiness, or anger when studying feelings. Encourage outdoor movement activities such as jumping, skipping, and running as well.

From *Creating the Multiage Classroom* published by Good Year Books. Copyright © 1996 Sandra J. Stone.

Using Arts-Related Themes

The arts are often overlooked when it comes to thematic study. Try choosing plays, musicals, or dance as the classroom themes. For example, the children could study the play and music of *Peter and the Wolf,* the art of children's artist Eric Carle, or the music and dance of the *Nutcracker Suite.* From the center of the web, the arts expand to the other curricular areas such as reading, writing, social studies, and math. Review the example of a webbing with the theme of artist Eric Carle on p. 158.

Creative Arts Projects

Using the creative arts as the center of the curriculum prompts ideas for interesting and exciting projects. Children may engage in putting on a play or musical. They might design an art museum featuring different styles of art. Consider the following example of the way small cooperative groups might work on a single project.

PROJECT TOPIC: *Cinderella*
Group 1: Write the play
Group 2: Create the costumes
Group 3: Create the scenery
Group 4: Plan publicity

INTEGRATED
CURRICULUM WEBBING

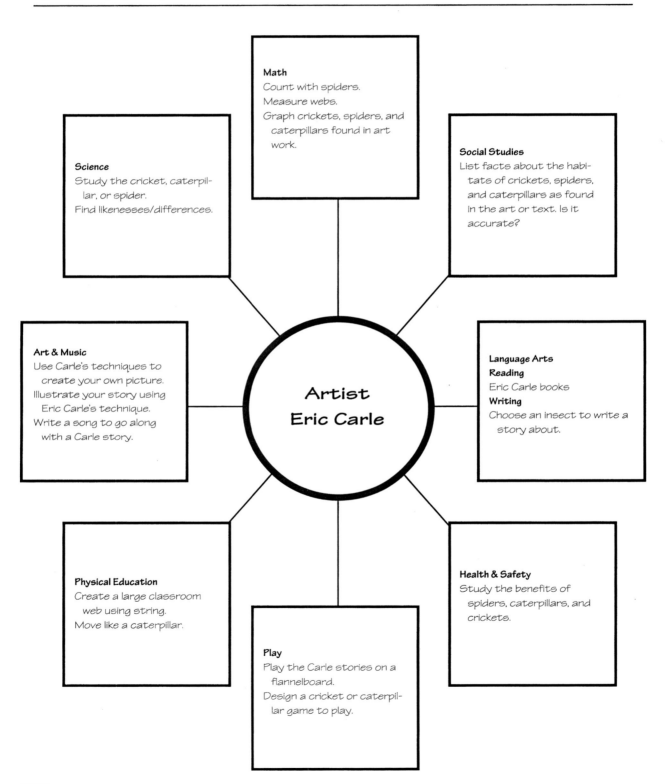

Math
Count with spiders.
Measure webs.
Graph crickets, spiders, and caterpillars found in art work.

Science
Study the cricket, caterpillar, or spider.
Find likenesses/differences.

Social Studies
List facts about the habitats of crickets, spiders, and caterpillars as found in the art or text. Is it accurate?

Art & Music
Use Carle's techniques to create your own picture.
Illustrate your story using Eric Carle's technique.
Write a song to go along with a Carle story.

**Artist
Eric Carle**

Language Arts
Reading
Eric Carle books
Writing
Choose an insect to write a story about.

Physical Education
Create a large classroom web using string.
Move like a caterpillar.

Play
Play the Carle stories on a flannelboard.
Design a cricket or caterpillar game to play.

Health & Safety
Study the benefits of spiders, caterpillars, and crickets.

From *Creating the Multiage Classroom* published by GoodYear Books. Copyright © 1996 Sandra J. Stone.

CHAPTER SIX

SAMPLE CURRICULUM PLANS

This chapter suggests five curricular plans, each covering a two- to three-week period of time. The plans demonstrate how to integrate the curriculum, make use of open-ended centers and projects, and teach broad-based skills in context. Use them as guides for your own creative planning based on the needs and interests of your children.

Each plan begins with a general planning web that presents many ideas around each theme. Three of the plans are based on literature themes, one plan has a social studies theme, and the last is based on a science theme. The plans follow the instructional day models discussed in Chapter 4.

PLAN 1-MODEL 1:

LITERATURE THEME

WHERE THE WILD THINGS ARE (MAURICE SENDAK)

Science
Real "monster" in biology (boa
    constrictor, rhinoceros, igua-
    nas)
Jungle vegetation
Rain forest
Ocean pollution
Teeth

Math
Counting/adding monsters
Graphing monster types
Measuring monsters
Making calendars
Sorting monster types

Social Studies
Land and sea concepts
Oceans of the world
Islands
Feelings
Family relationships
Kings/government
Monster traditions / Monster
    culture / Monster habitats

Art & Music
Paper-bag monster masks
Monster paintings
Monster clay sculptures
Monster mosaics
Design a crown
Monster music/rumpus

Where the Wild Things Are

Language Arts
Reading
Monster books/poetry
Real monster stories
Writing
Research real monsters
Fiction: monster story

Physical Education
Re-create wild rumpus
Monster march

Play
Home Center
Where the Wild Things Are
    (drama)
Play story on flannelboard
Create monster play center

Health & Safety
Make healthy menus for
    breakfast, lunch, dinner
Boat safety
Safety when carrying utensils

A.M.

___ **Large Group Opening**

Calendar

News from home

Shared Big Book

Week 1: *THE HOBYAHS* (Brenda Parkes/Judith Smith)

Skills: Capitals, commas in a series, adjectives, blends, -ing words, sight word *the*,
capital *H*

Culminating Activity: Design a Hobyah Machine.

Week 2: *WHO'S IN THE SHED?* (Brenda Parkes)

    Skills: Contractions; blends; *-ing* words; question marks; rhyming words; sight words *in, the*

    Culminating Activity: Do an innovation. Change the final character to a monster or have monsters peeking in the shed.

Shared Poem

Week 1: "Hobyah Chant" from book

    Skills: Exclamation points, blends, contractions, capital *T*

Week 2: *I Thought I Saw a Monster* (Sandra J. Stone)

    Skills: Contractions, rhyming words, syllables

Guided Reading Groups/Centers

Small Guided Reading Groups: Select books appropriate for each group. Choose extended activities to tie in with the Monster theme, if possible.

Centers

Big Book: Children read *The Hobyahs* or *Who's in the Shed?* in pairs as well as other favorite Big Books or Shared Reading books.

Listening: Children choose to listen from a selection of books that represents fact and fiction about monsters: *There's a Nightmare in My Closet; A Special Trick* (both by Mercer Mayer).

Writing: Children write a fiction story about their own adventure to a faraway land, a story about a monster, a letter to the mother from Max, or monster rules. They first design a book cover from materials at the Writing Center.

Letters: Children manipulate letters at the Letter Center.

Notes: Children write notes to an imaginary friendly class monster. The imaginary monster writes back to the children.

Printing: Children make thumbprint monsters and then write about their creation. Children also use stamp printing letters to label the monsters.

Flannelboard: Children retell the story *Where the Wild Things Are* using flannelboard story figures.

Drama: In the stage area, children act out the story *Where the Wild Things Are*. The children use the paper-bag masks they made at the Art Center.

Home: Children pretend they are in Max's house.

Play: Children play with boats in a water tub.

Science: Children will classify various types of real "monsters" by type (i.e., reptile, mammal). Children research facts about a "monster" of their choice.

Social Studies: Children draw face pictures to match feelings expressed in the book *Where the Wild Things Are* (i.e., lonely, sad, happy, angry). Children write about a sad or happy time in their lives.

Children also find the oceans and landmasses on a globe and flat map. Children color the oceans and landmasses on a flat map.

OHP: Children read overhead stories created by classmates during Guided Reading.

Art: Children make paper-bag monster masks to use at the Drama Center. Children also paint monsters at the art easel. Paintings will be added to a class mural on monsters and used for a measuring activity during math.

Music: Children create a new chant to be sung by the Hobyahs or write a song to be used during the "wild rumpus" in *Where the Wild Things Are*.

Computer: Children use available software. If a printer is available, children type the stories they created at the Writing Center.

Poetry: Children read the poem card for the week as well as other poetry cards. Each child will then illustrate his own copy of the weekly Shared Poem and add it to his poetry book.

Library: Children choose from a variety of books to read. Some of the books reflect the Monster theme, both fact and fiction. Children use the library books to research the social studies topic.

Read-the-Walls: Children walk around the room with a friend, reading the wall print in the literacy-rich classroom.

From *Creating the Multiage Classroom* published by GoodYear Books. Copyright © 1996 Sandra J. Stone.

___ **Recess**

Children have monster races or reenact the story from *Where the Wild Things Are*.

___ **Modeled Writing (large group)**

Teacher will discuss monsters throughout the two weeks. The following are possible topics to discuss and write about:

- If you went to a faraway land, what would be on the island?
- Choose a monster picture from *Where the Wild Things Are* and write a descriptive paragraph.
- Write about the monster you chose, describing what he is like and what he does.
- Tell about a time when you were "getting into mischief."
- Write a descriptive paragraph about the land Max visited.
- Write about a monster who comes to live with you.
- Write about a time when you were lonely like Max.
- Discuss the Loch Ness Monster. Write some facts that interest you.
- Discuss the Abominable Snowman. Write some facts that interest you.
- Discuss Big Foot. Write some facts that interest you.

During Journal Writing, children use the discussion content to write a fact or fiction story. The teacher conferences individually with children as they complete their journal entries.

P.M.

___ **Read to Children (large group)**

The teacher reads both fact and fiction monster-related books as well as favorite stories. Children participate as guest readers during this time, reading a favorite book and/or a book from Guided Reading to the group.

___ **Independent Reading**

Children read books from the library or book baskets. Children choose from a variety of books including fact and fiction monster books. Reading may be individual or social. Social reading occurs in pairs and small groups.

___ ## Guided Math/Centers

Teacher meets with small groups of children based on need while the rest of the class is at centers with a focus on math, science, and social studies.

General Centers: Geoboards, tangrams, puzzles, blocks, Lego®, math games, flannelboard, manipulatives

Math Theme Centers:

Research: Children research the size of famous monsters such as the Loch Ness Monster, Big Foot, and the Abominable Snowman, and then use rulers to create life-sized murals.

Measuring: Children measure painted monsters created at the Art Center. Children make Big Foot tracks with their own feet and then measure the footprints.

Weighing: Children weigh healthy food items such as a bag of potatoes, a bag of carrots, or a bag of oranges.

Counting: Younger children count monster cutouts and then graph them by color or type. Older children add or subtract monsters to get various math combinations. Children create their own Monster Math problems or word problems. For example, a monster has six teeth on top and three teeth on the bottom. How many teeth does he have in all? Monsters with large mouths and packing peanuts can be used as manipulatives for the problem.

Estimation: Children estimate how many teeth and claws appear on the art-only page in *Where the Wild Things Are* (without counting). At the end of the week, the children will then count to see whose guess was the closest.

___ ## Sharing Time

Children share items they completed at centers.

Plan 2 - MODEL 1:

LITERATURE THEMES

The Carrot Seed (Ruth Krauss); The Enormous Watermelon (Brenda Parkes/Judith Smith); Jack and the Beanstalk (Paul Galdon)

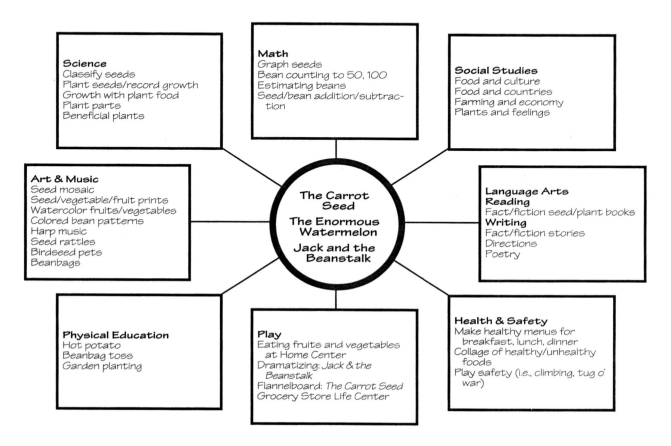

Science
Classify seeds
Plant seeds/record growth
Growth with plant food
Plant parts
Beneficial plants

Math
Graph seeds
Bean counting to 50, 100
Estimating beans
Seed/bean addition/subtraction

Social Studies
Food and culture
Food and countries
Farming and economy
Plants and feelings

Art & Music
Seed mosaic
Seed/vegetable/fruit prints
Watercolor fruits/vegetables
Colored bean patterns
Harp music
Seed rattles
Birdseed pets
Beanbags

**The Carrot Seed
The Enormous Watermelon
Jack and the Beanstalk**

**Language Arts
Reading**
Fact/fiction seed/plant books
Writing
Fact/fiction stories
Directions
Poetry

Physical Education
Hot potato
Beanbag toss
Garden planting

Play
Eating fruits and vegetables
   at Home Center
Dramatizing: *Jack & the
   Beanstalk*
Flannelboard: *The Carrot Seed*
Grocery Store Life Center

Health & Safety
Make healthy menus for
   breakfast, lunch, dinner
Collage of healthy/unhealthy
   foods
Play safety (i.e., climbing, tug o'
   war)

A.M.

___ **Large Group Opening**

Calendar

News from home

Shared Big Book

Week 1: *THE CARROT SEED*

Skills: Sight words *she, said;* -ed endings; quotation marks; contractions; double
ee sound; family names *Father, Mother, Brother*

Culminating Activity: Plant an outside garden.

Week 2: *THE ENORMOUS WATERMELON*

Skills: Quotation marks; capital *G*; sight words *she, said*; blends *gr*; *ed* endings; capitals

Culminating Activity: Eat a watermelon; estimate the seeds and then count.

Week 3: *JACK AND THE BEANSTALK*

Skills: Capital *B, J*; periods; quotation marks; *ea* words

Culminating Activity: Do a retell. As a group, have the children tell the story in their own words. Make a Big Book. Write the new text and have the children illustrate the book.

Shared Poem

Week 1: "Peter, Peter, Pumpkin Eater"

Skills: Rhyming words; capital *P*; periods; contractions

Week 2: "Old Mother Hubbard"

Skills: Rhyming words; sight word *went*; r-controlled vowel

Week 2: "Jack Sprat"

Skills: Rhyming words; long vowel/silent *e*; capital *J, S*; irregular spelling *could*

Guided Reading Groups/Centers

Small Guided Reading Groups: Select books appropriate for each group. Choose extended activities to tie in with the Plant theme, if possible.

Centers:

Big Book: Children read *The Carrot Seed, The Enormous Watermelon,* and *Jack and the Beanstalk* in pairs as well as other favorite Big Books or Shared Reading books.

Listening: Children choose to listen from a selection of books that represents fact and fiction about seeds, plants, fruits, vegetables, farming: *The Tiny Seed; The Very Hungry Caterpillar* (both by Eric Carle).

Writing: Children write an innovation on *The Carrot Seed,* choosing a different seed/plant and different characters. The children design a book cover in the shape of the fruit or vegetable they choose and also illustrate their own books. The children also write directions on how to plant a seed, create a book entitled *My Book of Favorite Foods* (using descriptive adjectives), or write a story beginning "If I had a magic seed. . . ."

Letters: Children manipulate letters at the Letter Center.

Notes: Children write notes to each other.

Printing: Children make vegetable print notepaper for writing letters to friends and family.

Flannelboard: Children retell the stories *The Carrot Seed* and *Jack and the Beanstalk* using flannelboard story figures.

Drama: In the stage area, children act out the story *Jack and the Beanstalk* with simple props.

Home: Children pretend they are going shopping at the grocery store next to this center. Provide some cooking utensils, pans, etc., for this center so children can pretend they are cooking food such as pizza.

Grocery Store: Have the children bring in empty boxes, cans, and grocery sacks. Provide a cash register and play money. Children label shelves of food and determine the prices.

Play: Create an outdoor Play Center with plastic gardening tools, buckets, empty seed packets, etc. Children also play Hot Potato with the beanbags made at the Art Center.

Science: Children classify seeds by type. Children examine the parts of a plant and make an illustration of its parts (with labels). Children should also plant a seed, possibly in a plastic bag with a wet paper towel. The children will record what they see every day for several weeks. The seeds may be replanted in soil after the roots have developed. The children also experiment with their plants. Some plants can be treated with plant food and some not. Children should write their hypotheses and draw conclusions.

Social Studies: Children taste the foods of different cultures throughout the week. Children invite their parents in to provide the food for this center and then monitor the center as children stop by to enjoy the selections. Parents should engage the children in a discussion of the food and the culture. Children also match certain foods to their corresponding country.

OHP: Children will read overhead stories created by classmates during Guided Reading.

Art: Children make seed mosaics. Some children also draw certain fruits and vegetables such as the carrot and watermelon and then watercolor the drawings similar to the artwork in *The Enormous Watermelon*. Children may also want to create their own garden pets. For example, a child may make an elephant from salt dough. After the elephant dries, the child spreads a seed paste over the animal and sprays it with water periodically until the seeds sprout. Grass or birdseed is inexpensive.

Children hand sew beanbags for the Play Center.

Music: Children listen to harp music. An actual harp would be a wonderful addition to this center. Possibly a parent who plays or someone from a local orchestra would donate time to spend at this center.

Children make seed rattles or "rain sticks" with birdseed.

Computer: Children use available software. If a printer is available, children type the stories they created at the Writing Center.

Poetry: Children read the poem card for the week as well as other poetry cards. Each child will then illustrate his own copy of the weekly shared poem and add it to his own poetry book.

Library: Children choose from a variety of books to read. Some of the books reflect the seed/plant theme, both fact and fiction.

Read-the-Walls: Children walk around the room with a friend, reading the wall print in the literacy-rich classroom.

Recess

Children use the outdoor play gardening materials. Children may actually do real gardening.

____ **Modeled Writing (large group)**

Teacher will discuss seeds, plants, and magic throughout the two weeks: The following are possible topics to discuss and write about:

The Carrot Seed

- Discuss the feelings of the little boy. Write how you would feel.
- Change the story. Rewrite with a different fruit or vegetable. Put in your own family as the characters.
- Tell about a time when you planted seeds or what you would do if you planted seeds.
- Describe your favorite fruit or vegetable (color, size, weight). Use descriptive words.
- Innovate the poem, "Peter, Peter, Pumpkin Eater."

The Enormous Watermelon

- Write about the biggest thing you ever saw.
- Write about another nursery rhyme character who came along to pull out the watermelon.
- If you were going to pull out the watermelon, who would you get to help you and why?
- Innovate the poem, "Old Mother Hubbard."
- Make a grocery list for your mom or dad.

Jack and the Beanstalk

- What would you do with all the riches from the giant's castle?
- If you had a magic bean, where would it take you? How?
- Tell the story from another perspective such as the giant or cow. Use dialogue.
- Describe the setting (home, castle).
- What if Jack was evil and the giant was good? How would the story change?

During Journal Writing, children use the discussion content to write a fact or fiction story. The teacher conferences individually with children as they complete their journal entries.

P.M.

____ **Read to Children (large group)**

The teacher reads both fact and fiction seed/plant-related books as well as favorite stories. Children participate as guest readers during this time, reading a favorite book and/or a book from Guided Reading to the group.

____ **Independent Reading**

Children read books from the library or book baskets. Children may choose from a variety of books including fact and fiction seed/plant books. Reading may be individual or social. Social reading occurs in pairs and small groups.

___ ## Guided Math/Centers

Teacher meets with small groups of children based on need while the rest of the class works at centers with a focus on math, science, and social studies.

General Centers: Geoboards, tangrams, puzzles, blocks, Lego®, math games, flannelboard, manipulatives

Math Theme Centers:

Measuring: Children measure plant growth of their own plants.

Weighing: Children weigh fruits, watermelons, vegetables, and beans.

Counting: Children count beans to 50, 100.

Estimation: Children estimate how many seeds/beans are in a jar.

Graphing: Children graph seeds by kind.

Word Problems: Children decide how much each seed in a packet of seeds will cost. Children find out which seeds are the most expensive.

Addition/Subtraction: Children engage in bean addition and subtraction.

___ ## Sharing Time

Children share items they completed at centers.

From *Creating the Multiage Classroom* published by GoodYear Books. Copyright © 1996 Sandra J. Stone.

Plan 3 - MODEL 2:

LITERATURE THEME

SYLVESTER AND THE MAGIC PEBBLE (WILLIAM STEIG)

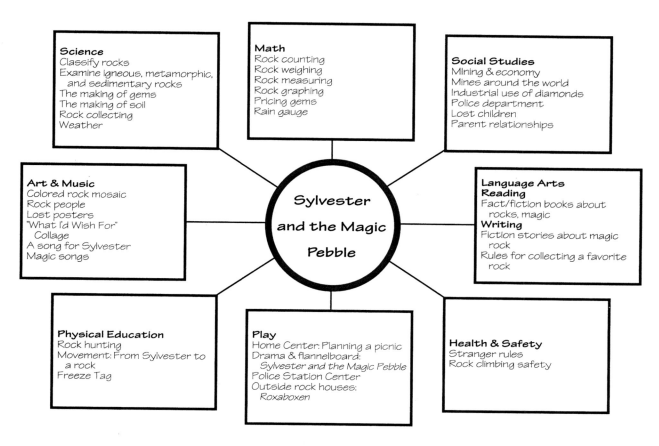

Science
Classify rocks
Examine igneous, metamorphic, and sedimentary rocks
The making of gems
The making of soil
Rock collecting
Weather

Math
Rock counting
Rock weighing
Rock measuring
Rock graphing
Pricing gems
Rain gauge

Social Studies
Mining & economy
Mines around the world
Industrial use of diamonds
Police department
Lost children
Parent relationships

Art & Music
Colored rock mosaic
Rock people
Lost posters
"What I'd Wish For" Collage
A song for Sylvester
Magic songs

Sylvester and the Magic Pebble

Language Arts
Reading
Fact/fiction books about rocks, magic
Writing
Fiction stories about magic rock
Rules for collecting a favorite rock

Physical Education
Rock hunting
Movement: From Sylvester to a rock
Freeze Tag

Play
Home Center: Planning a picnic
Drama & flannelboard:
   Sylvester and the Magic Pebble
Police Station Center
Outside rock houses:
   Roxaboxen

Health & Safety
Stranger rules
Rock climbing safety

A.M.

___ **Large Group Opening**

Calendar

News from home

Shared Book

Week 1: *Sylvester and the Magic Pebble* (overhead)

Skills: Descriptive words, using commas in a series, beginning sounds, syllables

Culminating Activity: Create a mural of wishes that do not cost anything or write a class book of own rules for collecting special rocks.

Week 2: *Everybody Needs a Rock* (Byrd Baylor)

Skills: Free verse; describing words; adverbs; capitals; sight words *rock, is*

Culminating Activity: Choose a special rock and make a special box for it.

Shared Poem

Week 1: "Parents"

    Skills: Rhyming words, capital P, periods

Week 2: "Something Special"

    Skills: Rhyming words, sight word *and*

Independent Reading/Centers

Children monitor own progress with Reading Logs. After children complete reading, they choose literacy-based centers. Teacher works with individuals or small groups based on need.

Centers

Big Book: Children read *Sylvester and the Magic Pebble* and *Everybody Needs a Rock* in pairs as well as other favorite Big Books or Shared Reading Books.

Listening: Children choose to listen from a selection of books that represents fact and fiction about rocks, magic, and weather, along with other favorite books.

Writing: Children write *A Journal of Rock Collecting*, *Rules for Finding a Special Rock*, or a *Rainy Day* story.

Letters: Children manipulate letters at the Letter Center.

Notes: Have parents write notes for the week to their children. Place a note each day for each child to read and then respond to. The notes from the parents do not have to be long.

Printing: Children print a title for the Lost Poster created at the Art Center.

Flannelboard: Children retell the story *Sylvester and the Magic Pebble* using flannel-board story figures.

Drama: In the stage area, children act out the story *Sylvester and the Magic Pebble*. Provide simple props.

Home: Children pretend to prepare for a picnic. Provide simple picnic props.

Play: Create an outdoor Play Center where the children create "rock" house areas such as illustrated in *Roxaboxen* (Alice McLerran).

From *Creating the Multiage Classroom* published by Good Year Books. Copyright © 1996 Sandra J. Stone.

Social Studies: Children research mining and locate mines around the world, and then create a mural. Children also create different land formations such as a volcano, mountains, hills, and so on.

OHP: Children read overhead stories created by classmates during Guided Reading.

Art: Children make rock people or a colored rock mosaic. Some children make posters for something that has been lost.

Music: Children create a song for Sylvester. Children listen to songs about magic such as "Puff the Magic Dragon."

Computer: Children use available software. If a printer is available, children type the stories they created at the Writing Center.

Poetry: Children read the poem card for the week as well as other poetry cards. Each child will then illustrate his own copy of the weekly Shared Poem and add it to his own poetry book.

Library: Children may choose from a variety of books to read. Some of the books reflect the Rock theme, both fact and fiction.

Read-the-Walls: Children walk around the room with a friend, reading the wall print in the literacy-rich classroom.

___ Literature Circles

Children work in small groups. Teacher may direct one group a day. Literature selections may focus on theme.

___ Recess

Children may play *Roxaboxen* outside or go rock hunting.

___ Writers' Workshop (large group)

Teacher first models writing strategies. Children then begin the process of developing their own stories. Suggested story themes may revolve around *Sylvester and the Magic Pebble*. The teacher edits with children. Children illustrate their own texts.

P.M.

___ Read to Children (large group)

The teacher reads both fact and fiction rock-related books as well as favorite stories. Children participate as guest readers during this time, reading a favorite book and/or a book from Guided Reading to the group.

___ ### Independent Reading

Children read books from the library or book baskets. Children choose from a variety of books including fact and fiction rock books. Reading may be individual or social. Social reading occurs in pairs and small groups.

___ ### Guided Math/Centers

Teacher meets with small groups of children based on need while the rest of the class works at centers with a focus on math, science, and social studies.

General Centers: Geoboards, tangrams, puzzles, blocks, Lego®, math games, flannelboard, manipulatives

Math Theme Centers:

Measuring: Children measure rocks.

Weighing: Children weigh rocks.

Counting: Children count rocks.

Estimation: Children estimate the weight of rocks before weighing them.

Graphing: Children graph rocks by type.

Word Problems: Children decide how much gems would cost when given the cost per carat.

Addition/Subtraction: Children engage in using small rocks as manipulatives in adding and subtracting experiences.

___ ### Project Time

Children work in small cooperative groups. Children choose the topics they wish to explore. Suggested topics: rock formations, gems, minerals, land formations, rock/mineral use (murals, displays, demonstrations)

___ ### Sharing Time

Children share items they completed at centers.

From *Creating the Multiage Classroom* published by GoodYear Books. Copyright © 1996 Sandra J. Stone.

PLAN 4 - MODEL 2:

SOCIAL STUDIES THEME

FEELINGS

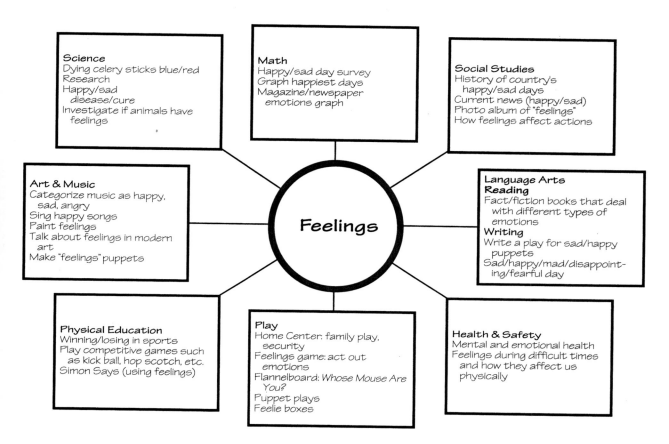

Science
Dying celery sticks blue/red
Research
Happy/sad
  disease/cure
Investigate if animals have
  feelings

Math
Happy/sad day survey
Graph happiest days
Magazine/newspaper
  emotions graph

Social Studies
History of country's
  happy/sad days
Current news (happy/sad)
Photo album of "feelings"
How feelings affect actions

Art & Music
Categorize music as happy,
  sad, angry
Sing happy songs
Paint feelings
Talk about feelings in modern
  art
Make "feelings" puppets

Feelings

Language Arts
Reading
Fact/fiction books that deal
  with different types of
  emotions
Writing
Write a play for sad/happy
  puppets
Sad/happy/mad/disappoint-
  ing/fearful day

Physical Education
Winning/losing in sports
Play competitive games such
  as kick ball, hop scotch, etc.
Simon Says (using feelings)

Play
Home Center: family play,
  security
Feelings game: act out
  emotions
Flannelboard: *Whose Mouse Are
  You?*
Puppet plays
Feelie boxes

Health & Safety
Mental and emotional health
Feelings during difficult times
  and how they affect us
  physically

A.M.

___ **Large Group Opening**

Calendar

News from home

Shared Big Book

Week 1: *WHOSE MOUSE ARE YOU?* (Robert Kraus)

Skills: Question mark; wh sound; sight words you, your, is, my; blends br, sh, fr, tr;
period; capital M, Y

Culminating Activity: Do an innovation. Choose a different animal. Focus on the
feelings.

Week 2: *CLIFFORD THE SMALL RED PUPPY* (Norman Bridwell) (Big Book or overhead)

Skills: Capital C, P, E; contractions; syllables; -ed endings; compound words; periods; question marks; sight words *big, little*

Culminating Activity: Clifford Mural. Have children paint different versions of Clifford with tempera paint—some small, some medium, and some large. Each should also reflect emotions—sad, happy. As a class, write a poem to accompany the mural.

Shared Poem

Week 1: "There Was a Little Girl"

Skills: Sight words *she, was*; double consonants; commas

Week 2: "Little Miss Muffet"

Skills: Capital M; rhyming words; syllables *away, along*

Independent Reading/Centers

Children monitor own progress with Reading Logs. After children complete reading, they choose literacy-based centers. Teacher works with individuals or small groups based on need.

Centers

Big Book: Children read *Whose Mouse Are You?* and *Clifford the Small Red Puppy* in pairs as well as other favorite Big Books or Shared Reading Books.

Listening: Children choose to listen from a selection of books that represents fact and fiction about situations that involve emotion.

Writing: Children write a play to go along with the emotion puppets from the Art Center; a story to go along with the photographs of children's emotions taken at the school or pictures from magazines; a book of personal emotions.

Letters: Children manipulate letters at the Letter Center.

Notes: Children write notes to encourage each other. Each "happy" note should reflect something positive about the child to whom it is written.

Flannelboard: Children will retell the stories *Whose Mouse are You?* and *Clifford the Small Red Puppy* using flannelboard story figures.

Drama: In the stage area, children act out different emotions using paper-plate puppets. The children write scripts at the Writing Center.

Home: Children pretend that someone is having a birthday (surprise, happiness), someone is sick (sadness), and so on.

Play: Children play Simon Says using emotions as the directions. Children play situations using paper dolls: someone is missing, someone is going to Disneyland, someone is going to school on the first day, and so on. Paper dolls may be made from magazine pictures glued to oaktag.

Science: Children tie a science experiment into the Feelings theme. Each child places a stalk of celery in either a glass with red food coloring (for happiness) or blue food coloring (for sadness). Children will see how the celery stalk draws the coloring into the stalk. An analogy can be made to positive and negative environments and our dispositions.

The children also research two or three diseases that have caused great unhappiness in our world and also the cures that have eliminated the fear of those diseases. Children also write about their fears of diseases that currently do not have cures and the efforts to find cures soon.

Social Studies: Children write about how feelings affect our social actions. Children also put together a picture album of emotions depicted in magazines.

Art: Children paint their feelings with tempera paint. Modern paintings may be displayed for inspiration. Have children discuss the paintings in pairs and decide which emotions they seem to express before children do their own emotion paintings.

Children create "feelings" puppets using small paper plates and frozen juice sticks. These puppets will be used at the Writing and Drama Centers.

Music: Children listen to mood music on tape. With a friend, each child should discuss how the music makes him or her feel (happy, sad, excited, mad).

Children choose to sing a happy song with friends from a selection of three or four records or tapes. The words to the songs should be printed for the children to read.

Computer: Children use available software. If a printer is available, children type the stories they created at the Writing Center.

Poetry: Children read the poem card for the week as well as other poetry cards. Each child will then illustrate his own copy of the weekly shared poem and add it to his own poetry book.

Library: Children choose from a variety of books to read. Some of the books reflect the Feelings theme, both fact and fiction.

Read-the-Walls: Children walk around the room with a friend, reading the wall print in the literacy-rich classroom.

___ Literature Circles (small groups)

Children work in small groups. Teacher may direct one group a day. Literature selections should focus on different emotions.

___ Recess

Children use the outdoor time to dramatize stories that might reflect fear or surprise, such as *The Three Little Pigs* or *The Big Bad Wolf*.

___ Writers' Workshop (large group)

Teacher demonstrates focus skills such as webbing a story; mapping a beginning, middle, and ending; or writing with descriptive words. For younger children, the focus may include using beginning and/or ending sounds, adding periods and capitals, and writing with several sentences.

Writing topics would include some emotional content. The teacher should encourage the children to ask themselves questions about how they feel at certain times during the story and to reflect those feelings in the writing. Suggested topics could be: a family story such as a trip taken; an imaginary story about a big or little pet and how you feel about it; a feeling story such as a happy, sad, angry, surprised, or fearful day.

P.M.
___ Read to Children (large group)

The teacher reads both fact and fiction feelings-related books as well as favorite stories. Children participate as guest readers during this time, reading a favorite book and/or a book from Guided Reading to the group.

___ Guided Math/Centers

Teacher meets with small groups of children based on need while the rest of the class works at centers with a focus on math, science, and social studies.

General Centers: Geoboards, tangrams, puzzles, blocks, Lego®, math games, flannelboard, manipulatives

From *Creating the Multiage Classroom* published by GoodYear Books. Copyright © 1996 Sandra J. Stone.

Math Theme Centers:

Measuring: Children measure their own growth. Small groups of children measure themselves along a wall of butcher paper. Children also discuss how they felt when they were younger and smaller and how they feel now that they are older and bigger. Children should write their feelings along with the measurement.

Weighing: Children weigh themselves on a scale throughout the week and record any changes.

Counting: Children will count and classify the different emotions expressed in a literature book's pictures or in a magazine.

Estimation: Children estimate how many happy faces are on a poster. Small happy face stickers may be used or happy faces can be drawn.

Graphing: Children graph the emotions found in a book or magazine.

Word Problems: Children write their own word problems. The word problem should contain some type of emotional event. Each child should write one problem and add it to a container of problems and solve at least three other problems. The problem writing and solving may be done with other children.

Addition/Subtraction: Children use happy face chips made from milk carton tops as manipulatives for addition and subtraction problems.

___ Project Time

Children plan and implement a project plan based on the topic of feelings. The project will focus on feelings in the news. Each day the group reviews newspaper articles from a local paper looking for news that represents or elicits an emotion. Each story should be rewritten and summarized so that the basic elements of the story are told and the group should add the emotion. Stories may be added to a class bulletin board where the stories are categorized by type of emotion. A class graph may be made later.

An extension of this project would be to create a class newspaper of school and community news focusing on "good news." Children gather their items from the newspaper, TV, and personal interviews at school and in the community. The class publishes the newspaper at the end of the week.

___ Sharing Time

Children will share items they completed at centers.

Plan 5 - MODEL 3:

SCIENCE THEME

LIFE-CYCLE OF THE FROG

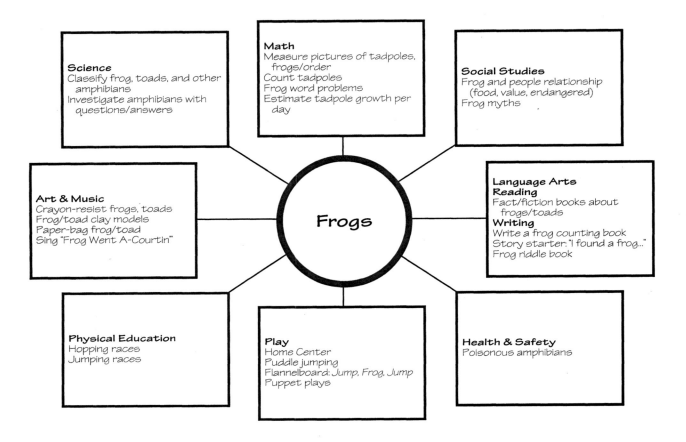

Science
Classify frog, toads, and other amphibians
Investigate amphibians with questions/answers

Math
Measure pictures of tadpoles, frogs/order
Count tadpoles
Frog word problems
Estimate tadpole growth per day

Social Studies
Frog and people relationship (food, value, endangered)
Frog myths

Art & Music
Crayon-resist frogs, toads
Frog/toad clay models
Paper-bag frog/toad
Sing "Frog Went A-Courtin"

Frogs

Language Arts
Reading
Fact/fiction books about frogs/toads
Writing
Write a frog counting book
Story starter: "I found a frog..."
Frog riddle book

Physical Education
Hopping races
Jumping races

Play
Home Center
Puddle jumping
Flannelboard: *Jump, Frog, Jump*
Puppet plays

Health & Safety
Poisonous amphibians

From *Creating the Multiage Classroom* published by GoodYear Books. Copyright © 1996 Sandra J. Stone.

A.M.

__ **Large Group Opening**

Calendar

News from home

Shared Big Book

Week 1: *JUMP, FROG, JUMP* (Robert Kalan)

Skills: Sight words *jump, frog;* capital *J;* commas; exclamation point

Culminating Activity: Write and illustrate a class poem.

Week 2: *FROG AND TOAD TOGETHER* (Arnold Lobel) (Big Book or overhead)

Skills: Capital *F, T;* syllables; *-ed* endings; compound words; periods

Culminating Activity: Do a story retell in the form of a Big Book.

Shared Poem

Week 1: "Polliwog" (author unknown)

   Skills: blends; short *o*; rhyming words

Week 2: "Frog Went A-Courtin'" (John Langstaff)

   Skills: Capital F, A; apostrophes; sight word *went*; periods

____ Project Time

Children plan and implement project plans based on the life-cycle of a frog topic. Each group works on the life-cycle. Group comparisons will be made at the end of the project. Small, cooperative groups set up a frog hatchery tank. Each group has access to resource books on frogs and magnifying glasses. Each group researches frogs, makes frog models, creates frog life-span charts (five developmental stages), creates a vocabulary list (tadpole, embryo, toad), completes observation sheets, and writes a factual report on frogs.

___ Recess

Children enjoy hopping and jumping races.

____ Literature Circles/Centers

Children work in small groups. Literature selections include frog fairy tales. Teacher may direct several groups a day. Children also engage at literacy-based centers.

Centers

Big Book: Children read *Jump, Frog, Jump* and *Frog and Toad Together* in pairs as well as other favorite Big Books or Shared Reading Books.

Listening: Children choose to listen from a selection of books that represents fact and fiction about frogs/toads.

Writing: Children write a frog counting book, "I Found a Frog . . . ," or a frog riddle book made from lunch-sized paper bags.

Letters: Children manipulate letters at the Letter Center.

Flannelboard: Children retell the story *Jump, Frog, Jump* using flannelboard story figures.

Drama: In the stage area, children act out frog/toad dialogue. Children use paper-bag puppets made in the Art Center.

Home: Children pretend that a frog prince or princess is coming for dinner.

Play: Children play a frog board game.

Science: Children write and answer frog/toad questions. Each child writes a question and answer to add to question-and-answer containers. Children try to match the questions and answers.

Social Studies: Children investigate frog myths and create a collage.

Art: Children make frog drawings. Children make paper-bag frog/toad puppets.

Music: Children listen to and then sing with a recording of "Frog Went A-Courtin'."

Computer: Children use available software. If a printer is available, children type the stories they created at the Writing Center.

Poetry: Children read the poem card for the week as well as other poetry cards. Each child will then illustrate his own copy of the weekly shared poem and add it to his own poetry book.

Library: Children choose from a variety of books to read. Some of the books reflect the Frog/Toad theme, both fact and fiction.

Read-the-Walls: Children walk around the room with a friend, reading the wall print in the literacy-rich classroom.

P.M.

___ ### Read to Children (large group)

The teacher reads both fact and fiction frog-related books as well as favorite stories. Children participate as guest readers during this time, reading a favorite book and/or a book from Guided Reading to the group.

___ ### Writers' Workshop (large group)

Teacher demonstrates focus skills such as webbing a story; mapping a beginning, middle, and ending; or writing with descriptive words. For younger children, the focus may include using beginning and/or ending sounds, adding periods and capitals, and writing with several sentences.

Children create their own frog fairy tales.

___ ### Guided Math/Centers

Teacher meets with small groups of children based on need while the rest of the class works at centers with a focus on math, science, and social studies.

General Centers: Geoboards, tangrams, puzzles, blocks, Lego®, math games, flannelboard, manipulatives

Math Theme Centers:

Measuring: Children measure pictures of tadpoles/frogs and put in order.

Counting: Children count tadpoles.

Graphing: Children classify and graph amphibians.

Word Problems: Children write their own word problems.

Addition/Subtraction: Children use toy frogs as manipulatives for addition and subtraction problems.

___ ### Sharing Time

Children share items they completed at centers.

CHAPTER SEVEN

ASSESSING THROUGH PORTFOLIOS

Assessment is a critical component in the multiage classroom. Assessment should document children's progress, guide and support instruction, and inform children and parents of the children's successes. The National Association for the Education of Young Children (NAEYC) suggests that young children should only be assessed if it benefits them. The new ways to implement learning that a multiage education offers call for new ways to assess that learning. Multiage teachers find that portfolio assessment is a highly effective tool for assessing mixed-age learners, allowing teachers to see each child as an individual and to document her growth.

Because assessment is essential to the successful multiage classroom, teachers must understand why it suits those classrooms and traditional assessment does not. Understanding the difference will strengthen your role as an advocate for children and their successful adventure in learning.

In this chapter we will examine the characteristics of traditional assessment compared to the highly successful portfolio assessment technique. Following will be an exploration of how you can easily implement portfolio assessment in your multiage setting, along with forms for your convenience.

Traditional
Assessment

ASSESSMENT BASED ON CURRICULUM. Traditional assessment measures children's knowledge of the curriculum instead of their learning development. Based on the belief that all children are the same in their development and needs, a curriculum-centered instruction expects all same-age children to master the curriculum and be on "grade level." The curriculum gets harder and more complex each year, regardless of the children's needs and abilities. The children who master the skills assessed by the tests receive passing marks and move to the next grade, where some find the level of skills not challenging enough. Among children who do not master the skills, some are labeled as failures and retained. Others are promoted and continue to struggle with the more difficult work.

TESTS CAN BE UNRELIABLE. Standardized tests, textbook tests, and teacher-made tests have traditionally been used to assess the mastery of skills and knowledge of the curriculum. Testing of this sort is problematic. First, tests are only *one* form of assessment, not the *only* form. Second, testing is not always a reliable tool for assessment. The testing process can create undue anxiety and misunderstanding; many children, especially young children, do not test well. Third, tests rely heavily on memorized knowledge and isolated skills easily forgotten after a test. And, fourth, some tests are biased. Furthermore, many teachers use dittos and worksheets to practice skills to be tested, thereby creating an inappropriate learning environment.

Tests and paper-and-pencil tasks convey a limited and sometimes inaccurate view of what children can do and what they understand. The testing and grading process reduces a child to a number, thus giving an impersonal, narrow profile of how she is learning.

Assessment by tests and grades reflects a philosophy contrary to that of multiage education. Traditional methods assume that a curriculum will be taught and tests will assess the children's success at learning the curriculum. Test scores determine children's grades and are used to rank and label them. Because the multiage classroom focuses on teaching the children not the curriculum, curriculum-centered assessment techniques are inappropriate.

Portfolio Assessment

PORTFOLIOS ASSESS EACH CHILD INDIVIDUALLY. Multiage teachers have changed how they teach to match the way children learn best–as active participants in real and meaningful contexts. Assessment should be made within those contexts and should reflect how children learn. Portfolios do both while focusing on each child individually and what she can do or understand. Portfolio assessment enables the teacher to tailor the curriculum to fit each child's needs.

PORTFOLIOS REFLECT THE PROCESS OF LEARNING. We know that every child constructs her own knowledge as she actively and meaningfully engages in the world. Each child is on her own continuum of learning. Children are not all the same; they vary in their developmental rates of learning and in their learning styles. Multiage teachers are facilitators of each child's individual growth, with each growth step being a success for the child. Multiage teachers help children in the process of becoming readers, writers, problem solvers, scientists, and artists.

Multiage teachers focus on the natural processes of learning similar to how parents support and nurture their own children's growth. When a young child learns to talk, parents know their child is in the process of learning language. They accept the initial babbling and are overjoyed when their child first says "Ma ma" or "Da da." Then the child begins to put words together, such as "more milk," and eventually speaks in complete sentences, such as "Mom, may I have more milk, please?" Parents praise their child along the way.

Parents naturally give their child real, meaningful experiences to talk about; they talk with their child. The child gradually builds her knowledge of language. She does not do worksheets and tests along the way, and yet amazingly, she learns how to talk. We do not grade her in her language development. Instead, we praise and nurture her development. Multiage teachers know this natural process of learning needs to be continued in school. With portfolios, multiage teachers can document and support each child's successful growth in this learning process.

PORTFOLIO ASSESSMENT HIGHLIGHTS STRENGTHS.

Multiage teachers use portfolio assessment as a tool to benefit children by asking the question, "How can we assess children to help them grow, rather than test, rank, and sort them?" Portfolio assessment answers this query by evaluating children's strengths and guiding instruction to support future success. Traditional assessment focuses more on what children cannot do, rather than on what they can do, which undermines the confidence of many children.

Portfolio assessment evaluates children based on their past achievements and their own potential, not by comparison to group norms. Because the approach supports continuous progress, children can see themselves as competent, successful learners.

I want to put this report on planets in my portfolio. It shows I'm using paragraphs now in my writing.

Portfolio assessment benefits children and teacher in many other ways as well, by

- Respecting the learning process. Learning is a continuous process and not a final product. Portfolios illustrate the process.

- Respecting each child's individuality. Each child's portfolio reveals her progress as an individual on her own continuum of learning. While expectations are high, they reflect each child's own learning rate and style.

- Documenting each child's growth. A portfolio documents each child's growth in the learning process so that each step can be celebrated as a success.

- Supporting a child's chance for success, competence, and self-worth. Focusing on a child's strengths allows her to see herself as a successful, competent learner.

- Encouraging children to value the learning process. Because portfolios help children to participate in their own learning and endow them with ownership of the process, children value learning as an exciting, positive, personal experience. They experience the joy of learning.

- Encouraging children to be thoughtful evaluators of their own work. Portfolio assessment encourages children to reflect on their own work, instead of always relying on someone else to make judgments. As thoughtful evaluators of their own work, children set goals and continue learning.

- Supporting and guiding instruction. Portfolio assessment helps the teacher know where each child is and where she needs to go next. Knowing this, the teacher can adjust his instruction to meet the learning needs of each child.

- Increasing teacher's awareness of how children learn. Making observations and documenting growth enables the teacher to see how children construct or build their knowledge. This vitally important information supports the teacher's ability to nurture each child's successful development.

- Serving as a vehicle for communicating with child and parent. As a tool for reporting the child's growth and development to the child and parent, the portfolio gives both the opportunity to see the child as a successful learner and to celebrate successes together.

- Promoting lifelong learning. Seeing herself as a competent learner motivates a child to continue learning. Learning does not stop in the classroom, but continues throughout life as a reward in itself.

The following chart, based on "Understanding Portfolio Assessment" (Stone 1995), summarizes the differences between portfolio assessment and traditional assessment.

PORTFOLIO ASSESSMENT VS. TRADITIONAL ASSESSMENT

Portfolio Assessment	Traditional Assessment
• Multiple forms of assessment	• One form of assessment
• More complete picture of child's learning	• Narrow view of child's learning
• Assessment made within context of learning	• Assessment made in contrived context (i.e., test)
• Child-centered	• Curriculum-centered
• Ongoing	• One-time test on particular task
• Supports the process of learning	• Isolated task, separate from the process of learning
• Focuses on what children can do	• Focuses on what children cannot do
• Evaluates on child's past achievements and own potential	• Evaluates by comparison to norms
• Benefits children by supporting their growth	• Labels, sorts, ranks children
• Provides teacher information to extend child's learning	• Provides little information teacher can use to help child
• Provides opportunity for child to evaluate own learning	• Evaluation done by teacher only

Stone, S. J. *Understanding Portfolio Assessment: A Guide for Parents.* Wheaton, MD: Association for Childhood Education International, 1995.

IMPLEMENTING PORTFOLIO ASSESSMENT

The Purpose of Portfolio Assessment

Portfolio assessment accomplishes three main objectives: To document student progress and growth, to support and guide instruction, and to communicate each student's successful growth to both child and parents.

DOCUMENTS STUDENT PROGRESS AND GROWTH. A portfolio comprises a purposeful collection of a child's work compiled by both teacher and child. Generated during ongoing, meaningful classroom activities, the pieces in the portfolio are systematically and purposefully selected to show a child's growth in the processes of learning over time. Portfolios are neither haphazard collections nor work folders of dittos and worksheets.

Just as a parent documents when their child first sits up, stands, and then walks, the portfolio documents the child's steps in becoming a reader, writer, and problem solver. Materials in a younger child's portfolio may illustrate her progress, from writing random letters, to writing letters for sounds, and then to writing words with all the syllables present. Finally, the child writes using sentences and conventional spelling.

For an older child, the portfolio may document how she first progresses from writing sentences without descriptive words, to writing with limited descriptive words, and finally to writing sentences with well-selected adverbs and adjectives.

In math, the portfolio may show how a younger child's understanding of number matures. The child may progress from using tally marks to count, to using numbers to represent quantity, to finally using numbers to add quantities.

An older child's portfolio may demonstrate her growth in understanding multiplication by using skills in real-life situations, such as class voting: from first adding a string of numbers from tally marks, to grouping numbers and adding, and finally to grouping numbers and multiplying.

In all of the preceding examples, the teacher actively assesses the pieces in the portfolio as it expands, helping the child continue to grow in knowledge and skills.

A portfolio reveals what a child can do and understand and how she thinks. It illustrates her process for writing a story, reaching a decision, forming a hypothesis, or solving a problem. Through her portfolio, the child demonstrates her growing ability to apply skills and understand concepts.

SUPPORTS AND GUIDES INSTRUCTION. The teacher uses a child's portfolio to support and guide instruction. Portfolio evaluations inform the teacher's practice since knowledge of the children's strengths and needs drives the multiage curriculum. As a result, the teacher can be highly selective of what he introduces in small- or large-group instruction.

COMMUNICATES EACH STUDENT'S SUCCESSFUL GROWTH TO BOTH CHILD AND PARENTS. Portfolios enable every child to see her own growth. Through frequent conferences, teacher, children, and parents can celebrate this progress and set goals together for growth.

THE CONTENTS OF A PORTFOLIO

A portfolio contains purposefully selected pieces representing a child's learning in reading, writing, math, social studies, science, and art, as well as items that reflect the child's social, emotional, aesthetic, and physical development. Some teachers treat each area within one portfolio. Others have multiple portfolios, one for each area.

From *Creating the Multiage Classroom* published by GoodYear Books. Copyright © 1996 Sandra J. Stone.

Sometimes a teacher integrates the various learning areas into a portfolio project. For example, a single science project may demonstrate a child's growth in working with a small group (social), her facility at writing a scientific report (writing), her ability to read research materials and understand the concepts (reading), her skill at painting a representative picture (art), and her ability to show how information from the science project may impact humans (social studies).

Generally, teachers use two kinds of portfolios: learning, or working, portfolios and showcase portfolios. Learning, or working, portfolios include work showing the learning process from the beginning to the final product. A learning portfolio paves the way to a showcase portfolio, which contains only finished works. Showcase portfolios can be displayed for an audience such as at a school open house.

A child's portfolio might include the following materials.

PERFORMANCE-BASED ASSESSMENTS. Performance-based assessments are made in a predetermined context. The teacher will give the same assessment activity to all of the students at various times throughout the school year. This allows the teacher to track each child's growth and understanding over time within the same context.

For example, the teacher may give a young child a letter/sound assessment to determine how many letters and sounds the child knows at the beginning of the year. The child repeats the assessment activity in the middle of the year and again at the end so that the teacher can see the child's growth in letter/sound identification and support her throughout the year with appropriate instruction.

For an older child, a writing exercise might define the predetermined context. In the beginning of the year, the child writes a personal narrative, repeating the exercise in the middle of the year and at the end. Based on appropriate criteria, the teacher uses this series of narratives to chart the child's growth throughout the year.

AUTHENTIC ASSESSMENT.
Authentic assessments are made on a child's performance on ongoing work and activity in the classroom rather than in a predetermined context. For example, a teacher may select a page from a child's personal classroom journal. If the child is younger, the piece may show how she is beginning to use letters for sound. A piece selected from an older child's personal journal may show how she is using quotation marks.

Both performance-based and authentic assessments measure what a child can actually do, rather than what has been memorized.

CHECKLISTS. A checklist summarizes a child's skills on a developmental continuum, providing a quick way to see where she is and where she should be going next. Teachers often use checklists for reading, writing, and math. Several examples are provided later in this chapter.

ANECDOTAL RECORDS. To compile anecdotal records, the teacher records observations about a child's strengths, interests, strategies, and needs while the child is engaged in meaningful classroom activities. Sometimes termed "kid-watching," anecdotal records give the teacher insight into the child's academic, social, and emotional development.

From Creating the Multiage Classroom published by GoodYear Books. Copyright © 1996 Sandra J. Stone.

Anecdotal Records Examples

1/21   During journal writing, Brandon is beginning to write with spaces between his words. He is still using capital letters instead of lower case for most of his words.

2/12   Brandon is writing with both capital and lower case letters.

10/15   Maria does not want to share her building materials with Tom today.

12/5   Maria brings a new pencil from home and asks Nancy if she would like to use it.

4/18   Jacob asks what he should do next for a science project. He is having difficulty making a decision about what to pursue.

5/20   Jacob decides on his own to use different weights of reflective paper in his science project in order to see if weight makes a difference in temperature.

VIGNETTES. Similar to anecdotal records, vignettes are more detailed accounts of significant milestones, meaningful events, or important understandings for the child. The teacher usually writes them after the observation, rather than during the observation.

STUDENT SELF-EVALUATIONS. Students are invited to add to their portfolios their own reflections on their work and progress, as well as their goals for future progress.

INFORMATION FROM QUESTIONNAIRES, INTERVIEWS, AND CONFERENCES. Teachers may also include information from questionnaires in a child's portfolio. Questionnaires can be designed to reveal a child's interests or dispositions. For example, questions might ask, "What is your favorite after-school activity?" or "How do you feel about math?"

A teacher may also include interviews or conferences with the child. In an interview, the teacher may ask the child to explain her understanding of a social studies concept, or her feelings about how well she did in a classroom debate. Dialogue during a teacher-child conference may reflect what the child knows and what goals she and the teacher wish her to pursue.

PARENT OBSERVATIONS AND CONFERENCES. Teachers value parent observations. Parents have insights that may not be apparent to the teacher. Perhaps parents fill out questionnaires regarding their child's interests, needs, and strengths, providing information on her daily reading interests or enthusiasm for an at-home project. Parents may review a child's portfolio on a regular basis and offer their written support of her successes. Some parents visit the school to observe their child.

During a portfolio conference, teachers and parents can derive valuable information from each other. As partners in portfolio assessment, parents and teachers can effectively support a child's growth both at home and at school.

PHOTOGRAPHS, AUDIOTAPES, AND VIDEOTAPES. Photographs, audiotapes, and videotapes can be an important part of a portfolio. Certain strengths that cannot be fully captured on paper can be beautifully expressed by a picture or tape. For example, when a young child designs a castle from wooden pieces, only a photograph can truly document the child's creativity. A videotape records an older child reasoning decisively during a class discussion. An audiotape captures a child's reading ability and expression.

PEER REVIEWS. Classmates can offer each other evaluation and support. Learning how to evaluate the work of others and offer suggestions makes children better critics of their own work as well. Peer reviews also help children see that their work is valued by others.

DECISIONS ON THE CONTENTS OF THE PORTFOLIO

Both teacher and child make decisions on what goes into the portfolio. Establishing ownership of a portfolio enables the child to "buy into" her own learning process.

Parents are also invited to place items in the portfolio, including supportive comments about their child's growth and development based on what they see in the portfolio, as well as suggestions and ideas to help support continual growth. Parents may also record observations that show how their child is using her skills and abilities at home.

PORTFOLIO CONFERENCES

Depending on each child's needs, teachers hold conferences with individual students on a regular basis, daily, weekly, or monthly. During these conferences, the teacher and child discuss the child's progress. The teacher praises the child for her successes and helps her set goals for her next growth step. Meanwhile, the child has the opportunity to be a partner in her own learning. The teacher may ask the child to evaluate a piece of writing, such as by asking, "Are you using descriptive words?" Children are encouraged to be thoughtful evaluators of their own work.

Conferencing helps a teacher learn what a child understands and where she is confused, and the child can talk about what she is learning. Conferencing promotes learning as a lifelong process and not just getting a score on a test. Conferences allow both child and teacher to understand each other and to collaborate for the benefit of the child.

Portfolio conferences that include both parents and children usually occur quarterly, often replacing the traditional report card or accompanying it. During the conference, parents and child review the contents of the portfolio as the teacher demonstrates the child's success through the portfolio. Dialogue focuses on the child's strengths, rather than weaknesses, and everyone has an opportunity to celebrate the child's progress, exchange information, and set goals.

Parents involved in portfolio assessment find that they discover much more about their child than they would from traditional tests and grades. Parents enjoy seeing what their child can do, such as write a book, plan a project, or solve a real problem, and they appreciate the personal and individual attention their child receives through portfolio assessment. When they know its benefits, parents become powerful advocates of portfolio assessment.

From *Creating the Multiage Classroom* published by GoodYear Books. Copyright © 1996 Sandra J. Stone.

TOOLS FOR ASSESSMENT

Appropriate tools are essential for effective assessment. The following forms will help you make performance-based and authentic assessments of reading, math, writing, science, and social studies skills from a developmental perspective. Use them to assess where the children are and apply the information to nurture their development. Examples of these forms begin on page 208.

ASSESSING READING

There are a number of ways to assess reading development.

STAGES OF READING DEVELOPMENT. The Stages of Reading Development Chart (p. 208) outlines the way children develop in their understanding of the reading process. In the primary multiage classroom, it is very important to attend to this process so you can encourage it. Study the chart and use it to determine where each child is on this continuum of reading development so that you can effectively guide your instructional strategies.

READING DEVELOPMENT CHECKLIST. Place a Reading Development Checklist (p. 209) in each child's portfolio to record progress in reading. Based on the stages of Reading Development, the checklist makes it easy to see where each child is on the continuum and how you can support the next stage of development. Be sure to use the checklist only as a guide. Remember that each child develops at her own rate. From the checklist, the teacher, the parents, and the child will quickly be able to see the progress.

LETTER/SOUND IDENTIFICATION. The Letter/Sound Identification Assessment (*Clay 1985*) should be given individually to emerging readers. Use the Letter/Sound Identification Chart on page 210. Ask each child to name each letter as it is pointed to. Then record the child's responses on the Letter/Sound Identification Form on page 211. Do the same for the letter sounds (only upper case). This assessment will reveal which letters and sounds each child knows and will identify areas of confusion. This knowledge will help you wisely choose focus skills for Shared Reading, Guided Reading, and Modeled Writing. Remember to focus on what the child knows, not on what she does not know. Encourage the child with what she already knows. Use this knowledge to support the child's feelings of competency.

Assess each child's letter and sound identification skills at the beginning, middle, and end of the school year. This way growth can be documented throughout the year. Letter/Sound Identification forms in a child's portfolio should be shared with parents and the child at conferences. This also serves as a check for the teacher on how well he has supported the child's development.

CONCEPTS OF PRINT. The Concepts of Print Form *(based on Clay 1985 and other research)*, assesses the emergent reader's book and print concepts, including letters, spaces, words, and punctuation. Teachers can informally assess a child's concept of print by interviewing her using the questions provided on page 212. This assessment helps teachers focus on what each child knows, thus giving a baseline for instruction within the context of books. Any beginning patterned book can be used. Check first to see if all the concepts appear in the book. Then sit down with each child individually and ask the questions from the assessment sheet as the book is read together. The child does not have to be and is most often not a reader to complete this assessment. Remember that this tool is an assessment of what the child knows and not a test. Administer it several times throughout the year to document each child's growth in book knowledge and concepts of print. Be sure to assess them first at the beginning of the year to establish baseline knowledge.

RUNNING RECORDS. Running Records (*Clay 1985*) effectively assess emerging, developing, or fluent readers. They can be used with any reading text. A Running Record is a sample of a child's reading of one or two hundred words from a reading text. For beginning readers, it may include only twenty-five words or less. Running Records analyze what cueing systems the child is using to read. A good reader uses three: meaning (meaning through the text and illustrations; what makes sense), grammar structure (knowledge of language patterns and grammatical structure), and visual graphics (phonics, letter-sound relationships). The cueing systems ask:

Meaning: Does that make sense?

Grammar: Does that sound right?

Visual graphics: Does that look right?

As a child reads, the teacher records what the child actually reads, including miscues. For example, the child may read as follows:

One day a lost girl went in the f - f - fast.
She saw a horse . . . house.
No one was in house . . . in the house.

Using the Running Record, the teacher would record the following:

✓✓✓✓✓✓
✓f-f-fast
   forest
✓✓✓horse
   house
✓✓✓✓___✓
      the

Based on the Running Record, the teacher can determine what cueing system the child was using when she made the errors. Knowing the answer guides the teacher to help the child examine her errors by asking: "Does it make sense? Does it sound right? Does it look right?" Asking these questions helps the child focus on using all three cueing systems and facilitates the child's progress toward independent reading.

Running Records are also used to evaluate whether the text is appropriate for the child. The child should be reading at the independent or instructional level. If the child continually reads at a frustrational level, the books are too hard and not appropriate. If the child always reads at the independent level, then the books are too easy. Children need to engage some text at the instructional level. The Running Record effectively supports children's reading development and enables the teacher to encourage it. The Running Record is an exceptional reading assessment tool that benefits children. See the third edition of Clay's *The Early Detection of Reading Difficulties* (Heinemann) for additional information on Running Records.

Take Running Records daily, usually during Guided Reading. After Guided Reading (or Literature Circles or Independent Reading), take a Running Record on at least one child from each group. Taking frequent Running Records during the week makes your assessments timely and allows you to use them to help each child. Place Running Records in each child's portfolio to show their successes in using the cueing systems and reading increasingly difficult texts.

RETELL. A Retell Form, see p. 213, is an excellent way of assessing a child's holistic comprehension of a story. Retelling requires the child to use higher-order thinking skills. The child must sequence the story; add details; and remember characters, plot, and the resolution. The story Retell also allows the child to personalize the story, adding her own thoughts and experiences. Retelling a story is often difficult for beginning readers, but with practice, children become quite adept. A story Retell can be done immediately following a Running Record.

At the beginning of the year, conduct an unaided Retell with each child to establish a baseline. Additional Retells may be enhanced by asking the child questions to help her focus on certain aspects of the story that she is missing. Aided Retells may also be done with flannelboard figures or photocopies of key story pictures. The Retell Form will help the teacher and the child see the progress she is making in story comprehension.

READING LOGS. Reading Logs can be simple records of a child's reading at home (often an extension of the Guided Reading or Literature Circles process), or Reading Logs can be a form of self-evaluation with guiding remarks made by the teacher during a portfolio conference. The child may record what she is reading and the pages read and then comment on certain aspects of the book such as vocabulary, plot, characters, setting, and so on. The teacher writes reflections and goals alongside the child's. Four examples of Reading Logs are provided on pp. 214–217.

ANECDOTAL RECORDS. As you conference with a child after Guided Reading, Literature Circle, or Independent Reading, write down anecdotes that focus on the child's strengths (what the child knows) and also on her needs (what the child should work on for the next step in her development).

Remember that the focus of all these assessments is the benefit of the child. Multiple assessments allow the teacher, the child, and parents to follow the child's progress throughout the year, so as to help her reach subsequent levels of development.

Assessing Writing

Make your writing assessments using the following tools.

STAGES OF WRITING DEVELOPMENT. The Stages of Writing Development Chart p. 218, outlines the way children develop in their understanding of the writing process. In the primary multiage classroom, it is very important to attend to this process so further development can be encouraged. Study the chart and use it to determine where each child is on this continuum of writing development so that they can be effectively guided by the proper instructional strategies to support each child's writing development.

WRITING DEVELOPMENT CHECKLIST. Place a Writing Development Checklist p. 219, in each child's portfolio to record progress in writing. Based on the Stages of Writing Development Chart, the checklist makes it easy to see where each child is on the continuum and how the teacher can support the next stage of development.

Remember that the checklist is only a guide; each child will develop at her own rate. The teacher, the child, and her parents will quickly be able to see the progress.

WRITTEN LANGUAGE SKILLS CHECKLIST. This checklist (see p. 220) is used to identify skills that can be encouraged in the context of writing as well as a child's experiences with various writing genres.

SENTENCE DICTATION. At the beginning of the year, take a writing sample from each child. Select a sentence or two to use throughout the year. Read the sentences slowly to the child first. Then read each word as the child writes down the sounds she hears. This process helps identify which sounds the child is able to hear and record, providing useful information on the child's ability to relate sounds and symbols. After using the Writing Development Chart to identify the child's writing stage, design instruction to support the child to the next stage of writing development. Conduct the Sentence Dictation Assessment at the beginning, middle, and end of the year, placing the results in the children's portfolios.

See the third edition of Clay's *The Early Detection of Reading Difficulties* (Heinemann) for additional information on using sentence dictation assessment.

WRITING VOCABULARY.
Writing Vocabulary is another assessment tool developed by Marie Clay for beginning writers. In this assessment, ask the child to write down as many words as she knows how to write in ten minutes. You may give the child suggestions such as your name, names of people in your family, names of friends, color and number words, food words, high-frequency words (e.g., *I, am, be, see, go, down, up, is, you, your, going, big, little, boy, girl, me, will, to, in, it, went, get, he, she, we, on, let, not*), and word families (e.g., *fat, hat, sat; look, book, cook; hit, fit, sit*). Younger children may only write two or three words and tire in a few minutes. Older children may use the entire ten minutes and write forty words or more.

See the third edition of Clay's *The Early Detection of Reading Difficulties* (Heinemann) for additional information on using the Vocabulary Assessment.

Remember that this is just an assessment, not a test. Your objective is to see how many words each child knows and can spell correctly. After the assessment, the child must read the words back to you correctly, receiving a point for every correctly read and spelled word. Administer this assessment at the beginning of the year to establish a baseline and then give it again in the middle and at the end of the year in order to document progress. Place these assessments in each child's portfolio.

WRITING SELF-EVALUATION CHECKLISTS. A Writing Self-Evaluation Checklist, see pp. 221–222, may be placed at the end of a child's journal or in the child's writing folder to use when you are conferencing after Modeled Writing, or while you are editing with the child during Writers' Workshop. The checklist will help the child to focus quickly on her writing and select the next goal to strive for. Checklist A is for beginning writers and Checklist B is for fluent writers.

WRITING LOG. The Writing Log, p. 223, offers another form of self-evaluation, enabling the child to assess her own compositions and set goals. The teacher also records his reflections and goals and uses the log during portfolio conferences.

AUTHENTIC WORK. Place selections from a child's journal or stories from Writer's Workshop in the child's portfolio to document writing progress. Research writing from projects may also be added. Both the teacher and child may select writing pieces.

ANECDOTAL RECORDS. As you conference with a child after Modeled Writing or during the editing process of a Writers' Workshop, write down anecdotes that focus on the child's strengths (what the child knows) and also on the child's needs (what you want the child to work on to advance her development). Anecdotal records provide valuable information for guiding your instruction and meeting the specific needs of the children in your multiage class.

From *Creating the Multiage Classroom* published by GoodYear Books. Copyright © 1996 Sandra J. Stone.

Assessing Math

The following tools will help you in assessing math development in your multiage classroom.

NUMBER TASKS (CONCEPTS AND PROPERTIES). Children who are constructing their logico-mathematical knowledge and understanding need to be assessed on what they know regarding numbers. The following simple tasks will supply baseline information and also indicate the kinds of experiences a child needs to help her improve number skills. Record the results on the Number Task Assessment Form provided on p. 224.

Ordering. Have the child count to 10 . . . 50 . . . 100 . . . 1000, and so on to document her emerging ability to order numbers. The child may begin with 1, 10, or 3 as a baseline counter until she counts sequentially by rote, increasing the numbers (1 to 10, 1 to 50, etc.).

One-to-one matching. Have the child match one item to another item. Put out five blue chips and five red chips and have the child pair them. The child may touch or move the objects as she matches them.

Conservation. Conservation is important for a child's understanding of number. Have each child match items such as blue chips and red chips. Next, move the blue chips apart and ask the child if there are more blue chips or red chips, or if there is still the same amount. A child who is "conserving number" will realize that the amount remains constant even if they are spread out. *Conservation* means "the ability to not fix on the physical characteristics of objects such as size or arrangement when determining if two sets are equal in number" *(Schultz, Colarusso, and Strawderman, 1989, pp. 50–51).*

Total number. Ask the child to count a number of objects and then to tell you how many objects are in the group. If the child understands total number, she will be able to say that the last number counted indicates how many there are in the group.

Different objects. Ask the child to count a group of different objects such as chips, money, and paper clips. The child should be able to see that objects do not have to be alike to be counted.

Ordinality. Ask the child to look at a series of objects and describe their positions in relation to one another: first, second, third, and so on.

Grouping. Ask the child to group objects by twos, fives, and tens and then tell you how many groups result.

Place value Ask the child to use frozen juice sticks (1s, 10s bundle, 100s bundle) to represent numbers such as 15, 63, or 114.

Commutative Property. The Commutative Property refers to the fact that whole numbers may be interchanged without changing their sum. Ask the child to show you how many ways she can arrange 3 and 2 to add up to 5, and how many ways she can arrange 4 and 6 to equal 2 (subtraction). The child should know that subtraction of whole numbers is not commutative.

Associative property. Ask the child to show you how many ways she can arrange 3, 6, and 1 to add up to 10. The child should know that changing the grouping of three addends does not change their sum.

Repeated addition (multiplication). Ask the child to arrange twenty beans in sets of five. How many sets result? How many beans are there altogether? The child may count by fives to show repeated addition.

Repeated subtraction (division). Ask the child to "deal" twelve cards to four players until the cards are all gone. How many are in each set?

Each of these number tasks helps you to assess the child's understanding of number and number operations. Establish a baseline and then provide experiences with number that will facilitate the child's number construction. Assess periodically using the Number Task Assessment Form.

MATH DEVELOPMENT CHECKLISTS. Math Development Checklists, pp. 225–227 help identify the concepts and skills that children move through in their development. Use the checklist to assess where each child is and where she needs support to reach the next stage of development. The checklists are only guides; each child will develop at their own rate. Place checklists in each child's portfolio.

AUTHENTIC WORK. Add children's authentic work to their portfolio. Authentic work may originate during centers or projects and demonstrate certain mathematical knowledge, skills, concepts, and/or problem-solving ability.

ANECDOTAL RECORDS. When working with small groups of children in Guided Math or at Math Centers, record observations and add them to the children's portfolios. Use these observations to plan math experiences to support the children's construction of math concepts and to nurture skill development.

From *Creating the Multiage Classroom* published by Good Year Books. Copyright © 1996 Sandra J. Stone.

Assessing Science

Assess progress in science according to the children's development in the science process skills: observing, comparing, classifying, measuring, discussing/reporting and predicting. These assessment tools will help.

AUTHENTIC WORK. The teacher and the children may choose work from centers and projects that reflect the children's increasing progress in the process skills. Label the work according to the process. Group work together that represents growth and continued skill in using these processes. During conference time, set goals for increasing competency in these skills.

SCIENCE PROCESS SKILLS CHECKLIST. A Science Process Skills Checklist, p. 228, will help you and the children focus on the process skills. The checklist may accompany the authentic work.

ANECDOTAL RECORDS. As the children work on projects and in centers, record observations that document their use of the process skills. Include the anecdotal records in their portfolios to share with children and parents.

SELF-EVALUATION: SCIENCE LOG. Invite the children to share their own awareness of using the process skills. Children may record their observations and reflections in a daily or weekly Science Log, such as that found on p. 229, and then set goals for themselves.

Assessing Social Studies

Assess children for growth in two areas in the social studies: (1) the process of becoming social beings and (2) the process of learning about the world in which we live. Use the following techniques.

AUTHENTIC WORK. Children demonstrate their facility with locating information, organizing information (classifying, comparing/contrasting, summarizing, graphing), and interpreting and reflecting on information through projects and centers across social studies content areas, such as history, geography, economics, ecology, and so forth. During conferences, identify these skills as they relate to a project and set goals for increasing a child's use of them. Label the projects with the skills that you identify.

SOCIAL STUDIES PROCESS CHECKLIST. A Social Studies Process Checklist, p. 230, will help you and the children focus on the process skills. Use it to document authentic work.

ANECDOTAL RECORDS. Write down your observations of children using social studies processes during project or center work and add to the children's portfolios.

Anecdotal records are also an effective way to document social development. Focus on certain social skills or attitudes for each child and then record your observations as children display them. Keep a record of each child's social needs to help you support specific behaviors (e.g., empathy, kindness, responsibility, helpfulness, generosity, sharing).

SELF-EVALUATION: SOCIAL STUDIES LOG. Invite the children to share their own awareness of using the social studies process skills. Children may record their observations and reflections in a daily or weekly Social Studies Log, such as that on p. 231, and then set goals for themselves.

I'm going to work on classifying this week. I'm going to classify types of habitats.

I'm working on summarizing.

Assessing Art, Music, Play, and Movement

Creative expression is also an important area in which to document growth. Are children developing in their abilities to discover, explore, prove, analyze, and test solutions? Are they aesthetically aware? Do they enjoy creative expression? Are the children continuing to seek new ways of doing things and figuring out their own ways of doing things? Assessing growth in these areas may be done through authentic work, anecdotal records, and self-evaluation.

AUTHENTIC WORK. Creative expression is an excellent medium for documentation. Portfolios may include artworks; photographs of art pieces, sculptures, and buildings; audiotapes of music pieces; and videotapes of expressive movement or dramatizations.

ANECDOTAL RECORDS. Anecdotal records are particularly useful in documenting children's creative ideas, attitudes, and risk taking.

SELF-EVALUATION. Elicit self-evaluation informally during conferences, creative expression centers, or projects. Encourage the child to consider different options or ideas with questions such as: "Have you considered another way? What else could you do? How did you do that?"

STAGES OF READING DEVELOPMENT

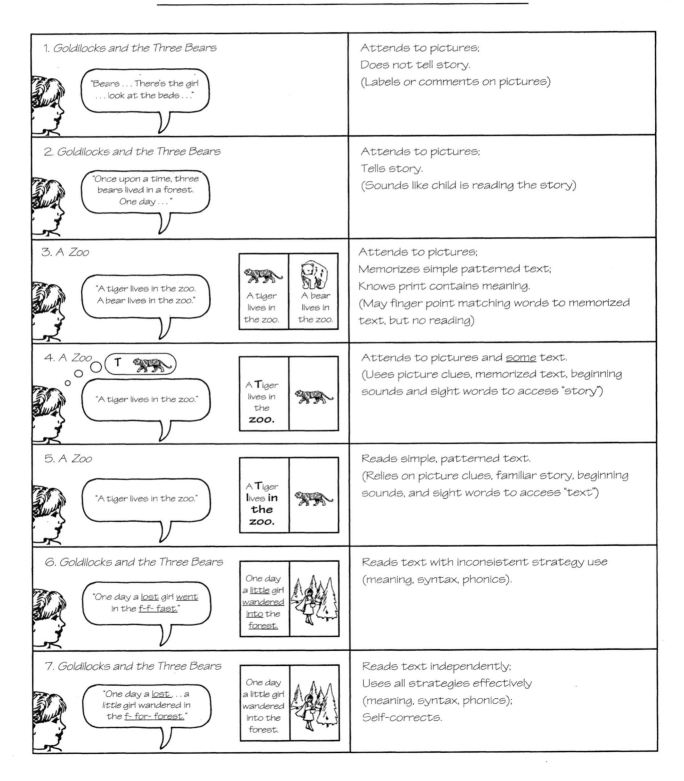

1. *Goldilocks and the Three Bears* "Bears . . . There's the girl . . . look at the beds . . ."	Attends to pictures; Does not tell story. (Labels or comments on pictures)
2. *Goldilocks and the Three Bears* "Once upon a time, three bears lived in a forest. One day . . ."	Attends to pictures; Tells story. (Sounds like child is reading the story)
3. *A Zoo* "A tiger lives in the zoo. A bear lives in the zoo."	Attends to pictures; Memorizes simple patterned text; Knows print contains meaning. (May finger point matching words to memorized text, but no reading)
4. *A Zoo* "A tiger lives in the zoo."	Attends to pictures and <u>some</u> text. (Uses picture clues, memorized text, beginning sounds and sight words to access "story")
5. *A Zoo* "A tiger lives in the zoo."	Reads simple, patterned text. (Relies on picture clues, familiar story, beginning sounds, and sight words to access "text")
6. *Goldilocks and the Three Bears* "One day a <u>lost</u> girl <u>went</u> in the <u>f-f- fast</u>."	Reads text with inconsistent strategy use (meaning, syntax, phonics).
7. *Goldilocks and the Three Bears* "One day a <u>lost</u> . . . a little girl wandered in the <u>f- for- forest</u>."	Reads text independently; Uses all strategies effectively (meaning, syntax, phonics); Self-corrects.

READING DEVELOPMENT
CHECKLIST

Name _____ Date_____

STAGE ONE	SEP	OCT	NOV	DEC	JAN	FEB	MAR	APR	MAY
Front/back of book									
Top/bottom of page									
Attends to pictures; Labels/comments									
Attends to pictures; Tells story									
Print contains meaning									
Differentiates letters/words									
Concept of word/space									
Identifies some environmental print									
One-to-one matching (voice to print)									
Knows where to begin									
Left-to-right/Return sweep									
Memorizes text									
STAGE TWO	SEP	OCT	NOV	DEC	JAN	FEB	MAR	APR	MAY
Attends to some print									
Identifies some letters									
Identifies sight words									
Uses picture clues									
Uses familiar story									
Uses beginning consonants									
Uses beginning and end consonants									
Uses some strategies (mean., syn., phon.)									
Expects reading to make sense									
Expects reading to sound right									
Uses knowledge of letter/sound relationships									
Takes risks without fear of making errors									
STAGE THREE	SEP	OCT	NOV	DEC	JAN	FEB	MAR	APR	MAY
Reads using all strategies (mean., syn., phon.)									
Uses decoding to confirm or disconfirm other strategies									
Self-corrects									
Rereads for meaning									
Reads on to gain meaning									
Retells story (set., char., theme, plot, res.)									
STAGE FOUR	SEP	OCT	NOV	DEC	JAN	FEB	MAR	APR	MAY
Reads with fluency (expression, rate)									
Silently reads new text independently									
Integrates all strategies (mean., syn., phon.)									
Reads different ways for different purposes									
Comprehends text (literal, inferential, critical)									

LETTER/SOUND
IDENTIFICATION CHART

Name _____ Date_____

upper case

A	K	F	W	P	X
B	O	H	U	J	
C	L	Y	M	Q	
D	S	N	I	Z	
E	R	G	T	V	

lower case

a	k	f	w	p	x
b	o	h	u	j	
c	l	y	m	q	
d	s	n	i	z	
e	r	g	t	v	

From *Creating the Multiage Classroom* published by GoodYear Books. Copyright © 1996 Sandra J. Stone.

LETTER/SOUND IDENTIFICATION FORM

Directions: Use the letter/sound identification chart. Ask the child to name the letter, both lower and upper case. Then go back and ask the child to give the sound of the upper case letters only. Record letters and sounds known or unknown, whichever is less. Record letter confusion.

Name _____ Date_____

	Letter	Sound	Incorrect Response		Letter	Sound	Incorrect Response
A				a			
K				k			
F				f			
W				w			
P				p			
X				x			
B				b			
O				o			
H				h			
U				u			
J				j			
C				c			
L				l			
Y				y			
M				m			
Q				q			
D				d			
S				s			
N				n			
I				i			
Z				z			
E				e			
R				r			
G				g			
T				t			
V				v			

Letters Known/Unknown:

Sounds Known/Unknown:

Letter Confusions:

CONCEPTS OF PRINT
FORM

Directions: Read an unfamiliar patterned picture book with the child. As you read, ask the following questions. Be sure all the concepts are in the book. The questions may be asked in any order except for questions 1–4.

Name _____ Date_____

		YES	NO
1.	Where is the front of the book? (Present book to child and observe how she/he handles it.)		
2.	Where should I start reading? (Child knows print contains meaning.)		
3.	As I read, which way do I go?		
4.	Can you point to the words while I read? (Child demonstrates word by word matching, one-to-one correspondence.)		
5.	Can you show me one letter, two letters?		
6.	Can you show me one word, two words?		
7.	Can you show me a space between words?		
8.	Look at the picture on this page. What is it? Can you find a word on this page that could be this word? (Child can use picture clues and beginning sounds to locate words.)		
9.	Can you count the syllables in this word? (read word) this word?		
10.	Can you show me a sentence?		
11.	Can you show me the first part of the sentence? last part?		
12.	Can you show me the first part of this word? last part?		
13.	Can you show me an upper case, capital letter?		
14.	Can you show me a lower case letter?		
15.	Can you show me a consonant?		
16.	Can you show me a vowel?		
17.	What is this for? (period)		
18.	What is this for? (question mark)		
19.	What is this for? (exclamation point)		
20.	What is this for? (quotation marks)		
21.	What is this for? (comma)		

RETELL

Title of Story or Book: _____

Check each element the child includes in the story retell. Evaluate the child by how much improvement the child is making "over time."

Begins Story Retell with an Introduction _____

Identifies Setting _____
      Identifies Time _____
      Identifies Place _____

Identifies Main Character _____

Identifies Other Characters _____

Can Retell Plot (Sequence of Events) _____

Identifies Problem _____

Identifies Solution (Resolution) _____

Identifies Theme or Moral _____

COMMENTS:

Name _____ Date_____

MY READING LOG

Book Title (Pages Read)	Reactions... Reflections... Vocabulary	Goals

Name _____ Date_____

From Creating the Multiage Classroom published by GoodYear Books. Copyright © 1996 Sandra J. Stone.

READING LOG
SELF-EVALUATION

_____ I can tell the main idea of a book.

_____ I can identify the theme/moral.

_____ I can retell a story.

_____ I can predict how a story will end.

_____ I can identify the main character and other characters.

_____ I can describe a character.

_____ I can identify character traits.

_____ I can describe the setting.

_____ I can describe the mood.

_____ I can identify the problem.

_____ I can identify the solution/resolution.

_____ I can connect the story to personal experience.

_____ I can compare/contrast stories.

_____ I can recognize types of stories.

_____ I can discuss the author's point of view.

_____ I can give my opinion of the book.

Name _____ Date_____

LITERATURE LOG

Child's Name _____ Book_____

My Response	Teacher Response

HOME READING
RECORD

NAME _____ DATE _____

Date	Title	Parent's Signature	Teacher's Initials

STAGES OF WRITING DEVELOPMENT CHART

1. (This is my house.)	Pictures
2. (This is my house.)	Scribble (Approximation)
3. AcMAOWA (This is my house.)	Random Letters
4. IVADAAO (I have a dog.)	Random and Initial
5. I L M B (I like my bike.)	Initial Consonants
6. I lk mi Bk. (I like my bike.)	Initial and Final Sounds
7. I lik to pla with my cat. (I like to play with my cat.)	Vowel Sounds Appear
8. My favorit dinosor is the stegosorus. (My favorite dinosaur is the stegosaurus.)	All Syllables Represented
9. Today I am going to the stor with my mothr. I am going to by a present for my brothrs brthday. He is thre yers old.	Multiple, Related Sentences and Many Words with Correct Spelling

From *Creating the Multiage Classroom* published by GoodYear Books. Copyright © 1996 Sandra J. Stone.

WRITING DEVELOPMENT CHECKLIST

Name _____ Date_____

STAGE ONE	SEP	OCT	NOV	DEC	JAN	FEB	MAR	APR	MAY
Pre-letter writing/pictures									
Approximation (scribble)									
Random use of letters									
Uses random and initial letters									
Random use of sight words									
Copies letters/words									
STAGE TWO	SEP	OCT	NOV	DEC	JAN	FEB	MAR	APR	MAY
Transfers thoughts to paper									
Uses initial consonants									
Uses initial and ending consonants									
Uses sight words									
Begins to form letters correctly									
Reads back accurately at conference									
Writes from left to right									
STAGE THREE	SEP	OCT	NOV	DEC	JAN	FEB	MAR	APR	MAY
Writes a complete sentence									
Beginning to use periods									
Leaves space									
Beginning to use vowels									
Beginning to use capital & lower case letters									
Beginning to represent all syllables									
STAGE FOUR	SEP	OCT	NOV	DEC	JAN	FEB	MAR	APR	MAY
Writes multiple sentences									
Uses vowels									
Represents all syllables									
More correct spellings than word approximations									
Sequences ideas									
Uses periods									
STAGE FIVE	SEP	OCT	NOV	DEC	JAN	FEB	MAR	APR	MAY
Can carry a story									
Uses punctuation (periods, commas, question marks, exclamation marks, quotation marks)									
Edits own writing (i.e., spelling, content)									
Uses a variety of genres (factual, imaginative, poetry, personal narrative, etc.)									
Organizes writing webs									
Writes with paragraphs									

WRITTEN LANGUAGE
SKILLS CHECKLIST

Name _____   Date_____

USES DIFFERENT GENRES	SEP	OCT	NOV	DEC	JAN	FEB	MAR	APR	MAY
Personal narrative									
Imaginative story									
Report									
Communication									
Poetry									
Retelling									
IDENTIFIES AND USES	SEP	OCT	NOV	DEC	JAN	FEB	MAR	APR	MAY
Subjects/predicates									
Nouns									
Adjectives									
Correct spellings of irregular plural nouns									
Common and proper nouns									
Action verbs									
Adverbs									
Subject-verb agreement									
Present tense verbs									
Singular and plural possessive nouns									
Subject pronouns/object pronouns									
Correct usage of possessive pronouns									
Subj.-verb agreement using subj. pronouns									
Correct spelling of pronoun contractions									
Correct usage of commas in sentences									
Correct usage of dialogue									
Apostrophes in possessive nouns									
Apostrophes in contractions									
Correct punctuation of titles									
Commas in dates									
Periods in abbreviations									
Commas in letter parts									
Capitals in letter parts									
Commas in a series									
Capital for proper nouns									

WRITING SELF EVALUATION
CHECKLIST A
Beginning Writers

Name _____ Date_____

I Can . . .

Write letters.				
Write the first letter in a word.				
Write the last letter in a word.				
Write some middle letters in a word.				
Write some vowels.				
Leave spaces.				
Write some whole words.				
Write one sentence.				
Write two or more sentences.				
Put periods at the end of sentences.				
Put a capital at the beginning of a sentence.				

WRITING SELF EVALUATION
CHECKLIST B
Fluent Writers

Name _____ Date_____

I Can . . .

I Can...				
Write complete sentences.				
Use question marks.				
Use exclamation marks.				
Use quotation marks.				
Plan before I write.				
Write a story with a beginning, middle and end.				
Use interesting and vivid words.				
Use describing words.				
Reread and revise my writing.				
Write paragraphs.				
Write with different genres.				

WRITING LOG

Child's Name _____ Selection _____

My Comments and Goals	Teacher Comments

NUMBER TASK
ASSESSMENT FORM

Name _____ Date_____

Ordering
One-to-One Matching
Conservation
Total Number
Different Objects
Ordinality
Grouping
Commutative Property
Associative Property
Repeated Addition (Multiplication)
Repeated Subtraction (Division)

MATH DEVELOPMENT
CHECKLIST 1
Ages 5-8

Name _____ Date _____

NUMBER AND NUMERATION	SEP	OCT	NOV	DEC	JAN	FEB	MAR	APR	MAY
One-to-One Correspondence									
Equivalent Sets									
Using Numerals (1-10, 1-20, 1-100)									
Counting (1-10, 1-20, 1-100)									
Counting to 100 (by 2's, by 5's, by 10's)									
Writing Numerals (1-10, 1-20, 1-100)									
Ordering Numerals (1-10, 1-20, 1-100)									
Number Lines									
Ordinal Numbers (1st-3rd, 1st-5th, 1st-12th)									
Set and Subset									
More than; Less than									
Odd and Even Numbers									
Reading and Writing Numerals									
Place Value (3 digits, 4 digits, 5 digits)									
Round Off (10's, 100's, 1000's)									
Estimation									
Roman Numerals									
OPERATIONS OF WHOLE NUMBERS	SEP	OCT	NOV	DEC	JAN	FEB	MAR	APR	MAY
Addition (Sums through 5, 10, 20)									
Associative Property of Addition									
Column Addition									
(Two digit, Three digit, Four digit)									
(Two digit w/regrouping, Three digit w/regrouping)									
Subtraction									
(One digit, Two digit, Three digit)									
Commutative Property of Subtraction									
(Two digit w/regrouping, Three digit w/regrouping)									
Commutative Property of Multiplication									
Multiplication (Basic Facts: 1-5, 6-10, 11-12)									
(Relation to Addition)									
(One digit, Two digit by one digit, Two digit)									
Division (Basic Facts: 2-3, 4-6, 7-9)									
(Relation to Multiplication)									
(Estimating Quotients)									

MATH DEVELOPMENT
CHECKLIST 2
Ages 5-8

Name _____ Date _____

RATIONAL NUMBERS	SEP	OCT	NOV	DEC	JAN	FEB	MAR	APR	MAY
Odd and Even Numbers									
Multiples and Factors									
Primes and Compounds									
Equal Parts									
Fractions (1/2, 1/4, 1/3, 1/8, 1/6)									
Decimals (Reading, Writing, Comparing)									
MEASUREMENT	SEP	OCT	NOV	DEC	JAN	FEB	MAR	APR	MAY
Money									
(Coins: penny, nickel, dime, quarter)									
(Bills: one, five, ten, twenty)									
(Adding and Subtracting)									
(Decimals with cents)									
(Making Change: simple, complex)									
Time									
(Sequence and Concepts of Time)									
(Clocks: kinds of clocks; clock faces; etc.)									
(Intervals: minute, hour, half-hour, quarter-hour)									
(Telling Time)									
Length									
(Concepts: shortest, longest)									
(Non-standard Units)									
(Standard Units: inches, feet, yards)									
(Measurement Instruments: ruler, yardstick)									
Weight									
(Measurement Units: ounce, pound, ton)									
(Measurement Instruments: balance, scale)									
Volume									
(Measurement Units: pint, quart, gallon)									
Temperature									
(Measurement Unit: degree)									
(Measurement Instrument: thermometer)									

From *Creating the Multiage Classroom* published by GoodYear Books. Copyright © 1996 Sandra J. Stone.

MATH DEVELOPMENT
CHECKLIST 3
Ages 5-8

Name _____ Date_____

GEOMETRY	SEP	OCT	NOV	DEC	JAN	FEB	MAR	APR	MAY
Shape									
(Square, circle, triangle, cube)									
(Congruent shapes)									
(Lines)									
(Symmetry)									
(Measurement: area, perimeter)									
Patterns									
(Matching: figure, number)									
(Completing: figure, number)									
(Making: simple, complex)									
PROBLEM SOLVING/MATH REASONING	SEP	OCT	NOV	DEC	JAN	FEB	MAR	APR	MAY
Observing									
Similarities and Differences									
Sorting and Classifying									
Sorting by Property									
Finding a Common Property									
Identify Attributes and Non-Attributes									
Use of More Than One Attribute									
Forming Subsets									
Estimating									
Making Predictions									
Making Problems									
Cause and Effect									
Explain Answers									
Develop New Strategies									
Create Word Problems									
Find and Record Data									

SCIENCE PROCESS
SKILLS CHECKLIST

Name _____ Date_____

Observing				
Comparing				
Classifying				
Measuring				
Discussing/Reporting				
Predicting				

SCIENCE LOG

Child's Name _____ Topic _____

My Comments and Goals	Teacher Comments

SOCIAL STUDIES
PROCESS CHECKLIST

Name _____ Date_____

Locating information				
Organizing information				
classifying				
comparing/contrasting				
summarizing				
graphing				
Interpreting and reflecting on information				

SOCIAL STUDIES LOG

Child's Name _____ Topics _____

My Comments and Goals	Teacher Comments

Integrating Assessment Into Your Instructional Day

Portfolio assessment can be overwhelming if tried all at once or forced into the end of the day. These guidelines will assist in the management of portfolio assessment so that the teachers and children enjoy the most benefit from it.

Start with one area of assessment and get comfortable with it before moving on to other areas. If new to portfolio assessment, trying to do it all at once may be discouraging.

Design personal portfolio assessment techniques. Techniques should fit the teacher's needs as well as the needs of the children. The tools included with this chapter are only guidelines for an assessment process. Each teacher must decide what is important to include and what is not.

Select the children's work that shows growth; don't just fill a folder with work. Effective portfolios document the children's development in all areas.

Integrate portfolio assessment into the instructional day. It is very important to take time to assess the children during instruction. Waiting until after school to work on portfolios is fruitless: there will be no time and there will be no children. Time must be taken during school, while there is teacher/student interaction.

Make assessment a part of your daily rather than monthly routine. Assess children's reading daily with Running Records during small-group times. Assess their writing daily as you conference or edit with them during journal writing or Writers' Workshop. Assess math skills during small-group Guided Math. Take time to observe on a daily basis and create anecdotal records. The time spent assessing need not be lengthy. In fact, frequency is favorable to length; frequent assessments take several minutes per child. More lengthy conferences may be scheduled every few weeks, if you wish. Frequent assessment is most effective in guiding instruction since it immediately conveys the needs of children, which can then be addressed promptly rather than waiting until after a conference at the end of the month.

Trust professional judgment. A teacher's expert knowledge of children and how they learn will assist him in assessing their needs. The more the teacher assesses, the more information he will have to make good instructional decisions. And the more one assesses, the easier it becomes!

From *Creating the Multiage Classroom* published by GoodYear Books. Copyright © 1996 Sandra J. Stone.

Reporting Progress Without Grades

Portfolios are a way to document a child's growth without labeling, sorting, and ranking children.

Some educators are trying to fit portfolios into a labeling format by introducing matrices to rank a child's work. Such matrices can then be used to issue grades. However, using this matrix to compare children violates the essence of portfolio assessment, and, indeed, the philosophy of the multiage classroom. Grades are given to establish who is successful in the class and who is not. In the multiage classroom, all children should be successful.

Documenting growth through portfolios is beneficial to the children, whereas grading them is not.

Many multiage teachers are moving away from the graded report card by reporting progress to parents without labeling children with a grade. Portfolio conferences are replacing report card conferences.

Some schools use narrative report cards describing a child's successes rather than grading her. Narrative report cards are very effective tools in multiage classrooms. Other schools issue report cards without grades, which are replaced with indicators such as "not yet," "developing," and "able," or "consistently," "frequently," "beginning," and "not introduced."

Portfolio conferences combined with new ways of documenting a child's progress make highly effective reporting systems that accurately reflect the underlying philosophy of multiage classrooms.

The following "report cards" are examples of the successful reporting systems currently being used by many multiage classrooms.

Primary Multiage Report Card, Tempe School District No. 3, Tempe, Arizona
used by permission

Primary Multiage Report Card pp. 234-237

Multi Age Primary Report Card

1994 - 1995

West Sedona Elementary School -- -- Sedona, AZ.

Philosophy

Emergent

The child is becoming aware of the basics of reading, writing, and math. These readers need predictable books which are high in interest and include rhyme, repetition, natural language flow and illustrations that match the text. As mathematicians they need hands on experiences.

Early

The child understands the basics of print and is learning to use various strategies to gain meaning. He/She is beginning to write meaningful stories. He/She is beginning to make the transfer from hands on to some abstract reasoning.

Fluent

The child is a confident reader. He/She is able to use many strategies to read a variety of reading materials for various purposes. He/She can read and write more detailed and complicated stories. He/She still needs to have hands on experiences, but is more able to make the transfer to the abstract concepts.

Marking Code

/ = Beginning to use this skill
X = Consistently using this skill
* = Independently using this skill

Color Code

1st Trimester = Purple
2nd Trimester = Green
3rd Trimester = Blue

Student _____

Teacher _____

1st Trimester Parent Signature	2nd Trimester Parent Signature	3rd Trimester Parent Signature

	1	2	3	Total
Absent				

From *Creating the Multiage Classroom* published by GoodYear Books. Copyright © 1996 Sandra J. Stone.

Sedona Primary Multiage Report Card, Sedona Elementary School, Sedona, Arizona

Emergent

I can sit and listen to stories.	
I can show the front, back, spine of a book and turn pages correctly.	
I know all the letters and sounds of the alphabet.	
I can match one to one.	
I can recognize some "heavy duty" words, for example: is, look, the, etc.	
I can recognize how words are alike.	
I can read in the Stage _____ Readers.	

Early

I can sit for awhile and read (alone, with a buddy, in a large group).	
I use meaning as a clue. I know that reading must make sense.	
I take risks. I "give it a go!"	
I am able to use text and pictures to sample, predict and confirm.	
I self correct errors.	
I can integrate strategies and cross check cue sources.	
I can retell stories.	

Fluent

I can read on my own with understanding.	
I can read with expression.	
I know the difference between fiction and nonfiction.	
I choose suitable reading material.	
I can tell the main idea.	
I can read with understanding a variety of styles:	
Personal Experience Narrative	
Story	
Informative Report	
Communication	
Poem	

Science

I investigate and experiment willingly.	
I can use field guides, resource books, encyclopedias, etc.	
I can use the following science processes:	

observe ☐   classify ☐   measure ☐   collect and organize data ☐
predict ☐   hypothesize ☐   process ☐   identify variables ☐

Personal Development

I stay actively involved in tasks until completed.	
I use initiative to resolve problems independently.	
I ask for help when needed.	
I respect rules/authority.	
I demonstrate self-confidence.	
I accept responsibility for my own behavior.	
I work cooperatively in a small group.	
I work cooperatively in a large group.	
I can work independently.	
I respect rights, feelings and property of others.	
I express feelings appropriately.	
I listen attentively and participate in group discussions and activities.	
I care for and clean up materials.	
I put forth my best effort.	

Sedona Primary Multiage
Report Card, Sedona
Elementary School,
Sedona, Arizona

used by permission

Emergent

I can count by 1's, 2's, 5's, and 10's.	
I can use numbers 0 - 100.	
I understand two number operations and place value 0 - 10.	
I can recognize equal and unequal concrete objects.	
I can recognize the dollar, quarters, dimes, nickels and pennies.	
I can tell time to the hour.	
I know what a circle, triangle, square and rectangle are.	
I can identify, extend and predict a pattern.	
I can make and read pictorial graphs.	
I know how to sort and classify objects.	
I know my colors.	

Early

I can solve oral story problems using addition and subtraction.	
I can use manipulatives for addition and subtraction.	
I can read number words 0 - 20 and match them to the numeral.	
I can identify numbers that come before or after a given number 0 - 99.	
I know the names and values:	
pennies ☐ nickels ☐ dimes ☐	
quarters ☐ half dollar ☐ dollars ☐	
I can identify numbers 0 - 99.	
I can identify ordinal numbers first through twentieth.	
I can use a calculator for single digit subtraction.	
I can recognize spheres, cubes and cylinders.	
I can read and write numbers when objects are grouped by tens and ones.	
I can identify place value for ones and tens.	
I can tell time to the hour and half hour.	
I can read Fahrenheit temperatures on the thermometer.	
I can identify, describe and extend a complex pattern.	
I know and can use the words:	
sum ☐ difference ☐ greater than ☐	
less than ☐ addition ☐ subtraction ☐	
equal ☐ pattern ☐ number sentence ☐	
graph ☐ table ☐	

Fluent

I can interpret word problems.	
I can write mathematical sentences to represent a situation.	
I can use manipulatives to make reasonable and logical conclusions.	
I can recognize and count money.	
I can use manipulatives to create pattern and then represent the pattern symbolically.	
I can use cardinal and ordinal numbers to compare and order.	
I can use manipulatives to demonstrate an understanding of place value:	
100 ☐ 1000 ☐	
I can read and write numbers that are grouped by 1's, 10's, 100's, 1000's.	
I understand the meaning of:	
+ ☐ - ☐ ÷ ☐ x ☐	
I can choose the appropriate operation to be used in a given situation.	
I have complete understanding and the ability to use:	
basic addition 0 -20 ☐ basic subtraction 0 - 20 ☐	
multiplication 0 - 5 ☐	
I can add or subtract two 3-digit whole numbers.	
I can use a variety of methods to estimate and measure length.	
I can read Celsius and Fahrenheit temperatures on thermometers.	
I can tell time to the minute.	
I can choose an appropriate unit of measure in a given situation.	
I can identify, describe and extend a two attribute pattern where the sequence is 4 or greater.	
I can determine a location by single ordered pairs of numbers on a rectangular grid.	

Sedona Primary Multiage Report Card, Sedona Elementary School, Sedona, Arizona

used by permission

Writing Skills

Emergent

I can write capital and lower case letters (handwriting, correct letter formation).	
I can write the first letter in a word (phonics, beginning consonant).	
I can write the last letter in a word (phonics, ending consonant).	
I leave spaces between words.	
I can write a few whole words.	
I can write one sentence.	
I can read back what I have written.	
I am able to spell correctly some high frequency words.	
I am able to distinguish between words that rhyme and words that don't.	

Early

I can use approximations (invented spelling, temporary spelling).	
I can use vowels.	
I can correctly spell many high frequency words correctly.	
I use periods and capital letters correctly.	
I can write two or more sentences.	
I can choose a topic for writing.	
I can use word sources to help with my spelling.	
I can remember the correct spelling of some words	
I can remember to have a beginning, middle and ending.	
I am able to brainstorm ideas for writing.	

Fluent

I can use editing skills.	
I can peer edit.	
I spell most of my words correctly.	
I vary sentence beginnings.	
I can sequence ideas.	
I use a wide vocabulary.	
I can choose a title for my story.	
I can use a dictionary correctly.	
I can publish correct pieces of written work.	
I can use spelling generalizations correctly.	
I can expand my story line	
I write on a variety of topics:	
Personal Experience Narrative	
Story	
Informative Report	
Communication	
Poem	

Art, Music, Physical Education, Computer, & Library

S = Satisfactory   I = Improving   N = Needs Improvement

	1	2	3
Art			
Music			
Physical Education			
Computer			
Library			

Sedona Primary Multiage
Report Card, Sedona
Elementary School,
Sedona, Arizona

used by permission

Sample Primary Multiage Narrative Report Card pp. 238-239

From Creating the Multiage Classroom published by GoodYear Books. Copyright © 1996 Sandra J. Stone.

STUDENT PROGRESS REPORT

READING

Mary has developed into a Fluent Reader. She uses strategies that good readers use. She has excellent comprehension skills as well. Mary is always prepared for Literature Circle. She often leads the study. Mary is also reading different kinds of books this year. She completes her Literature Log with great detail, which also shows a high level of understanding. Mary is becoming a dedicated, lifelong reader. I am thrilled with her progress.

WRITING

Mary eagerly participates in Writers' Workshop. She has published several books this semester. Her books continue to be of high quality. She is using more writing genres and becoming quite competent in establishing stories with a beginning, middle, and end. During Modeled Writing, she is learning to use adjectives and adverbs effectively. She is working on writing more complex sentences in her learning journal.

MATHEMATICS

Mary continues to develop in her math skills. She has mastered ordering numbers to 1,000 and place value up to five digits. She continues to develop in her skills of adding three-digit numbers. Problem solving is challenging for her, but she is a risk-taker, and does not give up trying. I see her mastering word problems very soon. Mary likes math and uses it effectively at centers and with projects.

SCIENCE

Mary has enjoyed our science centers this quarter. She is using science process skills effectively. Her skills in observing and communicating are particularly good. She completed a science experiment on soil composition. She is improving in her ability to hypothesize and control variables.

STUDENT PROGRESS REPORT

SOCIAL STUDIES

Mary has enjoyed studying geology this quarter. She and her classmates completed their project on gems and presented it to the class. Their research information was exceptionally well done. Mary contributed to this project by securing books from the library and writing several key reports. She was enthusiastic and creative and demonstrated strong leadership skills. She continually improves in locating and organizing information. I am particularly pleased with her interpretation of information.

SOCIAL GROWTH

Mary is a kind and caring person. When working at centers or in small, cooperative groups during projects, Mary is exceptionally good at mentoring younger children. She helps them find answers and solve problems for themselves without giving them the answers. The opportunity to mentor has helped Mary gain confidence in herself. Mary is becoming a quite competent leader. She also demonstrates excellent social skills. She is well liked by both younger and older classmates.

CREATIVE ARTS

Mary is demonstrating strong aesthetic awareness. She enjoys creating, discovering, and exploring with art, music, movement, and play. She created an outstanding painting for our theme on plants. She also demonstrates high imaginative abilities in our play center. She initiates elaborate stories and skillfully involves the other children. Music is a new area that Mary is exploring. I see her integrating music and movement in the near future.

CHAPTER EIGHT

GETTING STARTED

In their enthusiasm to implement multiage education, schools sometimes overlook the planning stage necessary for a successful multiage experience. Some schools have simply combined grades in an effort to create a multiage classroom without really understanding the concept. Starting a multiage classroom is truly a great adventure, but one must plan well before beginning. The route must first be known before the destination can be reached.

The Multiage Team

Recruit a team, including several teachers and the principal, to investigate the possibility of establishing multiage classrooms in your school. Such collegial and administrative support will serve the cause well. As part of your team, administrators can open doors to facilitate the process. If you are an administrator, your role in establishing successful multiage classrooms is invaluable.

Forming an investigative team does not mean teachers will team-teach when implementing the multiage classroom. This team's task is to conduct a thorough investigation that will include release time for research and on-site visits to explore models of multiage classrooms, including self-contained and team-taught. The investigation as well as the school's resources will help direct which model is chosen.

Preliminary Research

Read, read, and read some more.

In addition to using this book as a guide, do your own research. The Professional Resources section contains many resources for investigation. Individually and as a team, saturate yourself with what multiage classrooms are all about. Some multiage methodologies are appropriate and others are not. A thorough grounding in the literature will help in differentiating. As a team, discuss what each is reading.

MULTIAGE PHILOSOPHY, CHARACTERISTICS, AND APPROPRIATE PRACTICE.

Verse yourself in multiage philosophy, characteristics, and appropriate practice for young children in the primary grades before implementing in a multiage classroom. This will help establish a solid foundation for your multiage classroom and better prepare you to choose and refine effective learning environments for your children. Without this foundation, teachers sometimes mix conflicting philosophies of education with ineffective results.

VISIT EXISTING MULTIAGE PROGRAMS.

After you have read extensively and are saturated in multiage philosophy, characteristics, and appropriate practice, visit existing multiage classrooms in your area with your team. As you visit, note the ideas and processes that you believe work well. You may visit one classroom and say, "We really like what they are doing. It fits with what we know about multiage classrooms. We could use some of these ideas in implementing our own multiage classroom." You may visit another classroom and conclude, "We don't like what we see here. This classroom does not fit with what we know about multiage classrooms. We will not use these practices."

Visiting other programs will help you define what you want your classroom to look like. As a team, what you see will stimulate discussion and prompt decisions that will lead to an effective multiage program.

PLANNING TIME.

In addition to release time to read the literature and visit other schools, you will also need time to plan. The importance of administrative support cannot be stressed enough.

Regularly schedule days or half days when your team can read the literature, visit schools, and then plan together. Planning sessions may take place at school, at the district office, or even at someone's home. Again, even though your investigative team becomes your planning team, you will not necessarily be "teaming" in the classroom. During your planning sessions, you may decide to choose the self-contained model. If you do not "team" together in the classroom, this team will still exist for general planning and support. Your team will plan how to implement your multiage program, what it will look like, how you will involve parents and colleagues, what form your instructional day will take, how you will select the children, how you will conduct assessment, how the team will operate after implementation, and so forth.

From *Creating the Multiage Classroom* published by GoodYear Books. Copyright © 1996 Sandra J. Stone.

ESTABLISHING A TIME LINE

As an investigative and collaborative team, establish a time line for implementing your multiage classrooms. Don't just jump in by combining ages and then ask "Now what do we do?"! At the minimum, plan at least one semester before beginning. If possible, give the team at least one year to formulate a plan. The time line could be set along the following lines.

PHASE 1 (ONE TO TWO MONTHS): As a team, review the literature. Use this book as a guide. Establish a working knowledge of multiage classrooms, the philosophy, characteristics, and appropriate practice.

PHASE 2 (ONE TO TWO MONTHS): As a team, visit multiage classrooms in your area. Record effective and ineffective practices. Discuss your findings.

PHASE 3 (ONE TO TWO MONTHS): Do extensive planning for a general working scheme for your multiage program. Your planning should answer such questions as which ages to group, what model of multiage to implement (teaming or self-contained), whether the multiage program will involve the whole school or only some grades, how to gain parental support and involve parents, what your multiage philosophy will be, what your multiage classrooms will look like, and how to assess the children and report to parents.

PHASE 4 (ONE TO TWO MONTHS): Plan to involve parents as soon as possible. Once the goal is known and there is a plan for how to get there, then teachers can discuss the multiage program with parents intelligently. If possible, it would be advantageous to invite several supportive parents to be members of the investigative and collaborative team(s).

Plan several informational meetings for all parents. Be sure everyone is well prepared with a working knowledge of multiage classrooms and their benefits for children. Have pertinent literature available for parents to read. Encourage parents to ask questions. Be positive and confident. Your team is establishing a new model of schooling that supports and benefits children, families, and the learning process. Let enthusiasm and knowledge show.

PHASE 5 (ONE TO TWO MONTHS): Teachers should plan extensively for their own classrooms. This planning may be done with the multiage planning team if working on a self-contained model or the multiage teaching team. Classrooms need not be clones of each other. Each shares a common foundation and philosophy, yet also cultivates differences. Every teacher's style should be respected. During this time, plan the environment, daily schedule, instructional strategies, and management strategies. Collect materials that will facilitate the process approach to learning. Use this book and the team's research as a guide.

244

INVOLVING PARENTS

As already suggested, you may wish to involve supportive parents as members of your investigative and collaborative team(s).

When you call parent meetings, use information from this book. Make an overhead of your Philosophy Statement (derived from p. 28), How Children Learn (p. 17), Goals of Multiage Classrooms (p. 23) and Multiage Organization and Philosophy (p. 8). Let parents know how beneficial multiage classrooms can be for their children. Apprise them that other multiage programs have a waiting list. Once a multiage program begins, parents quickly see its advantages and strongly request that their children participate. Many schools are implementing whole-school multiage programs so that *all* their children will have the same advantage.

Parent involvement should not end with preliminary informational meetings. Because multiage classrooms include the same children for several years, the parents and families become an integral part of their children's education. This is extremely beneficial. You, as the teacher, will come to know the children and their families very well. Seek ways to extend the "multiage family" to the children's parents and families. Encourage parents to become more comfortable with attending portfolio conferences and school functions.

Send pertinent literature and classroom news home in a newsletter on a regular basis. Invite parents to write supportive comments in their child's portfolio. Extend regular invitations for parents to be involved in the classroom centers and projects. Design interesting "homework" that encourages parents to interact positively with their children, rather than the typical "worksheet" type of homework. Become true partners in validating each child's successful educational journey.

As each new year begins, many primary multiage teachers distribute attractive packets of information to new multiage classroom parents. This packet contains information on the benefits of multiage classrooms. Information meetings for new multiage parents are also conducted yearly. Some primary multiage programs involve parents on a weekly basis by sending home the children's portfolio work. The parents are invited to write only positive comments about their child's contributions.

The rewards of pursuing parents as partners in their children's education in multiage programs are many. Parental support will help you enjoy a successful multiage experience.

From *Creating the Multiage Classroom* published by GoodYear Books. Copyright © 1996 Sandra J. Stone.

SAMPLE PARENT BROCHURES AND PAMPHLETS

Used by permission

ANSWERING THE MOST FREQUENTLY ASKED QUESTIONS

The following questions represent some of the questions asked most frequently by teachers and parents alike. The answers are helpful in preparing concise answers to questions asked during informational meetings. They can also be used as informational items for multiage newsletters.

1. Will my child benefit from a multiage classroom experience?

Research strongly suggests that children benefit in many ways from multiage classrooms *(Miller, 1990)*. Academically, children usually do better in multiage classrooms than in traditional classrooms *(Anderson & Pavan, 1993)*. If they don't do better, then they do the same. Multiage classrooms clearly *do not negatively* affect academic achievement *(Miller, 1990)*. After reviewing twenty-one quantitative studies comparing the effects of multiage classrooms with single-grade classrooms, Miller *(1990, 6)* notes, "In terms of academic achievement, the data clearly support the multigrade classroom as a viable and equally effective organizational alternative to single-grade instruction."

In addition, the benefits for children, socially and emotionally, are consistently higher for multiage classrooms. The affective domain is greatly impacted by multiage classrooms. From his review of research, Miller *(1990, 7)* notes, "When it comes to student affect, the case for multigrade organization appears much stronger, with multigrade students out-performing single-grade students in over 75 percent of the measures used."

Multiage children often have a greater sense of belonging *(Sherman, 1984)* and more positive social relationships. Anderson and Pavan's *(1993)* review of research from 1977 to 1990 found that multiage children consistently like school more. Multiage children have more positive attitudes toward school than same-age children. The attendance rate in multiage classrooms is also significantly better than in same-age classrooms. Overall, multiage classrooms support children and their learning in much more positive ways than traditional classrooms.

2. Is the multiage classroom better for some children, but not for others?

This question assumes that traditional classrooms are the best way to educate children. As you investigate the philosophy of multiage classrooms, you quickly conclude that this child-centered approach is good for *all* children. Shouldn't all children be able to progress at their own pace? Shouldn't all children view themselves as successful, competent learners? Shouldn't all children be able to learn from their peers without competing? Shouldn't all children have the opportunity to be mentored and to mentor?

3. How are children selected for multiage classrooms?

In some schools, multiage classrooms have replaced all same-age classrooms. In schools where only some children can participate in the multiage program, the selection is a little more difficult. In both cases, children should be randomly selected. The selection should be heterogeneous. There should be a balance of ages, gender, and abilities. A balance of gender and abilities should be evident within each age. In schools where there are limited multiage classroom opportunities, parents often request their children to participate. Other children are randomly selected for the multiage program just as they are randomly selected for a particular teacher within a grade level. A caution should be noted that when parents request their children to be placed in the multiage classroom, a balance must be maintained across ages, gender, and abilities. Sometimes relying on merely parent request can skew the class so that the children represent only those with highest ability.

4. What is the best age range for a multiage classroom?

Usually the best age range is at least three years. Many schools do two-year combinations. Sometimes, if the teachers are not careful, a two-year program results in teaching each group rather than teaching the children as one group. With a three-year span, it is impossible to address grades separately with a graded-curriculum. With a three-year span, the children must be looked at as individual learners on their own continuum.

There are also social and emotional benefits that result from a three-year span. With a three-year span, there is greater opportunity for children to be mentors and to be mentored. There is less opportunity for competition between children. Children support one another and engage in more cooperation. Academically, three years allows for greater cross-age learning.

5. Do the older children benefit from the multiage classroom?

Sometimes parents and teachers worry that the older children may not benefit as much from a multiage classroom as the younger children. Obviously, the younger children are learning from the older children. With the older children mentoring younger children, do the older children not learn as much? In the multiage classroom every child, even the older child, is on his or her own continuum of learning. The curriculum is opened up for *all* the children. The older child is able to go as far as he or she is able to go just as the younger child is. Oftentimes in a same-grade classroom, some children, who have accomplished the curriculum, stagnate or get bored with learning things they already know. This does not happen in the multiage program. The older child is able to progress beyond the traditional curriculum limits.

Of course, the benefit for older children socially and emotionally is apparent. Older children have the opportunity to mentor younger children. This allows all the older children to gain confidence and increase their self-esteem. Older children also learn how to care for and nurture others. Without the strong competition of same-age classrooms, older children are free to cooperate and help others.

6. Do gifted children benefit from multiage classrooms?

Yes, gifted children benefit from multiage classrooms in much the same way that older children benefit. Gifted children are also on their own continuum of learning. They are not held back by a prescribed grade-level curriculum. Younger gifted children have the opportunity to interact with older children, increasing their level of learning. Older gifted children have the opportunity to increase leadership and mentoring skills. Self-concept and self-esteem are raised along with positive attitudes of helping others.

The open-ended curriculum in multiage classrooms encourages children to explore, discover, and invent. Gifted children, as do all children, have the freedom to pursue their interests and the opportunity to creatively expand their knowledge.

7. How does one manage to teach a multiage classroom when all the children are at different levels of learning?

One must keep in mind that even in same-age classrooms, the children are at different levels of learning. However, in a multiage classroom these differences are accepted and respected. A multiage teacher does not use the traditional approaches of a curriculum-centered classroom. The multiage teacher uses a child-centered process approach to learning.

Each child is able to participate in reading, writing, and problem-solving at his or her own level of development. The multiage teacher knows each child's needs and supports each child's development to the next stage by tailoring activities to expand to each child's level of understanding. Effective large- and small-group learning experiences are used, which allow for each child's continuous progress.

8. How are art, music, physical education, Chapter One, and special education classes accommodated in multiage classrooms?

Multiage programs should consider the multiage class as one class. If the children attend pull-out programs such as art, music, or physical education, they go to these classes together. They are not separated out by grade level. (Note: It is very important to include special class teachers in the information meetings about multiage classrooms, so they will support the multiage concept. Special class teachers usually are highly supportive of multiage classrooms. They find, as do the multiage classroom teachers, that it is very beneficial to have mixed-age children together. They enjoy the cross-age learning, the helpful older children, and the cooperative spirit.)

Classes, such as Chapter One and special education, are finding ways to incorporate their instruction into the multiage classroom, rather than pulling the children out for special services. It is very important that all special class teachers and multiage teachers communicate and collaborate for the benefit of the children.

From *Creating the Multiage Classroom* published by GoodYear Books. Copyright © 1996 Sandra J. Stone.

9. What happens if my child is in a primary multiage and then is not ready to go on to a traditional fourth grade?

Multiage teachers do not advocate retention. All teachers should be able to fit the curriculum to the child rather than the child to the curriculum. Multiage teachers will not hold children back a grade or in the multiage classroom.

It must also be noted that all children in multiage classrooms gain academically, socially, and emotionally. They see themselves as successful learners. This knowledge will empower them as learners in any classroom.

Children in multiage classrooms are truly given the gift of time to develop. Most children leave the multiage classroom ready to engage a graded classroom.

Wisely, many schools are now creating multiage classrooms for grades 3–5 or 4–6, and even establishing multiage middle schools. Many children are going from primary multiage classrooms into intermediate multiage classrooms.

10. What happens if my child goes from a multiage classroom to a traditional graded classroom as a transfer?

Sometimes children must relocate to another school that does not provide multiage classrooms. Both parents and teachers have concerns about how children will be able to manage in a graded environment after being in a nongraded environment. However, experience has shown that children who are in multiage classrooms are more confident learners and adapt quickly to same-age classrooms. One positive aspect is that they have had time to enjoy seeing themselves as competent learners. This knowledge holds them in good stead for days when they may encounter a comparative process. To have had some time in a multiage experience is better than none at all. We do not want to eliminate multiage classrooms because the children may eventually go into a graded classroom. This is like starving the children today, because some day they may encounter a famine!

CAUTIONS FOR TEACHERS AND ADMINISTRATORS

Teachers who successfully pursue multiage classrooms often say they have found multiage teaching to be the most rewarding and invigorating teaching experience they have ever had. They indicate that they would never return to same-grade teaching. However, some teachers, who have endeavored to be multiage teachers without adhering to some precautions, have decided they will never try multiage classrooms again. A poorly conceived or poorly supported multiage program is not only unrewarding to the teacher and children, but also detrimental to the multiage movement, in general.

The following are some words of wisdom to those teachers and administrators who are beginning multiage programs:

1. DON'T JUMP IN WITHOUT THOROUGH PLANNING. The preceding section on planning is important information to heed. Effective and thorough planning will help you move smoothly into a multiage program.

2. DON'T GO IT ALONE. Gain support for the multiage concept before implementing a multiage program. If you are a teacher, gain support from other colleagues and from the administration. If you are an administrator, gain support from teachers and other administrators. Gaining support also includes parental support. No one likes a "new" model imposed upon them. Gaining support also invites others to enjoy "ownership" of the process. Gaining support from all participants will create allies who will become your strongest advocates.

3. DON'T MIX PHILOSOPHIES. Don't try to implement a multiage philosophy and a same-grade philosophy at the same time. It just doesn't work. Adhere to the multiage philosophy and you will have smoother sailing.

For a successful multiage classroom, the multiage teacher must work hand and hand with the administration, parents, and her students.

4. DON'T USE A CURRICULUM-CENTERED APPROACH. Trying to teach a graded curriculum to each grade level within a multiage class is the least effective way to manage a multiage classroom as well as the hardest. Instead choose strategies that allow the teacher to facilitate learning through both whole-group and small-group instruction. Use a child-centered, developmentally appropriate, process-learning approach. Facilitate mixed-age learners in the process of real reading, writing, problem-solving, and so forth in order to have an effective program. Child-centered, hands-on learning, opportunities for socialization, and appropriate practices will maximize the learning and motivation for learning as well as provide a successful environment for mixed-age learners.

5. DON'T SELECT A HOMOGENEOUS MIXED-AGE GROUP. To gain the most benefit from mixed ages, you must have a heterogeneous group with mixed abilities and genders within each age range. An effective multiage program does not place all the low achieving children or all the high achieving children in a multiage classroom. A multiage classroom is not a transitional program to help children catch up, nor is it a form of a gifted program to expedite learning. Homogeneous groupings destroy one of the key foundations for multiage groupings, namely cross-age, cross-ability learning.

6. DON'T LABEL THE CHILDREN BY GRADE WITHIN THE MULTIAGE CLASSROOM. You may refer generally to older or younger children, but don't label the children as kindergartners or first, second, or third graders. Labeling children in the classroom creates barriers for cooperative, mixed-age interactions.

7. DON'T LABEL CHILDREN WITH GRADES. Respect every child's learning rate and style. Use authentic assessment that supports every child as a successful learner.

As you get started, know that many teachers have successfully implemented multiage classrooms. The work is not always easy, but, yes, it is very rewarding. One final word of advice is to BE KIND TO YOURSELF. As you begin, you will have many good practices in place, but don't try to establish the perfect multiage classroom in one year. Realize that a good multiage program is also a process. Just as children develop in their knowledge and experience, so do multiage teachers. Each year you will make changes and move forward. You will engage in continuous evaluation. The first year you may have language arts in place and the following year you will work on strengthening your math areas. Have high expectations, but temper high expectations with realistic expectations. Remember: Be kind to yourself and enjoy the journey!

CHAPTER NINE

EVALUATING YOUR PROGRAM

Ongoing assessment of your program allows you and your collaborative team to improve, revise, and validate your multiage program on a constant basis. Individually, you will evaluate your children's needs, your teaching strategies, assessment tools, and learning environment. Your multiage collaborative team should keep in touch with how the multiage program is addressing children's needs throughout the school; how parents and the community are being involved; what added supports are needed; what can be done better; and what is working well. Address issues, answer questions, and be sure to document the good things that are happening in your class and school. Remember that the focus on success works not only for children, but for teachers and administrators as well. Use "failures" as learning experiences and move forward. Don't be afraid to take risks and try out new ideas. Look at all your experiences as growth areas.

DOES YOUR PROGRAM FIT MULTIAGE GOALS AND CRITERIA?

As you evaluate your program, use multiage philosophy and characteristics as guidelines. Remember how children learn and the goals of a multiage classroom. Another resource for evaluation can be found in Anderson and Pavan's 1993 book, *Nongradedness: Helping It to Happen.*

If possible, evaluation and reflection should be done periodically, yet informally, throughout the year. At the end of each year, a more thorough evaluation may be undertaken. Remember that evaluation and reflection take time. Many schools provide teachers and administrators time during the school day to reflect and evaluate. Other schools pay teachers for additional time at the end of the school year to participate in this process.

SURVEYING CHILDREN AND PARENTS

Evaluation must include the children and their parents. Educators often implement programs that they assume are good for children but they never ask for the children's input. Respecting children in the learning process also means respecting their opinions about the process. Interviews during portfolio conferences are an excellent, informal way to ask children their opinions of the processes. A questionnaire can also solicit input from children. Two examples are provided for you on pp. 257–258. Gather parental input informally at portfolio conferences. A sample parent survey is included on p. 259 for your use as well.

Most often, the input from children and parents validates what you are doing as a teacher. This is important for you to know. Positive input strengthens your role as the teacher and the school's role in appropriately educating children.

CHILD QUESTIONNAIRE

MULTIAGE CLASSROOM

Child's name _____

1. When I am in my multiage classroom, I feel . . .

2. The best things about my multiage classroom are . . .

3. As a learner, I am . . .

4. The most interesting things I have learned are . . .

5. In my multiage classroom, I wish I . . .

MULTIAGE STUDENT
SURVEY

Child's Name _____

I have friends of different ages in my multiage class.	☺ ☺ ☹
I like to work with other students in my multiage class.	☺ ☺ ☹
This is how I feel about my multiage classes.	☺ ☺ ☹
I think more children should be in multiage classes.	☺ ☺ ☹
This is how I feel when I have to leave my multiage class and go to regular class.	☺ ☺ ☹
Someday I would like to be in another multiage class.	☺ ☺ ☹

The best thing about my multiage class is . . .

If I could change something in my multiage class, it would be . . .

From *Creating the Multiage Classroom* published by GoodYear Books. Copyright © 1996 Sandra J. Stone.

PARENT
QUESTIONNAIRE

MULTIAGE CLASSROOM

Parent's Name _____

1. What things do you like about the multiage classroom?

2. Is the multiage classroom performing as described
   in the parent meeting and brochure?

3. What would you like to see more of in the multiage classroom?

4. Were the themes interesting to your child?

5. Has your child shared information learned at school?

6. How has the multiage classroom benefited your child?

Additional comments:

(please write on the back)

LOOKING AHEAD

As you continue in the multi-age classroom, become an advocate for the multiage movement. Multiage classrooms provide an appropriate way to educate children that truly supports their learning as well as their social and emotional growth. Changing schools to benefit children is a worthy goal for all educators.

JOIN A MULTIAGE NETWORK. Your school support group should seek out other schools. Create a local or regional network if one does not already exist.

SHARE YOUR IDEAS. Let other multiage teachers know what practices you find effective. Present at conferences. Share your expertise with other schools. Invite teachers to visit your school.

PUBLICIZE YOUR PROGRAM. Let your community know the positive outcomes from your multiage program. Seek out opportunities to place items in your school district's newsletter and in your local newspaper.

ENJOY YOUR OWN LEARNING ADVENTURE AS YOU CHANGE SCHOOLS TO BENEFIT CHILDREN!

Professional Sources

Adair, J. H. "An attitude and achievement comparison between kindergarten and first-grade children in multi- and single-grade classes." (Ph.D. diss., 1978) *Dissertation Abstracts International,* 39, pp. 659A–660A.

Adams, J. J. "Achievement and social adjustment of pupils in combination class enrolling pupils of more than one grade level." *Journal of Educational Research,* 47 (1953), pp. 151–155.

Ames, G. J., and F. B. Murray. "When two wrongs make a right: Promoting cognitive change by social conflict." *Developmental Psychology,* 18 (1982), pp. 894–987.

Anderson, R. H. "Shaping up the shop: How school organization influences teaching and learning." *Educational Leadership,* 44 (5), (1987), p. 45.

Anderson, R. H., and B. N. Pavan. *Nongradedness: Helping It Happen.* Lancaster, PA: Technomic Press, 1993.

Azmitia, M. "Peer interaction and problem solving: When are two heads better than one?" *Child Development,* 59 (1), (1988), pp. 87–96.

Bandura, A. *Social Learning Theory.* Englewood Cliffs, NJ: Prentice-Hall, 1977.

Barbour, N. H. "Curriculum concepts and priorities." *Childhood Education,* 63 (5), (1987), pp. 331–336.

Barbour, N. H., and C. Seefeldt. *Developmental Continuity Across Preschool and Primary Grades: Implications for Teachers.* Wheaton, MD: Association for Childhood Education International, 1993.

Barker, B. "Teachers in the nation's surviving one-room schools." *Contemporary Education,* 57 (3), (1986), pp. 148–150.

Bellemere, E. "Scarborough's multiage program." *Journal of Maine Education,* 8 (1), (1991).

Bergen, D., ed. *Play As a Medium for Learning and Development.* Portsmouth, NH: Heinemann, 1988.

Biber, B. "A developmental-interaction approach: Bank Street College of Education. In *The Preschool in Action: Exploring Early Childhood Programs,* (2nd ed.), ed. M. Day and R. Parker, Boston: Allyn and Bacon, 1977, pp. 423–460.

Bizman, A., Y. Yinon, E. Mivitzari, and R. Shavit. "Effects of the age structure of the kindergarten on altruistic behavior." *Journal of School Psychology,* 16, (1978), pp. 154–160.

Boyd, W., and E. J. King. *The History of Western Education,* (10th ed.). London: Adams & Charles Black, 1972.

Bredekamp, S., ed. *Developmentally appropriate practice in early childhood programs serving children from birth through age 8.* Washington, DC: NAEYC, 1987.

Bredekamp, S., and L. Shepard. "How best to protect children from inappropriate school expectations, practices, and policies." *Young Children.* (March 1989), pp. 14–24.

Brooks, M. "Curriculum development from a constructivist perspective." *Educational Leadership,* 44 (4) (1986/1987), pp. 63– 67.

Brown, A. L., and M. J. Kane. "Preschool children can learn to transfer: Learning to learn and learning from example." *Cognitive Psychology,* 20 (4), (1988), pp. 493–523.

Brown, K. G., and A. B. Martin. "Student achievement in multigrade and single grade classes." *Education Canada,* Summer ETE, (1989), pp. 10–15.

Bruner, J., and H. Haste. *Making Sense: The Child's Construction of the World.* London: Methuen, 1987.

Bryan, B. "Rural teachers' experiences: Lessons for today." *The Rural Educator,* 7 (3), (1986), pp. 1–5.

Bunting, J. R. "Egocentrism: The effects of social interactions through multi-age grouping." (Ph.D. diss.: State University of New York at Buffalo, 1974). *Dissertation Abstracts International,* 35, p. 6356A.

Calkins, T. "The track: Children thrive in ungraded primary schools." *The School Administrator,* 49 (5), (1992) pp. 9–13.

Cambourne, B. *The Whole Story.* Auckland, NZ: Ashton Scholastic, 1988.

Carini, P. F. "Building from children's strengths." (Seminar address given at Take the Initiative in Early Childhood Education, Montpelier, VT. April 13, 1984).

Christie, J. F. "The effects of play tutoring on young children's cognitive performance." *Journal of Educational Research, 76* (6), (1983), pp. 326–330.

———. "Training of symbolic play." *Early Child Development and Care, 19,* (1985), pp. 43–51.

Clay, M. M. *Becoming Literate: The Construction of Inner Control.* Portsmouth, NH: Heinemann, 1991.

———. "Introducing a new storybook to young readers." *The Reading Teacher, 45* (4), (1991), pp. 387–396.

———. *The early detection of reading difficulties: A diagnostic survey with recovery procedures,* (3rd ed.). Auckland, NZ: Heinemann, 1985.

Cohen, D. "A look at multiage classrooms." *Education Digest, 55* (9), (May 1990).

Connell, D. R. "The first 30 years were the fairest: Notes from the kindergarten and ungraded primary (K–1–2)." *Young Children, 42* (5), (1987), pp. 30–39.

Cooper, C. R. "Development of collaborative problem solving among preschool children." *Developmental Psychology, 16,* (1980), pp. 433–441.

Cotton, K. *Nongraded Primary Education.* Portland, OR: Northwest Regional Education Laboratory, 1993.

Crisafi, M. A., and A. L. Brown. "Analogical transfer in very young children: Combining two separately learned solutions to reach a goal." *Child Development, 57* (1986), pp. 953–968.

Cuban, L. "The at-risk label and the problem of urban school reform." *Phi Delta Kappan, 70* (10), (1989), pp. 780–784 and 799–801.

Cushman, K. "The whys and hows of the multi-age primary classroom." *American Educator,* (Summer 1990), pp. 28–39.

Davis, R. *The Nongraded Primary: Making Schools Fit Children.* Arlington, VA: American Association of School Administrators, 1992.

Day, B., and G. H. Hunt. "Multiage classrooms: An analysis of verbal communication." *Elementary School Journal, 75* (1975), pp. 458–464.

Dewey, J. *Democracy and education.* New York, New York: Free Press, 1966.

Dodendorf, D. M. "A unique rural school environment." *Psychology in the Schools,* 20 (1983), pp. 99–104.

Doud, J. L., and J. M. Finkelstein. "A two-year kindergarten that works." *Principal,* (May 1985), pp. 18–21.

Drier, W. H. "The differential achievement of rural graded and ungraded school pupils." *Journal of Educational Research,* 43, (1949), pp. 175–185.

Elkind, D. *The Hurried Child.* Boston: Allyn and Bacon, 1982.

————. "Developmentally appropriate practice: Philosophical and practical implications." *Phi Delta Kappan,* 71 (2), (1989), pp. 113–117.

Ellis, S., B. Rogoff, and C. C. Cromer. "Age segregation in children's social interactions." *Developmental Psychology,* 17 (4), (1981), pp. 399–407.

Ellis, S., and S. F. Whalen. *Cooperative Learning: Getting Started.* New York: Scholastic Professional Books, 1990.

Ford, B. "Multiage grouping in the elementary school and children's affective development: A review of recent research." *The Elementary School Journal,* 78 (1977), pp. 149–159.

Foundation. (Pamphlet) Victoria, BC: Province of British Columbia Ministry of Education, 1990.

Freeman, J. "How I learned to stop worrying and love my combination class." *Instructor,* 93 (March 1984), pp. 48, 54–55.

Freund, L. S. "Maternal regulation of children's problem-solving behavior and its impact on children's performance." *Child Development,* 61 (1990), pp. 113–126.

Furman, W., D. F. Rahe, and W. W. Hartup. "Rehabilitation of socially withdrawn preschool children through mixed-age and same-age socialization." *Child Development,* 50 (4), (1979), pp. 915–922.

Galinsky, E. "Problem solving." *Young Children,* 44 (4), (1989), pp. 2–3.

Gardner, H. *Frames of Mind: The Theory of Multiple Intelligences.* New York, New York: Basic Books, 1983.

Gartner, A., M. Kohler, and F. Pressman. *Children Teach Children: Learning by Teaching.* New York: Harper and Row, 1971.

Gaustad, J. "Making the transition from graded to nongraded primary education." *Oregon School Study Council Bulletin,* 35 (7), 1992.

——. "Nongraded education: Mixed-age, integrated and developmentally appropriate education for primary children." *Oregon School Study Council Bulletin,* 35 (7), 1992.

——. "Nongraded primary education: Research roundup." *National Association of Elementary School Principles,* 9 (1), (1992), p. 1.

Gayfer, M., ed. *The Multi-Grade Classroom Myth and Reality: A Canadian Study.* Toronto: Canadian Education Association, 1991.

George, P. *How to Untrack Your School.* Alexandria, VA: Association for Supervision and Curriculum Development, 1992.

Goldman, J. "Social participation of preschool children in same- versus mixed-age groups." *Child Development,* 52 (1981), pp. 644–650.

Goodlad, J. I., and R. H. Anderson. *The Non-graded Elementary School,* (rev. ed.). New York: Teachers College Press, 1987.

Graziano, W., D. French, C. A. Brownell, and W. W. Hartup. "Peer interactions in same- and mixed-age triads in relation to chronological age and incentive condition." *Child Development,* 47 (1976), pp. 707–714.

Gulliford, A. *America's Country Schools.* Washington, DC: The Preservation Press, 1984.

Gutierrez, R., and R. E. Slavin. "Achievement effects of the nongraded elementary school: A best-evidence synthesis. *Review of Educational Research,* 62 (4), (1992), pp. 833–876.

Hansen, I. "Should we use bright children as untrained, unpaid teacher aides?" *Childhood Education,* 68 (5), (1992), pp. 308–309.

Hartup, W. W. "Cross-age versus same-age peer interaction: Ethnological and cross-cultural perspectives." In *Children as Teachers: Theory and Research on Tutoring,* ed. V. L. Allen. New York: Academic Press, (1976), pp. 41–55.

——. "Developmental implications and interactions in same- and mixed-age situations." *Young Children,* 3 (1977), pp. 4–14.

Harvey, S. B. "A comparison of kindergarten children in multigrade and traditional settings on self concept, social-emotional development, readiness development, and achievement." (Ph.D. diss.: Virginia Polytechnic Institute and State University, 1974) *Dissertation Abstracts International,* 35, p. 3340A.

Hillesheim, J. W., and G. D. Merrill. *Theory and practice in the history of American education.* Pacific Palisades, CA: Goodyear, 1971.

Hoffman, A. "A nice warm situation." *Teacher,* 91 (1973), pp. 42–45.

Holdaway, D. *The Foundations of Literacy.* Sydney, Australia: Ashton Scholastic, 1979.

———. "The structure of natural learning as a basis for literacy instruction. In *The Pursuit of Literacy: Early Reading and Writing,* ed. M. Sampson. Dubuque, IA: Kendall/Hunt, 1986.

Holmes, C. T., and K. M. Matthews. "The effects of nonpromotion on elementary and junior high school pupils: A meta-analysis." *Review of Educational Research,* 54 (2), (1984), pp. 225–236.

Hunter, M. *How to Change to a Nongraded School.* Alexandria, VA: Association for Supervision and Curriculum Development, 1992.

Iran-Nejad, A., W. J. McKeachie, and D. C. Berliner. "The multisource nature of learning: An introduction." *Review of Educational Research,* 60, (1990), pp. 509–517.

Isenberg, J., and N. L. Quisenberry. "Play: A necessity for all children." *Childhood Education,* 64 (1988), pp. 138–145.

Jacobs, H. H. "The integrated curriculum." *Instructor,* 101 (2), (1991), pp. 22–23.

Jacobsen, D., P. Eggen, and D. Kauchak. *Methods for Teaching: A Skills Approach.* Columbus, OH: Merrill Publishing Company, 1989.

James, H. F. "Small rural schools: A case study of a one-room school." (Ph.D. diss.: Northern Arizona University, 1990).

Johnson, J. E., J. F. Christie, and T. D. Yawkey. *Play and Early Childhood Development.* Glenview, IL: ScottForesman, 1987.

Kamii, C. "Leading primary education toward excellence: Beyond worksheets and drill." *Young Children,* (September 1985), pp. 3–9.

———. *Number in Preschool and Kindergarten.* Washington, DC: National Association for the Education of Young Children, 1982.

Kantrowitz, B., and P. Wingert. "How kids learn." *Newsweek,* (April 17, 1989), pp. 50–56.

Kasten, W. C., and B. K. Clarke. *The Multiage Classroom.* Katonah, NY: Richard C. Owen, 1993.

Katz, L. G., and S. C. Chard. *Engaging Children's Minds: The Project Approach.* Norwood, NJ: Ablex, 1989.

Katz, L. G., D. Evangelou, and J. A. Hartman. *The Case for Mixed-Age Grouping in Early Education.* Washington DC: (NAEYC) National Association for the Education of Young Children, 1990.

Katz, L. G., and D. E. McClellan. *The Teacher's Role in the Social Development of Young Children.* Urbana, IL: ERIC Clearinghouse on Elementary and Early Childhood Education, 1991.

Knight, E. E. "A study of double grades in New Haven City schools." *Journal of Experimental Education,* 7 (1983), pp. 11–18.

Kulik, J. A., and C-L. C. Kulik. "Effects of accelerated instruction on students." *Review of Educational Research,* 54 (1984), pp. 409–425.

Labinowicz, E. *Learning from Children: New Beginnings for Teaching Numerical Thinking.* Menlo Park, CA: Addison-Wesley, 1985.

Leeper, S. H., R. L. Witherspoon, and B. Day. *Good Schools for Young Children.* New York: Macmillan, 1984.

Lennon, R. T., and B. C. Mitchell. "Trends in age-grade relationship: A 35-year review." *School Society,* 82 (1955), pp. 123–125.

Lincoln, R. D. "The effect of single-grade and multi-grade primary school classroom on reading achievement of children." (Ph.D. diss.: University of Connecticut, 1981).

Lodish, R. "The pros and cons of mixed-age grouping." *Principal.* (May 1992), pp. 20–22.

Lougee, M. D., R. Grueneich, and W. W. Hartup. "Social interaction in same- and mixed-age dyads of preschool children." *Child Development,* 48 (1977), pp. 1353–1361.

MacDonald, P. A., and S. R. Wurster. *Multiple grade primary versus segregated first grade: Effects on reading achievement.* Bethesda, MD: ERIC Document Reproduction Service No. ED 094 336, 1974.

Martines, B. "Nongraded elementary schools: Restructuring and the future of education." (Unpublished paper, Morrison Institute for Public Policy, Arizona State University, Tempe, AZ, 1991).

Mayer, M. *There's a Nightmare in My Closet.* New York: Dial Press, 1968.

Mayesky, M. *Creative Activities for Young Children.* (5th ed.) New York, New York: Delmar, 1995.

Mazzuchi, D., and N. Brooks. "The gift of time." *Teaching K-8,* (February 1992), pp. 60–62.

McLean, L. "Student evaluations in the ungraded primary school." (Paper presented at 2nd Annual Conference on Classroom Testing, May 31– June 1 at the University of British Columbia, Center for Applied Studies in Evaluation, Vancouver, BC, 1990).

Meltzer, L. "Problem-solving strategies and academic performance in learning-disabled students: Do subtypes exist?" In *Subtypes of Learning Disabilities: Theoretical Perspectives and Research,* eds. L. V. Feagans, E. J. Short, and L. J. Meltzer. Hillsdale, NJ: Erlbaum, 1991.

Milburn, D. "A study of multi-age or family-grouped classrooms." *Phi Delta Kappan,* 64 (1981), pp. 306–309.

Miller, B. *The Multigrade Classroom: A Resource Handbook for Small, Rural Schools.* Portland, OR: Northwest Regional Educational Laboratory, 1989.

————. "A review of quantitative research on multigrade instruction." *Research in Rural Education,* 7 (1), (1990), pp. 1–8.

Mirsky, N. "Starting an interage full-time gifted class." *G/C/T,* 33 (1984), pp. 24–26.

Morrow, L. M. *Literacy Development in the Early Years.* Boston, MA: Allyn and Bacon, 1993.

Moving Toward a Primary Program. Kentucky Department of Education, Frankfort, KY, 1991.

Multi-age Classrooms: The Ungrading of America's Schools. Peterborough, NH: The Society for Developmental Education, 1993.

The Multiage, Ungraded Continuous Progress School: The Lake George Model. Peterborough, NH: Society for Developmental Education, 1992.

Muse, I., R. Smith, and B. Barker. *The One Teacher School in the 1980s.* Las Cruces, NM: ERIC Clearinghouse on Rural Education and Small Schools, 1987.

Mycock, M. A. "A comparison of vertical grouping and horizontal grouping in the infant school." *British Journal of Educational Psychology,* 37 (1966), pp. 133–135.

Nachbar, R. R. "A K/1 class can work wonderfully!" *Young Children,* 44 (5), (1989), pp. 67–71.

Nelson, D. and J. Worth. *How to Choose and Create Good Problems for Primary Children.* Reston, VA: NCTM (National Council for Teachers of Mathematics), 1983.

The Nongraded Primary: Making Schools Fit Children. Arlington, VA: American Association of School Administrators, 1992.

Oberlander, T. M. "A nongraded, multiage program that works." *Principal,* 68 (5), (1989), pp. 29–30.

Ogle, D. "The K-W-L: A teaching model that develops active reading of expository text." *The Reading Teacher,* 39, (1986), pp. 564–576.

Our Primary Program: Taking the Pulse. Victoria, BC: Province of British Columbia Ministry of Education, 1990.

Packard, F. A. *The Daily Public School in the United States.* New York: Arno Press, 1969.

Papay, J. P., R. J. Costello, and C. D. Spielberger. "Effects of trait and state anxiety on the performance of elementary school children in traditional and individualized multiage classrooms." *Journal of Educational Psychology,* 67, (1975), pp. 840–846.

Pavan, B. "The nongraded elementary school: Research on academic achievement and mental health." *Texas Tech Journal of Education,* 4 (1977), pp. 91–107.

————. "The benefits of nongraded schools." *Educational Leadership,* 2 (1992), pp. 22–25.

Pavan, B., M. Stanfill, R. Anderson, and M. McCall. *Nongradedness: A Model for Transforming Schools into Nurturing Learning Communities.* Alexandria, VA: Association for Supervision and Curriculum Development, 1993.

Pellegrini, A. D., and L. Galda. "Children's play, language and early literacy." *Topics in Language Disorders,* 10 (3), (1990), pp. 76–88.

Perlmutter, M., S. D. Behrend, F. Kuo, and A. Muller. "Social influences on children's problem solving." *Developmental Psychology,* 25 (5), (1989), pp. 744–754.

Piaget, J. "Symbolic play." In *Play: Its Role in Development and Evolution,* eds. J. S. Bruner, A. Jolly, and K. Sylva. New York: Basic Books, 1976.

Piaget, J. and B. Inhelder. *The Psychology of the Child.* New York, New York: Basic Books, 1969.

Piers, M. W., ed. *Play and Development.* New York, New York: Norton, 1972.

Pratt, D. "On the merits of multiage classrooms: Their work life." *Research in Rural Education,* 3 (3), (1986), pp. 111–115.
Primary Program Foundation Document. Victoria, BC: Province of British Columbia Ministry of Education, 1990.

"Repeating a Grade: Does It Help or Hurt?" *Research and Practice,* 1–5. Far West Laboratory, 1989.

Resource. (Pamphlet) Victoria, BC: Province of British Columbia Ministry of Education, 1990.

Rhoades, W. M. "Erasing grade lines." *The Elementary School Journal,* 67, (1966), pp. 140–145.

Rippa, S. A. *Education in a Free Society: An American History,* (6th ed.). New York: Longman, 1988.

Roopnarine, J., and J. Johnson. "Socialization in a mixed-age experimental program." *Developmental Psychology,* 20 (4), (1984), pp. 828–832.

Rule, G. "Effects of multigrade grouping on elementary student achievement in reading and mathematics. (Ph.D. diss.: Northern Arizona University, Flagstaff, AZ, 1983). *Dissertation Information Service No. 8315672.*

Schrankler, W. J. "Family grouping and the affective domain." *Elementary School Journal,* 76 (1976), pp. 432–439.

Schroeder, R., and R. E. Nott. "Multi-age grouping—it works!" *Catalyst for Change,* 3 (1), (1974), pp. 5–18.

Schultz, K. A., R. P. Colarusso, and V. W. Strawderman. *Mathematics for Every Young Child.* Columbus, OH: Merrill, 1989.

Seefeldt, C. *Social Studies for the Preschool-Primary Child.* (4th ed.) New York, New York: Merrill, 1993.

Sendak, M. *Where the Wild Things Are.* New York: Scholastic Book Services, 1963.

Shepard, L. A., and M. L. Smith. "Synthesis of research on school readiness and kindergarten retention." *Educational Leadership,* 44 (3), (1986), pp. 78–86.

———. eds. *Flunking Grades: Research and Policies on Retention.* London: Palmer, 1989.

———. "Synthesis of research on grade retention." *Educational Leadership,* 47 (8), (1990), pp. 84–86.

Sherman, L. W. "Social distance perceptions of elementary school children in age-heterogeneous and homogeneous classroom settings." *Perceptual and Motor Skills,* 58 (1984), pp. 395–409.

Shores, E. F. *Explorers' Classrooms.* Little Rock, AR: Southern Early Childhood Association, 1992.

Slavin, R. E. "Ability grouping and student achievement in elementary school: A best-evidence synthesis." *Review of Educational Research,* 57 (1987), pp. 293–336.

———. "Cooperative learning and the cooperative school." *Educational Leadership,* 45 (3), (1987), pp. 7–13.

Slavin, R. E. "Developmental and motivational perspectives on cooperative learning: A reconciliation." *Child Development,* 58, (1987), pp. 1161–1167.

Smith, M. L., and L. A. Shepard. "What doesn't work: Explaining policies of retention in the early grades." *Phi Delta Kappan,* 69 (2), (1987), pp. 129–134.

Sorohan, E. G. "Schools try mixed-age approach to class assignment." *School Board News,* (December 17, 1991).

Steig, W. *Sylvester and the Magic Pebble.* New York: Simon and Schuster, 1969.

Stone, S. J. "Integrating play into the curriculum." *Childhood Education,* 72 (2), (1995/1996), pp. 104–107.

———.*The Multiage Classroom: A Guide for Parents.* Wheaton, MD: Association for Childhood Education International, 1995.

———. *Playing: A Kid's Curriculum.* Glenview, IL: GoodYearBooks, 1993.

———. "Strategies for teaching children in multiage classrooms." *Childhood Education,* 70 (2), (1995), pp. 102–105.

———. "Wanted: Advocates for Play in the Primary Grades." *Young Children,* 50 (6), (1995), pp. 45–52.

Stone, S. J. *Understanding Portfolio Assessment: A Guide for Parents.* Wheaton, MD: Association for Childhood Education International, 1995.

Stone, S. J., and J. F. Christie. "Collaborative literacy: Exploring informal scaffolding in a primary multiage classroom (K-2) within a sociodramatic play context." (Paper presented at Annual Meeting of the National Reading Conference, New Orleans, 1995).

Sylva, K., J. S. Bruner, and P. Genova. "The role of play in the problem solving of children 3–5 years old." In *Play: Its Role in Development and Evolution,* eds. J. S. Bruner, A. Jolly, & K. Sylva. New York: Basic Books, 1976.

"Teaching combined grade classes: Real problems and promising practices." Virginia Education Association and Appalachia Educational Laboratory. In *Multiage Classroom: The Ungrading of America's Schools.* Peterborough, NH: The Society for Developmental Education, 1993.

Teale, W. "Toward a theory of how children learn to read and write naturally." *Language Arts,* 59 (1982), pp. 902–911.

Theilheimer, R. "Something for everyone: Benefits of mixed-age grouping for children, parents, and teachers." *Young Children,* 48 (5), (1993), pp. 82–87.

Trudge, J., and D. Caruso. "Cooperative problem solving in the classroom: Enhancing young children's cognitive development." *Young Children,* 44 (1), (1988), pp. 46–52.

"Ungraded classrooms: Fail-safe schools?" In *Multiage Classrooms: The Ungrading of America's Schools*. Peterborough, NH: The Society for Developmental Education, 1993.

"Ungraded primaries begin to take over Kentucky." *Teaching K-8*, 28 (2), (October 1992).

Ungraded Primary Programs: Steps Toward Developmentally Appropriate Instruction. Kentucky Education Association and Appalachia Educational Laboratory. Washington, DC: Office of Educational Research and Improvement, U.S. Department of Education, 1990.

Ungraded Primary Programs: Steps Toward Developmentally Appropriate Instruction. Charleston, WV: Appalachia Educational Laboratory, 1991.

Veenman, S., M. Voeten, and P. Lem. "Classroom time and achievement in mixed age classes." *Educational Studies*, 13 (1), (1987), pp. 75–89.

Villa, R., and J. S. Thousand. "Enhancing success in heterogeneous classrooms and schools: The power of partnerships." *Teacher Education and Special Education*, 11 (4), (1988), pp. 144–154.

Vygotsky, L. S. "Play and its role in the mental development of the child." *Soviet Psychology, 5* (1976), pp. 6–18.

———. *Mind in Society: The Development of Psychological Processes*. Cambridge, MA: Harvard University Press, 1978.

Wasserman, S. "Serious play in the classroom." *Childhood Education*, 68 (3), (1992), pp. 133–139.

Way, J. W. "Verbal interaction in multiage classrooms." *The Elementary School Journal*, 79 (3), (1979), pp. 178–186.

———. "Achievement and self-concept in multiage classrooms." *Educational Research Quarterly*, 6 (2), (1981), pp. 69–75.

Whiting, B. B. "The genesis of prosocial behavior." In *The Nature of Prosocial Development*, ed. D. Bridgeman. New York: Academic Press, 1983.

Wild, P. "What's the choice?" *Equity and Choice*, 2 (2), (1986), pp. 64–68.

Williams, L. R. "Determining the curriculum." In *The Early Childhood Curriculum: A Review of Current Research*, ed. C. Seefeldt. New York: Teachers College Press, (1987), pp. 1–12.

Wortham, S. *Early Childhood Curriculum*. New York, NY: Macmillan, 1994.

Index

From *Creating the Multiage Classroom* published by GoodYear Books. Copyright © 1996 Sandra J. Stone.

List of Forms and Assessment Tools

Printed in the United States
218159BV00002B/10/P

9 781596 470248